The Vertical Solitude:
Managing in the Public Sector

The Vertical Solitude:
Managing in the Public Sector

by

David Zussman
and
Jak Jabes

The Institute for Research on Public Policy
L'Institut de recherches politiques

Printed in Canada

Legal Deposit Fourth Quarter
Bibliothèque nationale du Québec

Canadian Cataloguing in Publication Data

Zussman, David.

The vertical solitude

Prefatory material in English and French.
ISBN 0-88645-094-2

1. Civil service—Canada—Personnel
management.   2. Government executives—
Canada.   3. Canada—Officials and employees.
I. Jabes, Jak, date.   II. Institute for
Research on Public Policy.   III. Title.

JL108.Z87   1989   351.1'00971   C90-097504-0

Camera-ready copy and publication management by
PDS Research Publishing Services Limited
P.O. Box 3296
Halifax, Nova Scotia   B3J 3H7

Published by
The Institute for Research on Public Policy
L'Institut de recherches politiques
P.O. Box 3670 South
Halifax, Nova Scotia   B3J 3K6

Contents

Foreword

The federal public service is an important national institution; the values and attitudes which those in that institution bring to their work are critically important determinants of public policy in Canada. Yet we know very little about this subject compared, for example, to our knowledge of the workings of Parliament, federal-provincial relations or virtually any public policy field. This book examines the challenges which managers face in the public sector and seeks a better understanding of their work environment. Its theme is found in the results obtained in a survey undertaken in 1986 with public and private sector managers. The findings from this survey are developed to explain individual differences, leadership practices, the working environment, organizational culture and rewards, with an emphasis on the public sector management environment itself.

The Vertical Solitude is written for managers and students of public management and policy. Although the arguments developed in the book derive from existing management theory and literature, there is no attempt to draw novel theoretical conclusions. Rather, the aim is to describe the difficulties faced in the management environment in the public sector and put forth the arguments about the existence of the phenomenon which gives this book its title.

The 1986 study, around which this book is written, was quickly followed by a second survey of managers in the Public Service of Canada. Conducted in the summer of 1988, the second survey included all federal government senior managers and executives in 65 departments and agencies—as compared to the 1986 survey, in which a random sample of managers and executives from only 20 departments participated.

The analysis of the 1988 data led to two general observations. First, in comparison with the 1986 data, the 1988 results indicated that in most areas surveyed managers' attitudes and perceptions were even less positive. Second, the 1988 survey confirms that job level is a powerful determinant of respondents' attitudes and perceptions towards their work and organization. This finding, which is detailed in this book and named "the vertical solitude", is the key feature of the 1986 survey findings. The summary of the 1988 survey results, which was distributed to the senior management cadre in the federal government and reinforces the importance of this phenomenon, forms the Afterword to this volume.

The present study has its origins in the entrepreneurial efforts of David Zussman, the financial support of the Office of the Controller General of the Government of Canada, and the willing participation of private sector supporters. The Institute welcomed and nurtured proposals for this survey initially as part of its program of work on public management, based on the conviction that the processes and structures of public management, as well as the attitudes and values of public officials, are in themselves important determinants in the formation of public policy. More than ever, perhaps, attitudes within and towards government shape the prospects for national policy and even national survival.

The original Zussman proposals for this analysis thus were seen as a key part of an on-going program of Institute work on values, leadership, and structures in the public sector—closely related to Tim Plumptre's study, *Beyond the Bottom Line*, and John Langford's television series and monograph (with Professor Kenneth Kernaghan), *The Responsible Public Servant*, and several other works dealing with organization, process, or people in public administration.

This present study started germinating in the late fall of 1984. In the hope of conducting a comparative analysis of management in the public and private sectors, the authors contacted over a dozen private companies in the summer of 1985. Most were willing to participate in such a survey of senior management attitudes. Convincing the public sector to participate was not so easy, despite the fact that a number of senior officials were keenly interested in the problems. The encouragement of Paul Tellier, Clerk of the Privy Council, finally provided the impetus.

Using a Social Sciences and Humanities Research Council seed money grant and modest supplementary Institute funding, the authors developed the first version of a survey instrument. The last months of 1985 and first months of 1986 were spent testing the questionnaire, especially at Touraine where senior managers were undergoing initiation courses. By the spring of 1986, the survey was ready to go into the field.

Once the data were collected, the authors devoted considerable effort to discussion of the results with senior officials. They also had review sessions with private sector companies. The latter half of 1986 and first half of 1987 were spent analyzing, understanding, interpreting, feeding back, and discussing data and analytical results, and developing an overall view of their meaning and significance. (As a footnote, it should be observed that formal statistical tests were applied to the survey results; any particular findings which are discussed or highlighted in this book were statistically significant.)

Then, in the summer of 1987, Jak Jabes took a postponed sabbatical and went to Europe. There was interest in the study results in a number of European countries, as well as in organizations such as the OECD. In addition to presentations of the results of the 1986 study, Jabes found himself involved in a mini-survey along the same lines for the Metropolitan Municipality of Istanbul.

In the spring of 1988, when the authors were finishing first drafts of the book, the federal government commissioned the second survey mentioned above and described in the Afterword. The spring, summer and fall of 1988 were spent revising the questionnaire, going to the field and collecting data, then analyzing it. Meanwhile, Zussman had become Dean at the Faculty of Administration and Jabes was taking up daily academic chores.

All this to say that it took longer than the authors had hoped to finish the study. The result, however, is a more polished and more readily understood analysis, with major significance for the management of the public sector. The Institute is happy to support this publication as one milestone in a continuing process of public debate on these key issues.

Rod Dobell
President   October 1989

Avant-propos

La fonction publique fédérale est une institution nationale importante; les valeurs et les attitudes de ceux qui y travaillent jouent un rôle essentiel dans l'élaboration de la politique générale au Canada. Pourtant, nous savons bien peu de choses sur ce sujet, en comparaison de ce que nous connaissons, par exemple, du mode de fonctionnement du Parlement, des relations fédérales-provinciales ou de pratiquement n'importe quel autre domaine en politique générale. Dans cet ouvrage, les auteurs examinent les défis auxquels doivent faire face les gestionnaires du secteur public et cherchent à préciser le milieu dans lequel ceux-ci travaillent. Le thème du livre émane d'une enquête entreprise en 1986 auprès d'un certain nombre de responsables des secteurs public et privé. Les résultats de cette enquête sont exploités de manière à expliquer les différences individuelles, les pratiques en matière de leadership, le milieu de travail, les concepts organisationnels et les stimulants; et cela, principalement par rapport aux conditions de gestion dans le secteur public.

The Vertical Solitude ("La Solitude verticale") a été écrit à l'intention des administrateurs et des étudiants en gestion publique et en politique générale. Bien que les arguments présentés dans ce livre dérivent de systèmes de gestion et d'écrits déjà connus, les auteurs n'essaient pas de suggérer de nouvelles théories. Leur but est plutôt de faire une description des difficultés rencontrées dans la gestion du secteur public et de dégager les arguments relatifs à l'existence du phénomène qui donne son titre à l'ouvrage.

L'étude de 1986, qui a servi de base à ce livre, a été suivie d'une seconde enquête menée durant l'été de 1988 et portant sur les gestionnaires de la fonction publique du Canada. Cette seconde enquête a inclus tous les hauts fonctionnaires et cadres de 65 ministères et agences gouvernementales, alors que celle de 1986 n'avait porté que sur un certain nombre de directeurs et de cadres de 20 ministères, qui avaient été sélectionnés au hasard.

L'analyse des données recueillies en 1988 a abouti à deux observations générales. Premièrement, dans la plupart des domaines examinés, les données de 1988, comparées à celles de 1986, révèlent une dégradation dans les attitudes et les perceptions des gestionnaires vis-à-vis de leur travail et de leur administration. Deuxièmement, l'enquête de 1988 confirme que le niveau du poste occupé joue un rôle primordial dans la manière dont les personnes interrogées perçoivent leur emploi et l'organisme au sein duquel elles travaillent. Cette découverte, qui est analysée dans ce livre et résumée dans l'expression "la solitude verticale", constitue l'élément clé des résultats de l'enquête de 1986. Le résumé des résultats de l'enquête de 1988 a été distribué aux hauts fonctionnaires et aux cadres du gouvernement fédéral; il vient confirmer l'importance de ce phénomène et est repris dans la postface de cet ouvrage.

La présente étude est due à l'initiative de David Zussman, et elle a bénéficié du soutien financier du Bureau du contrôleur général du Canada et de la participation active de certains éléments du secteur privé. L'Institut a, dès l'abord, accueilli et encouragé les propositions relatives à cette enquête dans le cadre de son programme sur la gestion publique, étant bien convaincu que les processus et structures de gestion publique, ainsi que les attitudes et les valeurs de ceux qui en ont la responsabilité, sont d'une grande importance dans l'élaboration des règles de politique générale. Aujourd'hui peut-être plus que jamais, les attitudes à l'intérieur de la fonction publique et celles envers le gouvernement conditionnent l'avenir de la politique nationale et même la survie du pays.

C'est pourquoi les propositions initiales de David Zussman ont été perçues comme étant un élément essentiel des travaux en cours de l'Institut portant sur les valeurs, le leadership et les structures du secteur public. Elles étaient en rapport étroit avec l'étude de Tim Plumptre, *Beyond the Bottom Line*, la série télévisée de John Langford et sa monographie (en collaboration avec le professeur Kenneth Kernaghan) intitulée *The Responsible Public Servant*, ainsi qu'avec plusieurs autres travaux sur la fonction publique traitant d'organisation, de méthodes ou de personnel.

Le travail que nous présentons a commencé à s'ébaucher à la fin de l'automne 1984. Dans l'espoir de pouvoir entreprendre une analyse comparative de la gestion dans les secteurs public et privé, les auteurs ont d'abord pris contact, au cours de l'été 1985, avec une douzaine d'entreprises du secteur privé qui ont, pour la plupart, accepté d'y participer. Il n'a pas été aussi facile de convaincre le secteur public, en dépit du fait qu'un bon nombre de hauts fonctionnaires étaient très intéressés par ces questions. L'appui de Paul Tellier, greffier du Conseil privé, s'est finalement révélé déterminant.

À l'aide d'une subvention de démarrage du CRSH et d'un modeste supplément financier fourni par l'Institut, les auteurs ont pu mettre au point la première version de leur instrument d'enquête. Les derniers mois de 1985 et les premiers mois de 1986 ont été consacrés à l'essai du questionnaire, spécialement à Touraine où les hauts fonctionnaires étaient en train de suivre des cours d'initiation, si bien qu'au printemps de 1986, le questionnaire de l'enquête était prêt à être utilisé.

Une fois les données recueillies, les auteurs ont consacré un temps considérable à la discussion des résultats avec des cadres supérieurs. Ils ont également organisé des sessions d'examen avec des entreprises du secteur privé. La deuxième moitié de 1986 et le premier semestre de 1987 ont ensuite été employés à l'analyse, à la compréhension et à l'interprétation des données, aux réactions que celles-ci provoqueraient ainsi qu'à la discussion des données et des résultats analytiques et à l'élaboration d'une vue d'ensemble de leur signification et de leur portée. (Il est à noter que les résultats ont été soumis à des tests statistiques en règle; tous les résultats particuliers discutés et soulignés dans ce livre sont pertinents d'un point de vue statistique.)

Ensuite, au cours de l'été 1987, Jak Jabes a pris un congé sabbatique et s'est rendu en Europe : un certain nombre de pays européens et d'organismes comme l'OCDE se sont montrés intéressés par les résultats de l'enquête. Outre la présentation des résultats de l'étude de 1986, Jak Jabes a également participé à la mise en oeuvre d'une mini-enquête du même genre, pour le compte de la municipalité métropolitaine d'Istanbul.

Alors que les auteurs terminaient la première version de ce livre, au printemps de 1988, le gouvernement fédéral a décidé de commissionner la seconde enquête mentionnée plus haut et que nous décrivons dans la postface. Aussi, le printemps, l'été et l'automne de 1988 ont-ils été employés à revoir le questionnaire, à se rendre sur le terrain pour recueillir les données et à analyser ces dernières. Entre-temps, David Zussman était nommé doyen de la faculté d'administration et Jak Jabes reprenait la routine universitaire quotidienne.

Tout ceci pour dire que l'achèvement de cette étude a pris plus de temps qu'escompté. Il en résulte cependant qu'elle se présente sous un aspect beaucoup plus élaboré et plus facile à comprendre, et qu'elle offre par ailleurs un intérêt considérable pour la gestion du secteur public. L'Institut est heureux d'apporter son soutien à cette publication qui constitue un nouveau jalon sur la route qui mène, par le débat public, à une meilleure compréhension de ces questions clés.

Rod Dobell
Président   Octobre 1989

Acknowledgements

Studies of this kind are difficult to do without the cooperation of many individuals, especially those who take the time to fill out the questionnaires. Over the last months, we have learned to appreciate, even more than in the past, the dedication and commitment of public servants. To all who completed the survey instrument which forms the nucleus of this study, from both the public and private sectors, we dedicate this book. While the results do not paint a rosy picture of the Canadian public service, we believe that they are representative of how managers perceive their current situation. The challenge to the public service is to find ways in which managerial behaviour is developed to the point where all managers can maximize their potential and serve the public and their clients in the most efficient and effective ways.

The Institute for Research on Public Policy helped in many ways. Rod Dobell, the president of IRPP provided constant encouragement from the beginning. Tim Plumptre, while a fellow at IRPP, made research funds available which allowed us to have students help with background research. John Langford, then in charge of the governability and public management publications of IRPP, and Steve Rosell, currently in charge of this program, both concurred with us that the study should be written up as a monograph. The commitment of the Institute to notions of governability is strong evidence of its continuing interest in understanding how this country works.

The IRPP published a summary of preliminary findings from the survey as part of its series of publications on problems of governability and public management. Many in the Institute provided much needed prodding, courage and leadership so that we could finish this work. Their help is much appreciated.

The Social Sciences and Humanities Research Council provided seed money which helped the project get underway. Our students, Pat Lemay, Gerry Tessier, Celia Smith, and France Leclair, got involved in various aspects of the project and their eagerness has been very much appreciated.

We acknowledge the help received from individuals within both sectors who felt that a study of this kind had to be done because good managers want this kind of information. In the federal government, we thank Paul Tellier, Jack Manion, Huguette Labelle, Gérard Veilleux, Doug Rowland, Phil Fay, George Post and especially Guy Leclerc, who provided so much of the support. Very special thanks also go to Michael Rayner, who was Comptroller General of Canada, and Gaetan Lussier, who was Deputy Minister at the Department of Employment and Immigration, at the time the study was undertaken, and who are now in the private sector. They provided the help and inspirational leadership that is often necessary in such work.

In the private sector, we particularly thank Jim Burns of Power Corporation, Torrance Wylie of Imasco, and the CEOs of the 13 participating companies who had the courage to give us the opportunity to survey the attitudes and values of their senior managers.

Michael Hicks, as principal of the Staff Development Centre at Touraine, always welcomed us and graciously provided the time of senior managers who were undergoing training, so that we could pretest various versions of the questionnaire.

Many people read parts of the manuscript at different times and made valuable suggestions. We especially thank Professor James C. McDavid from the University of Victoria and two anonymous reviewers who provided comments, asked questions, pointed to omissions and forced us to critically look at our own conclusions. We are grateful to Kathryn Randle, who commented on an earlier draft of the manuscript. Finally, special thanks go to Sheila Protti, who did a wonderful job of editing what we always felt was the last version. In the end, of course, each of the authors puts the responsibility for all errors and misinterpretations on the other.

Chapter 1

Managing in the Public Service and the Survey of Managerial Attitudes

As an ex civil servant I hold your country in very high regard. You have the finest civil service in the world today. It was based on ours, I know, but it has surpassed it considerably. I suspect most Canadians don't realize it, but it is a fact recognized by civil servants everywhere in the world.

—C.P. Snow[1]

Introduction

This book is about management in the Canadian federal public service as seen by its senior managers. The story is developed through a survey of managerial attitudes, and includes a private sector component to give readers a benchmark against which to consider the findings about the public sector. It relates impressions about managing in the public and private sectors as told to us by almost 2,000 senior federal managers in 20 departments and 1,300 private sector managers in 13 companies who responded to our survey during the summer of 1986. The emphasis in this book is on public sector management, with occasional references to the private sector data in order to signal the relevance and magnitude of the results. It was

1

decided that it was not possible to interpret and explain the management practices of both sectors in the same publication.

The federal public service is a massive, multi-faceted organization operating in a particularly difficult environment, buffeted by changing public expectations and philosophies of political leaders. In the 1960s and 1970s, public service organizations in general, and the federal public service in particular, grew at a very rapid rate in order to provide the new policies and services being promised by their governments.[2] This cycle was fuelled largely by improved economic growth in Canada and rising public expectations that led, in turn, to the popularity of grand policy designs aimed at solving society's ills.

More recently, politicians and the public at large have come to realize that society's problems have become more complex and that massive policy initiatives can have only limited effects. As a consequence, growth in the federal public service has been slowed by expenditure restraint, downsizing, and related measures. Doing more with less has become the operating maxim of governments throughout the western world. Leaders have renounced big government and embraced greater reliance on market mechanisms and private enterprise. Inherent in these new operating principles is the notion that less government intervention in regulation, economic development and social programming is more effective public policy than previous interventionist efforts.

Despite the decrease in the emphasis being placed on government activities, the federal public service remains the primary source of policy advice to ministers, principal contact between the government and the public, and the major vehicle of service delivery. As a consequence, a healthy public service is critical in ensuring that Canadians are well served by their government officials.

Unfortunately, our research has noted a serious discrepancy between the perception public and private sector managers have of the quality of management practices in their own organizations. The wide gap in perceptions between public and private sector managers was consistent throughout our study.

As well, our data revealed consistent differences of perception within the public service between those working at the highest levels of the organizational structure and those working four and five levels below them. This situation, which we have termed the "vertical solitude", was found to exist on a consistent basis within the public service, although not among the private sector managers and executives.

Our data, for example, indicate that the executives (known as EXs) in the federal public service appear to have a different set of work values, express higher levels of job satisfaction, and regard management practices in a more generous light, than the managers (known as

SMs and SM-1s) who work for them (see Appendix 1-1). This finding occurs in almost all our analyses of responses from public sector managers and is in marked contrast to the situation in the private sector where there is a consistency in the responses of managers regardless of job level.

There appears to be a serious breakdown in the communication flow between the executive ranks and the managerial cadre in the federal public service. This breakdown suggests that it is unlikely that public servants working below the managerial level, and who are in constant contact with the public and client groups, will develop a valid understanding of the expectations of their ministers and the other people who set the tone and direction of their departments. It is unreasonable to expect that employees can function effectively without a clear appreciation of the organization's goals and direction, its reward structure, and its corporate values.

The vertical solitude is only a symptom of what ails the public service today. Our analyses have yielded insights into the nature of the relationship between a manager's job level and work satisfaction, showing the relevance of factors such as the fairness of reward systems, corporate culture, and leadership. Despite the pervasiveness of the vertical solitude, as well as other difficulties explored in this book, we discovered levels of job commitment, loyalty to the client group and general job satisfaction at all levels in the senior management cadre that were much higher than might be expected from managers with so many negative things to say about their management environment.

The study concludes with the argument that, despite the current pressures on the public service, most of the problems identified in this study can be remedied, provided those responsible for management matters are prepared to embrace a new philosophy of public sector management—one that emphasizes management skills and the nurturing of human resources.

Some Constraints to Strengthening Public Service Motivation and Productivity

From a management perspective, "Let the managers manage!" became the inspirational cry of public sector planners after the Glassco Royal Commission reported on the state of the federal public service in 1963.[3]

As a consequence of the Commission's admonition to give public sector managers more management responsibilities, the federal public service underwent significant changes in scope and orientation. During the 1960s and '70s, public sector management became associated with the development of new systems for controlling inputs and outputs. Governments in general, and the federal government in particular, embarked on a series of initiatives to cope with increased demand for services.

Despite the emphasis on planning in both sectors, by the time the recession of the early 1980s took hold there was already a widely held belief that the federal public service was ill-prepared to deal with a changing environment. The Lambert Commission, the D'Avignon Committee, and the Auditor General of Canada reported, within a short period in the late 1970s, that the management of human resources needed considerable restructuring.[4]

In addition to weaknesses in its overall management of human resources, the federal public service over the last ten years has undergone a number of external and internal shocks. Among the most significant of the pressures have been successive governments' attempts to decrease the number of federal public servants through layoffs and early retirement incentives, to cut program expenditures, and to privatize several Crown corporations.[5] Government efforts to limit the role of the public service have also contributed to a decline in public confidence in government institutions, a deterioration in the relationship between the political superstructure and the public service, and a significant revamping of parliamentary rules on the appointment of senior officials.[6]

During the last decade, politicians and senior public servants appear to have lost confidence in their ability to solve the types of problems they tackled so eagerly in the 1960s and 1970s. The failure to improve the lot of the poor, the disadvantaged, and native Canadians; the persistence of regional disparities despite massive efforts to improve regional imbalances; the difficulty of lowering the unemployment rate substantially; and the failure to manipulate economic levers with any degree of certainty have all served to undermine the confidence government policy-makers once had in the tools of their trade. It is difficult to measure the actual impact of this situation on the public service, but the failure to generate dramatically effective public policy or to implement good policy effectively has undoubtedly sapped the energy of many who joined the public service during the early 1970s when there was a sense of optimism about what government could achieve. Anecdotal evidence suggests that, having been unable to deliver what was promised, many senior public servants have retreated from the activist roles they played only a few years ago to more administrative ones.

As government gets more complicated, politicians seek more simplistic explanations for problems, and government programs and employees are obvious and easy scapegoats. In his 1984 Annual Report, the Chairman of the Public Service Commission argued that "The phenomenon referred to as 'bureaucrat bashing' escalated during the heat of the (1984) election campaign. While such attacks usually fail to distinguish between what is the result of a political decision and what is due to administrative practices, the result is destructive to the morale of public servants who have no way of defending themselves."[7]

One-sided media coverage, reports of auditors and other investigators whose duty it is to note weaknesses and imperfections, declarations by interest groups which require publicity for their own causes—all contribute to producing a rather negative image of the public service. When this climate persists, talented people are increasingly dissuaded from joining, while those within the public service are inclined to become discouraged. The reality moves toward the image.

We are concerned that the sense of pride in service is being eroded. We fear that the Canadian situation is approaching that in the U.S., where

> our last two presidents have led the way in campaigning against the very government they need to lead, undermining their ability to govern once in office by reducing the morale of the career civil service and limiting their ability to recruit others to come into government. No corporate leader would denigrate his or her employees in this way. The irony is that the civil servants are badmouthed by the presidents whose inadequate management skills and political over-promising are often more responsible for negative public attitudes than anything that career government employees do.[8]

The nature of the parliamentary system further impedes good management. Among the characteristics of Canadian government are: the relative frequency of elections, which creates uncertainty within the public service while political parties campaign for public support, and reorientation when a new party gains office; the problem of dealing with neophyte ministers who are ignorant of their departments' mandates and who feel little obligation to the public service; the difficulty in measuring performance in a public sector environment where objectives are often unstated or contradictory and multifaceted; the traditional public service values of anonymity and neutrality which tend to mute creative and innovative solutions; and occasional political interference in the activities of the public service.

All these factors have made managing in the public service extremely difficult. They have created enormous pressures on an increasingly fragile system at the very time that the public service is being asked to do "more with less". It seems that the cumulative effects of these conflicting pressures on the public service have contributed to the vertical solitude.

Several internal changes in the federal public service have compounded these problems. Figure 1-1 shows that the number of person years authorized by the Treasury Board has been relatively stable over the last ten years, despite the public's demand for more government services. Taking various personnel adjustments into account, which reflect restraint, efficiency measures and withdrawal from certain policy areas, there was a decrease of more than 3,000 employees between 1985-1986 and 1986-1987.[9] While the number is not large in relation to the total employee base of 230,000, downsizing efforts have cut off a vital source of new blood at the job-entry level and have reduced promotion opportunities for those in the middle of the hierarchy.

Figure 1-2 reveals another serious internal constraint in the federal public service: the age structure of the senior management category. It shows a severe compression between managers working at the SM (senior manager) level and those working about five levels higher, i.e. at the EX5 level. Between the lowest level of management and the highest there is less than a four-year age gap (an average of 47.3 years compared with 51.1). As well, the slight increase in age between 1985 and 1986 suggests that the management category is growing older because there are few younger managers being introduced into the system, or that the most senior are relatively young and not ready to retire.[10]

A further source of compression is found in Figure 1-3, which displays the number of senior managers in the federal public service working at the various management levels in 1986. It is clear that the number of senior management positions decreases dramatically as one moves up the hierarchy. For example, in 1986 there were 5,600 individuals working one level below the senior management cadre (SM-1); there were 1,560 EX1, EX2 and EX3 positions and 190 EX4 and EX5 positions. One expects a steep fall-off in pyramidal organizations, but the federal public service has a larger proportion of senior managers and executives than comparable organizations in the private sector. At the lower ranks of the management hierarchy, there appear to be limited promotion opportunities for the SMs and SM-1s, given the fairly young age profile of the EX5s in addition to the aforementioned lack of growth of the EX and SM group since 1983 (see Figure 1-4).

In an environment of downsizing and growing public cynicism towards the ability of government to deliver the goods, we find a federal public service at an important point in its evolution. The public service will prevail, in that it will continue to provide services. Much less certain is the cost, measured in terms of responsiveness, turnover, absenteeism and job commitment, that the system will have to bear if it is to continue to provide what is generally viewed as an extremely good service.

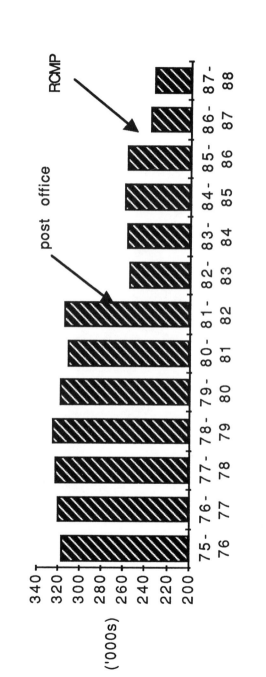

Figure 1-1
Person Years Authorized in the Main Estimates
(in '000s)

Sources: Public Service Commission, Annual Report, 1987

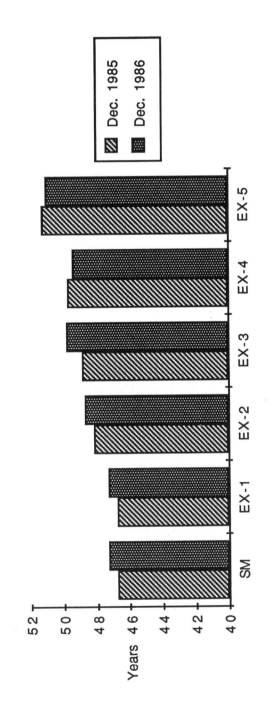

Figure 1-2
Average Age of the Management Category
(including Senior Managers and Executives)

Source: Public Service Commission, Annual Report, 1986.

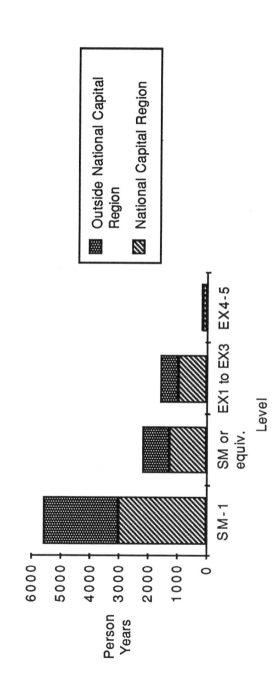

Figure 1-3
Size of the Management Category and SM-1 Group

Source: Public Service Commission, Annual Report, 1986

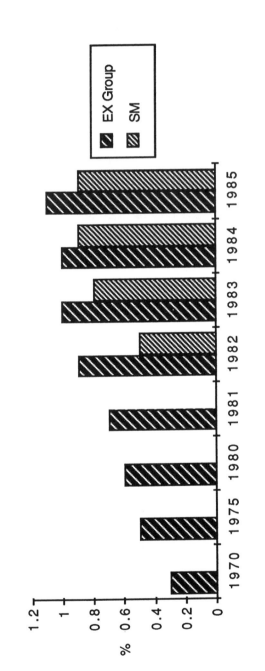

Figure 1-4
Distribution of Executives and Senior Managers
in the Federal Public Service

Source: Public Service Commission, Annual Report, 1986

In the words of Jack Manion, then Associate Secretary to the Cabinet and Deputy Clerk of the Privy Council, "It is not too great an exaggeration to suggest that public administration in Canada today is at an historic juncture. Some very fundamental questions are being asked, more and more urgently, about the role of government in society, and how government is organized, and about public servants, their roles and relationships and the skills and values they need to do their jobs."[11]

Management in the private sector also went through a fairly traumatic transition, particularly between 1981 and 1983. In the late 1970s most large private sector companies invested considerable effort in planning and other systems, to cope with expansion. However, while most public service efforts were directed to developing systems for managing expenditures and people, the private sector was looking for ways to increase motivation and employee participation so as to maximize productivity. Techniques such as T-groups, semi-autonomous work groups, matrix designs and quality circles have become part of the jargon of management in the last few years. The "search for excellence" route to providing quality products through a more productive and satisfied work force became the major objective of many private sector firms, especially during the 1981-83 recession, as they attempted to adjust to changing market conditions. The private sector may not yet have found the link between motivation and productivity, but its long-standing interest has given it a head start over the public service in dealing with the managerial issues on which we focus.

The Survey of Managerial Attitudes

Given the cumulative effect of pressures on the federal public service, one must consider whether the well-developed culture described by former mandarins is still in evidence in Canada. Are the traditional values of commitment to service and the public interest still shared by its employees? Is employment in the public service providing employees with satisfying jobs, and are employees reciprocating with feelings of loyalty to their departments or to the public service as a whole? Who are the principal culture carriers of the public service, and are their values similar to those of managers in higher positions? Finally, if there are differences among the various levels of management, to what extent can traditional sources of motivation such as leadership, rewards and cultural factors play a role in improving morale?

Various definitions of management exist, most of which point out the nature and importance of the management process. Some models of the management process describe management solely in terms of the personal characteristics of the leader; it is generally assumed that charismatic or powerful leaders are likely to manage successful organizations. More contemporary theories suggest that management is more often a function of environmental factors, political forces, world-wide economic issues, and the impact of competitors. Another strand of management theory focuses on the creation of a working climate that enhances productivity. Quality circles, incentive schemes, and reward structures are some examples of tools used to improve the working climate.

The most recent move toward integrating management theory is the contingency approach. In contrast to other theories, the contingency framework allows us to identify the internal and external variables that affect managerial actions and organizational performance. At the same time this approach acknowledges that one management style may be more effective than another depending on circumstances.[12]

This book defines management as the practice of planning, organizing, leading and controlling an organization's operations, in order to achieve a coordination of the human and material resources essential in the effective and efficient attainment of objectives. These functions must be performed by all persons in managerial positions, whether deputy ministers, vice-presidents, directors or senior managers. In addition, it should be recognized that the management process is best described by these functions, rather than by the status or rank held by certain members of the organization. Management is neither the privilege nor the responsibility of only a few members of an organization—it is the work of all individuals whose jobs are involved with reaching objectives through the coordination of available resources.

Applications of management functions must be considered within the context and confines of a given organizational setting. The functions are clearly not part of a mechanical process that produces equal degrees of success for all managers. Since the world is constantly changing, managers must deal with all kinds of uncertainty as they try to accomplish their organizational goals. Planning, organizing, leading, and controlling must be blended and applied as they relate to the situation. Therefore, managers must be knowledgeable of their day-to-day management needs, and informed about the possible impact of the environment, if they expect to be successful in meeting the challenges in their organizations.

The impact of the management practices on an organization is influenced by numerous factors, including (1) individual characteristics of the managers, (2) organizational climate, and (3) organizational forces that define the larger environment in which managers work.

To begin to address some of these problems, we approached the federal government in the fall of 1985 for permission to conduct a survey of managerial attitudes. During our initial contact we indicated that our interest lay primarily in middle managers, whom we viewed as the principal transmitters of information from their positions in the federal government.[13] As a consequence, we assumed that middle managers, situated a few levels below the deputy minister but, typically, in daily touch with clients, the public, and providers of service, were the critical players in inculcating their organizations with a culture or set of beliefs. These culture carriers are well placed to translate and interpret messages emanating from the minister, ministerial staff, and the deputy minister, as well as to inform senior management about attitudes and concerns in the lower ranks.

Since the culture of organizations has been such an important feature of the management literature during the last few years it was natural to consider it a point of departure in our study. As a consequence, we decided to look at those who occupied the pivotal role of transmitting the views and attitudes of the senior management cadre, as well as those of the minister, to employees whose jobs are to implement the plans and fulfill the expectations of federal organizations. For this reason the study compared the perceptions of lower levels of the federal government's senior management cadre (SMs, SM-1s) with those of managers working at more senior levels (EX1 to EX5).

The survey was designed to measure managerial attitudes and practices in the public and private sectors. Twenty federal government departments agreed to participate in the mail survey. They ranged from small central agencies of only a few hundred employees to service departments with more than 25,000 employees across the country.

In the private sector, of the 30 potential candidates chosen from the Financial Post 500, 13 very diverse companies agreed to participate.[14] The companies represented four of the major sectors of the economy (services, financial, resources, manufacturing) and ranged from membership in the Financial Post Top 10 to companies ranking between the 400th and 500th largest firms in the nation.

All but one of the private sector companies were Canadian-owned,[15] and they ranged in size from 3,000 to 35,000 employees. All had been profitable, on average, over a five-year period. To ensure meaningful comparisons between the two sectors, the last criterion was that participating companies have a work force that was not growing, given the stability in the size of the federal public service over the last few years.

The questionnaire was developed over a period of eight months, in consultation with public servants and private sector managers.

Draft questionnaires were tested on two occasions on groups of business executives and public servants.

In the public sector, participants were selected using a stratified random sample, based on population estimates provided by the Public Service Commission, with department, place of work, and job level as selection criteria. With one reminder to 2,703 potential respondents, as well as a letter from their deputy ministers, we received 1,981 completed questionnaires, for a response rate of 73 per cent.[16]

In the private sector, because of varying organizational structures and titles in the participating companies, firms were asked to define a stratified, random sample of up to 150 senior managers whose positions were one to five levels below the CEO, at the head office and in the regions.

In most cases, respondents returned the questionnaire by mail to the University of Ottawa to ensure anonymity and confidentiality. In other cases, questionnaires were returned on a confidential basis to a contact person in the company. Using one mailout of 1,784 questionnaires, we received 1,284 private sector completed questionnaires, for a response rate of 72 per cent.

The high response rates indicate the interest respondents have in managerial issues and provide substantial evidence that the results are representative of the respective groups of managers (see Table 1.1). A description of the sample is provided in Appendix 1-2.

The 1986 survey instrument contained 205 different items which measured 13 different variables related to (1) the individual characteristics of managers, (2) organizational climate, and (3) the larger environment in which managers work. These variables were selected because of their established value in previous research on management and the importance ascribed to them during our pretest and focus group discussions with public and private sector managers. Given the complexity of the analytical task due to the large number of variables, it was imperative that a model be developed to help shape the direction of the analysis. That model, which is still preliminary, is summarized in Figure 1-5.

It was important that the study conform to a theoretical or conceptual model of management reflecting the reality of everyday public service management. By imposing a working model of management on the data we would avoid, to the extent possible, spurious or irrelevant findings.

To assess the context of public sector managers' attitudes and perceptions, it was critical to establish benchmarks against which these observations could be measured. In the absence of trend data from the public sector, we felt it would be unfair to consider the results of a public sector survey in the abstract measured against a theoretical

Research Design

We suggest that there are four fundamental factors to consider in understanding the outcomes of the management process in an organization: the individual characteristics of the manager; the organizational climate which defines the day-to-day working relationship; the organizational forces, which include the history, traditions and cultural aspects of the organization; and the managerial practices of the managers. This complex model, to the extent possible, portrays the competing factors which determine employee perceptions of work satisfaction. In the simplest case, all have some impact on work satisfaction. For example, those who perceive the current reward system as fair will perceive their work as more satisfying than those who do not feel that rewards are fairly distributed. The model suggests that all 17 variables in Figure 1-5 relate to work satisfaction.

There is a more complex way of examining this model and that is by assuming that managerial practices, individual characteristics, and organizational forces have some impact on organizational climate before affecting work satisfaction. (The dotted arrows represent these relationships.) There is also the possibility that high levels of work satisfaction are not only the direct result of some of these factors but that work satisfaction might also affect the way in which respondents perceive the previous four factors. As an illustration, it is possible that when people are particularly satisfied with their work they might be more disposed to perceive the level of leadership more favourably. This expanded model is not part of the analysis in this book although it does represent an interesting line of research.

Since this book is a first attempt at integrating the data from the Survey of Managerial Attitudes, we decided to analyze the simple links between work values, leadership, culture, rewards, and work environment with work satisfaction—without reference to the possible effects of interactions among these variables (see Figure 1-5a). These five variables were chosen from the set of 13 variables to represent the four major factors of the management model and because, in earlier multivariate analyses, they were found to be particularly good predictors of work satisfaction.

This book analyses public sector management from two perspectives. First, it demonstrates that there are significant differences in the perceptions of public and private sector managers with regards to (a) the extent to which certain management practices are used on the job, (b) the organizational climate, (c) the organizational forces, and (d) their personal characteristics.

The degree to which the public and private sectors are similar or different in their management practices is of critical importance for two reasons. First, there is a commonly held view in Canadian society that "the private sector does it better" when one assesses the relative competencies of public and private sector managers. As a consequence, there is considerable pressure on the public sector to borrow private sector practices for its own use even though the environments are very different and specific management practices may not always be transferable.

The purpose of this analysis, therefore, is not only to establish whether differences in management practices exist between the two sectors but also to measure whether the differences between them are so large as to threaten the successful transfer of any of them. It is therefore of critical importance for us to know if environmental, organizational, and personal factors—as well as managerial practices—differ between the two sectors.

The second perspective, established through analysis, is that there is an important link between elements of the organization's climate, managerial practices, organizational forces, and the individual characteristics of the manager with work satisfaction. In the absence of productivity measures, it was seen as imperative that this linkage be established to firmly denote that good management practices, the creation of a favourable work environment, and the existence of positive organizational forces are important not only for their own sake but also because they produce more satisfied employees. Although management research has not consistently established that job satisfaction is related to higher levels of productivity, as we argue in more detail in Chapter 5, there is plenty of evidence to suggest high levels of work satisfaction produce a more motivated and loyal workforce—two key factors in the maintenance of a professional public service.

At the outset, we hypothesized three different series of results. Our first hypothesis was that there would be significant differences in the perceptions of private and public sector managers with regard to the variables of the management model which were tested. While there was no reason to suggest that one sector would be consistently better, we felt confident, based on pre-test and focus group data, that differing goals would have produced variations in management methods in the two sectors.

Our second hypothesis was that each element in the management model would, on its own, have a significant linkage with work satisfaction. In some instances, such as leadership, we hypothesized that the more managers perceived that the deputy minister/CEO demonstrated leadership the greater would be their work satisfaction. In other instances we predicted, for example, that the fewer constraints on the manager the greater the work satisfaction. These linkages are explored in the following five chapters.

Finally, in addition to the first two hypotheses which dealt with general findings, we also predicted that job level would have some effect on the strength of the differences between the two sectors.* This hypothesis was based on our contention that a critical measure of an organization's health is the degree to which its management cadre share similar views. As a corollary, it was also recognized that communications within organizations are critical in creating the requisite flow of information which leads to good management practices, the establishment of a favourable work environment and supportive organizational forces. In the case of individual characteristics, it was also felt that people lower down the corporate ladder would, in some cases, have different characteristics than those working at the higher end, since the promotion process tends to reward those with certain work values and personality characteristics.

---

* We are indebted to George Post, who first suggested that we look at job levels. At present, he is the Federal Development Coordinator (Toronto) for the Department of Industry, Science and Technology and, during the planning phase of this study, was Associate Secretary to the Cabinet for Senior Personnel.

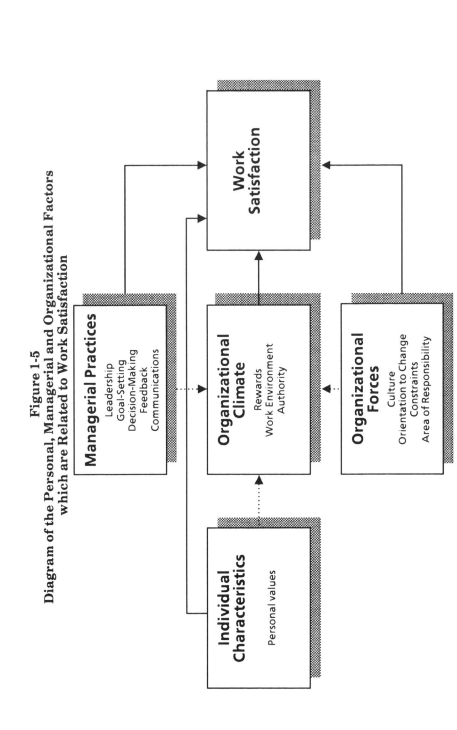

Figure 1-5
Diagram of the Personal, Managerial and Organizational Factors
which are Related to Work Satisfaction

Managerial Practices

Leadership
Goal-Setting
Decision-Making
Feedback
Communications

Work Satisfaction

Organizational Climate

Rewards
Work Environment
Authority

Organizational Forces

Culture
Orientation to Change
Constraints
Area of Responsibility

Individual Characteristics

Personal values

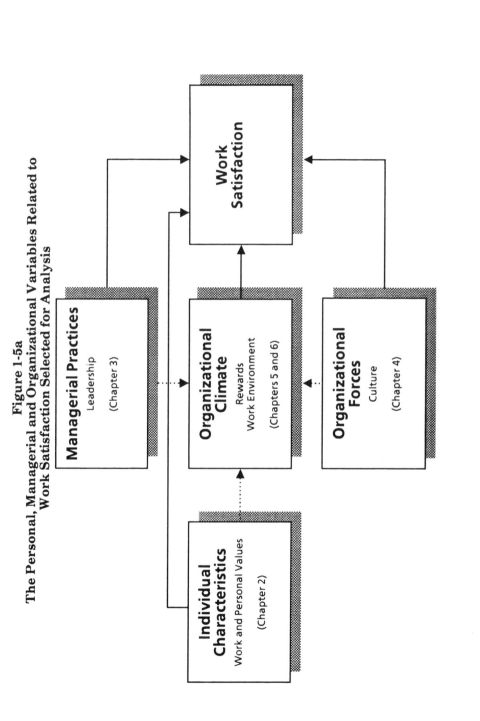

Figure 1-5a
The Personal, Managerial and Organizational Variables Related to Work Satisfaction Selected for Analysis

Work Satisfaction

Managerial Practices
Leadership

(Chapter 3)

Organizational Climate
Rewards
Work Environment

(Chapters 5 and 6)

Organizational Forces
Culture

(Chapter 4)

Individual Characteristics
Work and Personal Values

(Chapter 2)

norm, and decided that the private sector would serve as the best comparison. We therefore obtained information from senior managers with parallel responsibilities in the private sector.

We acknowledge at the outset that the private and public sectors are different, for reasons that have significant effects on how their constituent organizations are managed. First, the profit motive gives private sector executives a relatively clear view of long and short-term objectives, thereby helping to reduce the possibility of conflicting organizational goals. In the private sector, corporate goals tend to be defined, consistent and non-contradictory, whereas in the public sector the opposite is more likely the case. Similarly, the "output" of many government programs is difficult to identify in the absence of a benchmark like the private sector's bottom line. Also, the private sector generally is not subject to the same degree of public scrutiny as the public sector. Parliamentary committees, active interest groups, access to information, public curiosity, and media attention put public servants in a fish-bowl environment where all actions are potentially open to analysis and criticism. Another difference lies in the public sector's preoccupation with satisfying political imperatives—a notion foreign to the private sector where there is usually a clear understanding of corporate objectives.

Finally, conventional wisdom suggests that neither the board of directors nor the shareholders impose the same degree of administrative constraints on their private sector executives and senior managers as those imposed on public sector managers.

These differences in approach and environment may be critical in the institutional sense, but they really should have little to do with the type of management practiced by organizations. Managing should be part of the day-to-day activities of all individuals who have some responsibility for the performance of others in their organization whether it is in the public or private sector. In our view, the public sector, especially at senior levels, is a more complex environment in which to manage systems, work flow and human resources. Even so, we believe that the differences between the private and public sectors relate more to degree and emphasis than to kind.

Another reason for our reluctance to accept that the two sectors are inherently different is that when people speak of differences between the private and public sectors, they are usually comparing the activities of the deputy minister (DM) with those of the chief executive officer (CEO). There is no doubt that these two jobs require different skills, given the nature of the relationship between the DM and the minister and the political environment of the public service. However, our contention is that below the level of CEO/DM there is no evidence to suggest that the management practices of one sector should be significantly different, even after the sectors' fundamentally different objectives are taken into account.[17] For example, in both sectors responsible work units deliver products to clients and operate in layered environments subject to many external pressures. While their outputs vary considerably, both sectors attempt to serve clients within existing but often different constraints.

Finally, there is little doubt that management as a professional activity is more highly developed in the private sector. All major management theories have been preoccupied with private sector models and examples, with most having been tested in a private sector context. In those rare instances where the public sector or public management is discussed, it is almost always described in terms of public sector institutions (e.g., how the personnel system works) rather than management principles. This approach has tended to create a situation where the public sector, not having a managerial theory of its own, borrows from the literature arising from the private sector, often leading to unpredictable results and serious problems in implementation.

In the following chapters, the impact of a number of different factors in the management process on work satisfaction are analyzed as a function of respondents' job level in their private or public sector organization. In Chapter 2, work values, personality and perceptions of the public and private sectors are examined while chapter 3 is devoted to a look at the importance of leadership. The following chapters explore the relevance of organizational culture (chapter 4), the importance of rewards (chapter 5) and the significance of the work environment on work satisfaction (chapter 6). The last chapter (chapter 7) in this book is a synthesis of the results with some prescriptions for change in public sector management. Finally, the afterword provides an overview of the recently completed 1988 Survey of Managerial Attitudes.

Appendix 1-1
Federal Public Service Management Positions

For the purposes of this book the term "senior manager" refers to those public sector officials working one to five levels below the deputy minister in a federal department or agency. In the larger departments (e.g., Indian Affairs and Northern Development) there are also "associate deputy ministers" and "senior assistant deputy ministers" between the deputy minister and the assistant deputy ministers. Typically, those working four and five levels below the deputy minister can be referred to as "assistant directors" or "chiefs". The job classifications which carry a special job designation are most often categorized as shown in Table 1-1 below. It is impossible to summarize the organizational structure of the federal government in this table. But, for the reader who is interested in the typical federal department, it serves the purpose of associating the various job levels with the position of deputy minister, the highest ranking public servant in each department.

Table 1-1

	Executive			Senior Manager	Middle Manager
Title	Assistant Deputy Minister	Director General	Director	Assistant Director, Manager or Chief	Program Officer
Job Classification	EX4-5	EX2-3	EX1	SM	SM-1
Levels from Deputy Minister (DM)	1	2	3	4	5

Appendix 1-2
The Sample and Data Analysis

The Sample

A somewhat larger percentage of the public service participants worked in Ottawa (63 per cent) than those in the private sector who worked in head offices (51 per cent) (see Table 1-3). Private sector managers appeared somewhat younger but had less academic training than their counterparts. More than 40 per cent of public sector respondents claimed a graduate degree (MBA, MA, MSc, MPA, PhD) against 17 per cent in the private sector.

Only 6.8 per cent of respondents in the public sector were female, slightly below the 7.2 per cent in the private sector. Not surprisingly, 12 per cent of private sector respondents reported salaries of more than $90,000 (excluding bonuses and fringe benefits) while less than one per cent reported a similar level in the public sector. However, incomes between $50,000 and $70,000 were the most common level for both sectors, although a much larger percentage of public sector respondents (71 per cent) fell into this range than private sector (44 per cent).

As far as the span of the manager's control was concerned, the groups appeared similar. Sixteen per cent of public service managers indicated having more than 10 persons reporting directly to them, as opposed to 15 per cent of managers in the private sector.

The rate at which public sector managers progressed through the ranks when they compared themselves to their peer group is reported to be somewhat slower than for those in the private sector. As an example, 49 per cent of public servant respondents indicated that they had moved up through the federal government hierarchy at a faster rate than their peers, compared to 57 per cent of the private sector managers who responded to the survey.

Data Analysis

Since our interest is primarily in differences between public and private sector managers' perceptions of management practices in their own organizations, the basic unit of analysis is the individual respondent. While intercompany and interdepartmental comparisons would be fascinating, the small sample size would not yield reliable results.

All chapters present data from responses to closed and open-ended questions. In closed questions, respondents were given a five-point scale, although most of the tables summarize responses encompassing the two most favorable responses. That is, the tables represent the number of times respondents chose "4" or "5" on the five-point scale.

Tests were conducted to determine whether differences between the two sectors were attributable to chance or to differences in perceptions. The results in the body of the tables are statistically significant unless otherwise noted.

All the variables in the model described in Figure 1-5, such as culture and leadership, have been tested using bivariate analyses in terms of their relationship to the work satisfaction indices. Based on a factor analysis of the private and public sector samples, we have determined that there are five distinct work satisfaction indices from among the 15 satisfaction measures originally used. These measures are: intrinsic satisfaction; extrinsic satisfaction; job satisfaction; departmental satisfaction; and satisfaction with career progress. Intrinsic satisfaction is a composite of job independence, the degree of challenge in the work environment, and feeling of accomplishment. Extrinsic satisfaction was derived, again on the basis of factor analysis, from questions on pay, fringe benefits and job security.

In addition to these factors, three other indices were included as measures of satisfaction. The "job satisfaction" index was made up of items dealing with the degree to which managers agreed that their jobs were satisfying and the extent to which their jobs gave them feelings of personal satisfaction. The "departmental satisfaction" index (or company satisfaction index in the case of the private sector firms) was composed of answers to questions on the degree of pride respondents felt toward their organizations, the extent to which they perceived morale problems, and the overall departmental satisfaction they felt. In the private sector, satisfaction with one's company was measured in a similar way. Finally, answers to questions related to career progress as well as the perceived chances for advancement, made up the "progress satisfaction" index.

Since the job titles reported by respondents within and between the two sectors varied so much, it was imperative that a simple indicator be developed to make it relatively easy to compare the two sectors. As a result, tables display the results of comparisons between the public and private sectors, explained by a variable called "levels below CEO/DM". This variable was self-reported by respondents without any difficulty. As an example, when respondents said they worked one level below the DM/CEO, in most instances they occupied a senior vice president or assistant deputy minister position. Two levels below indicates a vice-president or director general position and so on.

Finally, each table contains an overall average result for each sector. This number, expressed in percentage terms, is a mathematical average of all responses. It does not reflect any weighing that may be used in future analyses of these data, which contain an over-sampling of the EX4 and EX5 groups. Although we believe that the study broaches an extremely important subject in the management of public sector organizations, there are limits to the depth to which one can interpret the data. For example, the attitudes of the vast majority of public servants who work below the level of SM-1 (or equivalent) in the federal government are not included. (See Table 1-2 for a breakdown of the sample.) As well, the nature of the sample does not allow comment on the attitudes of managers in individual departments or an explanation of whether interdepartmental differences are more important than intradepartmental differences. Moreover, it should be noted that the data represent the attitudes of managers during the summer of 1986, a particularly turbulent time in the federal public service when fears of downsizing were swirling in the heads of most public servants.

As mentioned in the preface, the 1986 study was followed in 1988 by a second survey of managers in the federal public service of Canada. The second survey included all federal government senior managers and executives in 65 departments and agencies—as opposed to the 1986 survey, which queried a random sample of managers and executives in 20 departments. The more recent study did not include a private sector component.

Our preliminary analysis of the 1988 survey indicates that there is little difference between the two data sets; where differences have been found they have tended to suggest that the managerial climate is somewhat worse than it was in 1986. The summary of the 1988 survey results, as distributed to the senior management cadre in the federal government, is included at the end of this publication.

Table 1-2
Public and Private Sector Respondents
Distributed by Levels Below the DM/CEO

| | Levels From the DM/CEO | | | | | | |
	1	2	3	4	5	Total	Respondents
Public Sector	18.4	25.5	26.8	19.4	10.1	100%	1981
Private Sector	22.6	25.3	27.3	12.9	10.9	100%	1284

Table 1-3
Characteristics of Public and Private Sector Respondents
(self-reported)

	Public Sector	Private Sector
Place of Work	(%)	(%)
Head Office/Ottawa	62.7	51.0
Not at Head Office/Not in National Capitol Region	37.3	49.0
Age		
Under 40	22.1	42.2
41-50	42.6	35.8
51-60	27.7	18.1
over 60	7.6	3.9
Sex		
Male	93.2	92.8
Female	6.8	7.2
Educational Attainment		
less than university	17.4	35.2
undergraduate degree	42.5	47.5
graduate degree	40.1	17.3
Salary		
less than 50k	5.8	22.6
50k-70k	81.0	43.7
70k-90k	12.4	21.4
greater than 90k	0.8	12.4
Progress through ranks		
slower than others	20.4	13.6
same as others	30.4	28.7
faster than others	49.2	56.8
Number of persons reporting directly to respondent		
none	12.6	8.2
1-5	45.5	51.1
6-10	25.9	26.2
more than 10	16.0	14.5
Work Experience		
1-10 years	2.2	11.3
11-20 years	35.2	39.0
more than 20 years	62.6	49.7

Notes

1. C.P. Snow, British novelist, and public servant, quoted by John Fraser in *The Globe and Mail*, (Toronto), 18 February 1975, p. 7.

2. S.L. Sutherland and G.B. Doern, *Bureaucracy in Canada, Control and Reform*, (Toronto: University of Toronto Press, 1985), p. 230.

3. Canada; Royal Commission on Government Organization (Chairman: John G. Glassco), vol. 1, (Ottawa: Queen's Printer, 1963).

4. Lambert, Canada; Royal Commission on Financial Management and Accountability, (Chairman: A.T. Lambert), *Final Report*, (Ottawa: Supply and Services Canada, 1979).

   D'Avignon, Canada; Special Committee on the Review of Personnel Management and the Merit Principle in the Public Service, (Chairman: G.R. D'Avignon), *Report of the Special Committee on the Review of Personnel Management and the Merit Principle*, (Ottawa: Supply and Services Canada, 1979).

   Minister of Supply & Services Canada, *Report of the Auditor General to the House of Commons*, 1983.

5. See D.R. Zussman, "Walking the tight rope: The Mulroney government and the public service in 1986-87," in M. Prince, ed., *How Ottawa Spends*, (Toronto: Methuen, 1987), pp. 250-282.

6. See D.R. Zussman, *Confidence in Canadian Government Institutions*, (Halifax, N.S.: Institute for Research on Public Policy, 1988), p. 80.

7. Public Service Commission, Annual Report, 1984, p. 14.

8. B. Adams, "The Frustrations of Government Service", *Public Administration Review*, vol. 44, no. 5, January 1984, p. 8.

9. In 1981-82 the Post Office moved from being a federal department to a Crown corporation, thereby decreasing the number of person-years in the public service by approximately 70,000.

10. N.S. Morgan, *Nowhere to Go? Possible Consequences of the Demographic Imbalance in Decision-Making Groups of the Federal Public Service*, (Halifax, N.S.: The Institute for Research on Public Policy, 1981).

11. J.L. Manion, "New challenges in public administration", The 1987 Donald Gow Memorial Lecture, Queen's University, Kingston, Ontario, September 25, 1987, p.1.

12. There are many theoretical discussions about the evolution of management thought and we suggest that the reader refer to the following for in-depth analysis: J. Pfeffer, *Organization and Organization Theory*, (Boston: Pitman, 1982); J.B. Miner, *Theories of Organizational Behavior*, (Hinsdale, Illinois: Dryden Press, 1980); J.B. Miner, *The Practice of Management*, (Columbus, Ohio: Charles E. Merrill, 1985); J.W. Lorsch (ed.), *Handbook of Organizational Behavior*, (Englewood Cliffs, N.J.: Prentice Hall, 1987).

13. In the lexicon of Ottawa, we were interested in people working at the SM and SM-1 levels.

14. The most common reason for not participating was that the companies were already conducting similar surveys for their own purposes.

15. The sole exception was a U.S.-owned subsidiary.

16. Job level was sampled according to these groupings: EX1 to EX3, EX4 and EX5, SM, and SM-1. Job location was defined as National Capital Region (NCR) and non-NCR.

17. Tim Plumptre has quoted Lyman who argues that the public sectors are "fundamentally similar in all unimportant ways" but he is referring to activities other than managerial ones. See T.W. Plumptre, *Beyond the Bottom Line: Management in Government*, (Halifax, N.S.: The Institute for Research on Public Policy, 1988), p. 458.

Chapter 2

Work Values, Personality Characteristics and Perceptions of the Public and Private Sectors

Introduction

One of the purposes in conducting this study was to consider whether some aspects of private sector management practices and techniques could be borrowed for use in the public sector. To gain some certainty that these practices would survive the transition, one would need an indication that the senior management cadres in both sectors share similar work values and personality characteristics.

By work values we mean a series of coherent, consistent and integrated attitudes to work-related issues. In particular, our interest is in those values which relate to respondents' decisions to work for their present employer, their feelings of personal responsibility, and the confidence they have in the role government can play in solving societal problems. All of these values should be important indicators of basic similarities and differences between managers in the two sectors.

Personality characteristics refer to "the dynamic organization within the individual of those psychological systems that determine his unique adjustments to his environment."[1] This definition stresses key notions, such as the "individuality of each person, the interplay of inner and outer forces, and the capacity of the system to change in response to demands from within and without."[2] In this instance, our interest is directed to those personality characteristics which could have impact on work-related behaviours or attitudes. In consequence, we chose to look at six personality traits that have been used in a number of work-related empirical studies. These will be described in detail in a later section of this chapter.

The last set of factors which attempts to tease out differences between public and private sector managers refers to respondents' perceptions of their counterparts in the other sector. The objective of this chapter is to determine, to the extent possible, whether there are basic differences in personality and work value characteristics between managers in the public and private sectors which would make it difficult to transfer management activities from one sector to the other. Therefore, it is important to know how each sector perceives the other.

The first part of this chapter discusses the influence of work values and personality on work behaviour. We then go on to examine perceptions of public and private sector respondents regarding their own work and personality values. The tables contain an analysis of respondents' feelings of responsibility for their work, their views on the role of the federal government in society, a discussion of the issues important to managers in their job choice and, finally, respondents' perceptions of those who work in the other sector.

The latter half of the chapter attempts to explain the linkage between work values and personality with the various indices of work satisfaction. In this way, we can weigh the importance of value and personality measures in predicting work satisfaction.

Influence of Work Values and Personality on Work Behaviour

It is worth taking a serious look at work values, since it has been established that they affect employee motivation which, in turn, has a significant impact on behaviour.[3] Through internalization, work and other types of values become incorporated into the individual's own value system—in effect becoming an expression of his or her self-image. Values affect not only perceptions of appropriate ends, but also perceptions of appropriate means to those ends. From the design and development of an organization's structure and processes, to the use of particular leadership styles and the evaluation of subordinates' performance, value systems are pervasive. Most theorists view values as stable and continuous. This assertion stems from the fact that it is not usually possible to obtain sudden and dramatic change in an individual.[4] As an example, one of the most influential theories of leadership is based on the argument that managers cannot be expected to adopt a particular leadership style if it is contrary to their "need structures" or value orientations.[5]

Work values are the sum of many attitudes and provide a reference for all future modes of conduct. Individuals differ both in the make-up of their value systems and in the weights they attach to them. Values are important because they underlie less stable attitudes and opinions and, as a consequence, have a profound influence on our behaviour. For example, it has been shown that someone who believes in pay for performance as the best form of compensation would have a difficult time working for an organization that rewards seniority over performance, despite all efforts to make the seniority equitable and transparent.[6]

As well, values are linked to attitude in the sense that a value serves as a way of organizing a number of attitudes. Values are defined as "the constellation of likes, dislikes, viewpoints, inner inclinations, rational and irrational judgments, prejudices, and association patterns that determine a person's view of the world."[7] Moreover, the importance of a value constellation is that, once internalized, it becomes a conscious or subconscious standard or criterion for guiding action. Thus, the study of work values is fundamental to the study of managing,[8] as well as to an understanding of managerial behaviour.

Another aspect of the importance of values is revealed when managers encounter different and potentially contradictory values. Studies have shown that assembly-line workers, scientists and those in various professional occupations are characterized by particular, if not unique, value orientations.[9] Day-to-day activities create numerous situations where managers must relate to others who have different ways of looking at common problems.

Personal values receive their share of attention in the management literature, but the issue of how employees' personality characteristics affect performance is perhaps one of the most complex and important matters managers have to deal with. An individual's personality is a "relatively stable set of characteristics, tendencies, and temperaments that have been significantly formed by inheritance and by social, cultural, and environmental factors. This set of variables determines the commonalities and differences in the behaviour of the individual."[10]

In considering each of the principal determinants that shape personality—such as heredity, culture, family composition and social class—we should note that the average individual has little control over or influence on these forces. The inability to influence the development of an employee's personality characteristics directly should not, however, lead the manager to conclude that personality is unimportant in the work place because it is largely determined outside the organization. The behavioural responses of an employee simply cannot be thoroughly understood without considering his or her own personality and values. In fact, personality and values are so inter-related with one's own perceptions and attitudes that any analysis of behaviour or any attempt to predict behaviour is incomplete unless these two factors are considered. This is the reason why the survey included a personality scale and a sense of work value questions. While one might assume that work values are commonly shared among managers, there are a lot of data which suggest that this type of generalization is invalid. For example, it is often noted that monetary rewards are the most highly valued aspect of a job. However, in a series of studies of managers conducted over a 40-year period by Kovach, it was found that what private sector employees want from their employers is, in order of preference: interesting work, full appreciation of work done, a feeling of being "in on things", job security, and good wages.[11] If we relate this list of employee ratings to Maslow's hierarchy of needs, or to Herzberg's two-factor theory, it becomes clear that private sector organizations, at least in the United States' industrial sector, have done a better job of satisfying the basic or "deficit" needs of their workers than they have of satisfying their ego or self-fulfilment needs.[12]

As an interesting expression of how managers' preferences can vary, each time Kovach conducted his study (1946, 1981 and 1986), supervisors were asked to rank job rewards as they believed their employees would rank them. Their rankings remained almost the same each year: good wages, job security, promotion opportunity, and growth in the organization. Of greatest relevance to our study is the fact that a comparison of the ranking shows that supervisors have a very inaccurate perception of what motivates employees. Why do managers continually place wages at the top of their hierarchy and the other motivators, which Maslow and Herzberg consider crucial, at the bottom? Several explanations are possible.

One reason could be that supervisors believe employees suspect that an interest in money and other basic needs is socially undesirable and, therefore, they pay lip-service to more socially acceptable factors, such as interesting work. On the other hand, it is also possible that employees are better witnesses to their own feelings than their supervisors. Another reason for the disparity may be that managers choose rewards for which they are less responsible, since few managers are directly responsible for compensation and other central personnel functions. Thus, they pass the buck and conveniently dismiss their managerial obligations as the responsibility of others.

Another theory that may explain this phenomenon can be called "self-reference." Managers offer rewards or behave toward employees in a way that would motivate themselves, but these are not necessarily the rewards and behaviours that will motivate their employees. David McClelland has argued that for managers, money is a quantifiable way of keeping score, although it may be of less relevance and importance to those working at lower levels.[13]

According to all three Kovach surveys, supervisors feel that money is the major motivator of their employees. But only three of almost 20 possible employee subgroups rated money as the most important reward. These groups were those under 30 years of age, those who earned under $12,000 (1986), and those who worked in the lower organizational levels.

From these data, it should be apparent that effective managerial practices require that individual differences be recognized and, where feasible, be taken into consideration in designing jobs, conducting performance evaluation interviews, and developing reward strategies to encourage improved performance. Some specific factors that contribute to individual differences in behaviour include personality and work values.

Work Values and Personal Attributes Surveyed
Joining the Public or Private Sector

Table 2-1 examines the differences between public and private sector respondents with regard to the factors that influenced their choice of employer. The reasons employees chose their employers have been grouped under intrinsic and extrinsic factors on the basis of a factor analysis, as a way of simplifying data presentation. Intrinsic factors are those affected by conditions or events under the control of the individual. Extrinsic factors subsume those imposed by external agents.

It appears that "challenge of work responsibilities" is significantly the most important of the nine possible factors considered as plausible reasons for choosing an employer. Almost 95 per cent of the public sector managers and 96 per cent of the private sector respondents indicated that work challenge was important or very important. This factor was clearly the most important of the possible choices, since it scarcely varied among the five levels of management and scored at least ten percentage points higher in the private sector and nearly 30 in the public than "opportunities for promotion", the second most important factor.

Among private sector managers, the next most important factors were all extrinsic (promotional opportunities, monetary rewards and fringe benefits). Within this grouping, there was some variation depending on location in the hierarchy. For example, the higher-ranking private sector respondents appeared less interested in job security or salary than those at the lower end of the managerial spectrum. As an example, 48 per cent of those working one level below the CEO said that job security was an important or very important factor in their decision to work for their present employer, as opposed

Table 2-1
Factors in Decision to Work for Present Employer
(per cent who chose "important" or "very important")

Factors:		1	2	3	4	5	Av.
		Levels below DM/CEO					

Factors:		1	2	3	4	5	Av.
Intrinsic							
Influence strategic	Public	64.8	51.3	42.4	37.8	40.3	47.7
decisions	Private	60.9	48.8	44.7	39.5	39.0	59.9
Further government/	Public	53.6	46.8	38.7	41.0	43.4	44.4
company goals	Private	73.9	59.4	54.1	47.3	52.6	61.0
Involved in public	Public	60.7	49.1	39.2	37.0	42.9	45.2
policy/company	Private	67.0	48.7	45.4	38.7	45.5	52.5
policy decisions							
Receiving recognition	Public	25.7	24.9	25.9	33.0	38.6	28.3
for work	Private	25.6	20.4	18.8	19.3	23.3	22.1
Challenge of work	Public	95.6	95.2	94.0	95.6	93.9	94.9
responsibilities	Private	97.2	94.7	95.9	97.0	94.9	96.1
Extrinsic							
Monetary rewards	Public	44.6	51.1	52.7	54.5	48.5	50.7
(salary)	Private	67.0	71.0	70.9	65.7	75.3	69.4
Job security	Public	39.9	52.1	57.7	63.6	68.1	54.1
	Private	48.2	58.0	59.4	62.5	69.7	56.8
Fringe benefits	Public	35.1	39.0	39.9	43.5	40.8	39.5
	Private	59.5	59.9	59.0	56.9	72.7	60.3
Opportunities for	Public	65.3	69.7	68.2	68.6	61.4	67.4
advancement at	Private	84.3	85.5	84.5	86.7	92.1	86.1
present level							

to 70 per cent of those working five levels below the CEO. This pattern was also found in the public sector data. Like their private sector counterparts, public servants suggested that opportunities for promotion were the second most important factor in their decision, although the strength of this choice was considerably less than in the private sector. This factor was followed in importance by job security and monetary rewards.

The least important of the factors was "recognition for work" which received a similar level of support in both the private and public sectors (28 per cent in the public sector, 22 per cent in the private sector). Having one's work recognized by peers and colleagues is usually seen as an important element in stimulating motivation in the work place. The generally low priority given to this option might reflect respondents' experiences in the work place where this work has not been recognized rather than their own personal preferences for some recognition. The low score might also be explained by arguing that, in choosing a job or career, prospective employees look at receiving recognition for work performed as a preferred but not an abstract concept with little expectation that it will matter.

The items that produced the largest differences between respondents from the two sectors were "furthering government/ company goals", "monetary rewards (salary)", "fringe benefits" and "opportunities for promotion". In each case, private sector respondents regarded these factors as more important than public sector respondents.

Within the public sector, two items showed some variation among job levels. First, job security was somewhat more important to those working five levels below the DM than to those working one level below the DM. Second, the only other factor that varied along hierarchical lines in the choice of employer was the index on the potential for involvement in public policy decisions. In this case, 61 per cent of respondents one level below the DM felt that being involved in a policy decision was important or very important in the decision to work for their present employer. In contrast, 43 per cent of those working five levels below the DM expressed the same degree of interest.

In the private sector, overall, the variation was larger between high-ranking executives and those at the lower end of the management cadre. Among the factors with the greatest variation were ability to "influence strategic decisions", "furthering company goals", "being involved in company decisions", and "job security". Except in the instance of job security, all items weighed more strongly with the high-level executives. Job security was of greater interest to the middle managers than to the executives.

In general, we are struck by both the similarities and the differences between public and private sector respondents in terms of the relative importance they ascribe to the factors in their decision to work for their present employer. Among the intrinsic factors, for example, both private and public sector respondents indicated their strongest preference for work offering challenging work responsibilities. This finding was consistent among all job levels regardless of sector.

Among private sector respondents, the second most important factor in the decision to work for their present employer was the opportunity for advancement at their present job level. More than 86 per cent of private sector respondents indicated that this factor was important or very important in their decision to accept employment. Ironically, this factor was also the second most important one for public sector managers although it was almost 19 per cent less valued than for private sector respondents. Other notable differences between the two sectors were the relative importance of fringe benefits, monetary rewards and furthering company or governmental goals, all of which were significantly less important for public sector managers than for private sector respondents.

Given the distribution of these findings between extrinsic and intrinsic factors, it is interesting to note that three of the four significantly different response patterns for public and private sector managers are to be found among the extrinsic factors. Public servants appear at this stage in the analysis to be relatively less motivated by extrinsic factors, such as salary, to seek employment in the public sector. Whether this finding reinforces the popular view that public servants are motivated to work in the interest of the public as opposed to private interest, is not altogether clear, although it does offer some supporting evidence.

Importance to Respondents of Intrinsic and Extrinsic Work Factors

The second table presents data on the importance of work-related factors in the respective environments. As in the previous table, these have been divided into intrinsic and extrinsic factors, on the basis of factor analyses of the public and private sector sample data. Table 2-2 indicates how "central" or important various work-related issues were to work satisfaction. We present these data in an attempt to unearth fundamental differences in values or motivation between managers in the two sectors.

It should be obvious from the data that public servants were not particularly different from their private sector counterparts on a large number of the items. For example, feelings of accomplishment, job challenge, respect from one's superiors, and independence and freedom

Table 2-2
Importance of Intrinsic and Extrinsic Motivational Factors
to Work Satisfaction
(per cent who indicate "important" or "very important")

Importance to you of:		Levels below DM/CEO					
		1	2	3	4	5	Av.
Intrinsic Factors							
Satisfaction with	Public	95.0	93.7	89.8	89.0	89.7	91.7
department	Private	98.9	98.7	95.9	96.4	97.1	97.8
Feelings of accom-	Public	98.9	99.0	98.5	98.9	99.0	98.9
plishment	Private	100.0	98.8	99.6	98.8	98.6	99.3
Independent thought	Public	98.9	99.2	98.8	96.9	98.4	98.5
and action on the job	Private	98.6	97.4	97.3	97.5	100.0	98.4
Amount of job	Public	98.9	98.5	97.9	97.5	98.2	98.2
challenge	Private	98.4	98.8	98.2	98.2	98.6	98.4
Respect received	Public	98.0	96.6	96.8	94.5	91.3	96.0
from superiors	Private	98.3	97.5	96.8	98.8	99.3	98.0
Opportunity to	Public	87.3	71.3	66.0	63.0	61.8	68.4
influence strategic decisions	Private	87.9	83.1	81.5	78.8	83.1	83.8
Furthering organiza-	Public	85.3	80.7	73.5	75.4	69.4	77.5
tion's goals	Private	97.9	96.9	91.3	90.3	94.3	95.1
Involvement in	Public	78.4	67.5	63.3	58.8	52.9	65.2
important policy decisions	Private	89.1	81.7	78.6	74.5	86.3	83.2
Extrinsic Factors							
Monetary rewards	Public	85.2	80.6	85.5	82.9	79.1	83.1
(salary)	Private	91.4	89.9	93.2	93.4	95.7	92.1
Fringe benefits	Public	70.2	69.5	69.7	67.2	60.7	68.4
	Private	85.4	84.9	82.9	86.7	91.4	85.7
Career progress	Public	86.8	86.3	84.4	81.2	80.0	84.3
made until now	Private	93.2	96.9	90.9	89.7	95.0	93.5
Opportunities for	Public	65.3	69.7	68.2	68.6	61.4	64.4
advancement at present level	Private	85.3	85.5	84.5	86.7	92.1	80.4
Public recognition	Public	43.0	40.0	46.6	51.8	51.1	45.7
	Private	44.2	41.6	36.7	35.4	42.5	40.9
Job security	Public	63.1	74.2	80.4	79.5	80.5	75.4
	Private	69.9	77.3	79.6	76.5	92.1	76.7

of action on the job were perceived in both sectors as extremely important in achieving work satisfaction.

Public servants were less interested in the opportunity to influence strategic decisions, to further organizational goals, and to be involved in important policy decisions, while these were considered very important factors by a large majority of private sector respondents. Similarly, public servants attached less importance to pay, fringe benefits, and chances for advancement than their private sector counterparts.

Within each sector, some factors varied considerably more than others, as one moved down the management hierarchy. For example, the importance of the "opportunity to influence strategic decisions", "furthering organization's goals", of "involvement in important policy decisions" and "job security" scored significantly differently, depending on a respondent's position in the organization. In the private sector, there was considerably less variation within the management hierarchy—save for "job security", which increased in importance as one moved down the managerial structure. As well, many of these findings displayed a curvilinear relationship between job level and the "importance" factors.

Facing Responsibility

Part of the survey dealing with personal values also contained items exploring differences between public and private sector managers' more general views of work and society. Table 2-3 lists items dealing with personal responsibility and the degree to which respondents value the role of government in solving the nation's problems. Few differences were noted among respondents with regard to feelings of personal responsibility and accountability. Overall, 94 per cent of public servants and 98 per cent of private sector respondents indicated that they "agreed" or "strongly agreed" with the statement that they felt personal responsibility for the work they performed. Almost an equal percentage of respondents suggested that they felt personally accountable for the results of their work. While there was some variation among the public sector managers in responding to the personal responsibility question, there was little within the private sector cadre.

Confidence in the Federal Government

In designing this study, we felt that tapping managers' perceptions of government efficacy might give us further insight into how managers went about choosing the sectors in which they work. We were intrigued to know if public sector managers might be motivated to work for the federal government because they felt that government could more effectively solve the nation's problems than did those who chose to work in the private sector. Despite the theoretical appeal of this item, however, neither group of respondents indicated much confidence in the ability of the federal government to solve the nation's problems (see Table 2-3). Their scepticism was most extreme at lower ends of the management structure, where five per cent of private sector managers agreed or strongly agreed that they were confident of the government's ability to solve the nation's problems; 12 per cent of public sector managers indicated the same sentiment. The group who expressed the greatest confidence in the federal government's ability to solve the nation's problems were the public sector executives (i.e., one or two levels below DM) but only 17 to 19 per cent of them agreed or strongly agreed with that viewpoint.

Table 2-3
Expressions of Personal Responsibility and Confidence in the Federal Government's Ability to Solve the Nation's Problems
(per cent who "agree" or "strongly agree")

		Levels below DM/CEO					
		1	2	3	4	5	Av.
Personal Responsibility							
Feelings of personal responsibility for work done on this job	Public	97.5	94.9	92.1	94.0	90.3	94.0
	Private	98.2	97.9	96.4	98.8	99.3	97.9
Personal accountability for the results of work done on this job	Public	89.0	90.0	86.9	88.7	87.2	88.6
	Private	92.1	93.2	92.3	81.6	93.5	92.5
Confidence in the Federal Government							
Confidence in the ability of the federal government to solve the nation's problems	Public	19.1	16.8	16.1	15.9	12.3	16.4
	Private	6.8	6.9	6.4	6.1	5.1	6.5

Motivational Traits

Turning to the personality characteristics of public and private sector managers, we found that the differences between average scores for each sector were, on an absolute basis, not very large, although the statistical tests did yield significant differences (see Table 2-4). For example, the "acquisitiveness" and "competitiveness" scales demonstrated that private sector managers were more competitive than public sector managers in their level of competitiveness, their desire to compete and their enjoyment in surpassing others in the work place. As well, they were more interested in material rewards than the public sector managers.[14] This means that private sector managers rated the need for economic gain significantly higher, seeing wealth as a good measure of success, than did their counterparts in the public sector.[15] These two characteristics, acquisitiveness and competitiveness, appear particularly to differentiate managers at the lower level in the two sectors.

Table 2-4
Personality Differences Between Public and Private Sector Senior Managers
(means and standard deviations)

Personality Scales:		Levels below DM/CEO						
		1	2	3	4	5	Av.	SD
Concern of excel-	Public	22.4	22.2	21.9	22.0	22.1	22.1	3.1
lence	Private	21.9	21.8	22.0	22.4	22.2	22.2	3.1
Acquisitiveness	Public	16.3	16.6	16.6	16.3	15.8	16.4	3.9
	Private	18.6	18.5	18.7	18.5	18.1	18.5	3.9
Status with peers	Public	18.3	17.8	17.7	17.7	17.3	17.8	3.2
	Private	18.4	18.2	18.1	18.4	18.0	18.2	3.2
Achievement via	Public	16.4	16.3	16.0	15.8	16.5	16.2	3.7
independence	Private	15.6	15.2	16.7	16.6	17.0	16.2	3.7
Status with experts	Public	18.6	18.6	18.2	18.4	18.1	18.4	3.4
	Private	19.2	18.8	19.0	18.6	19.3	19.0	3.3
Competitiveness	Public	17.2	16.8	16.4	16.4	16.6	16.7	3.8
	Private	18.0	17.6	18.0	17.8	18.2	18.0	3.7

*1   Av = Average on a scale of 3 to 27

2   SD = Standard Deviation

Within the two sectors, personality scores did not vary much among the various management levels. One possible exception involved "status with peers", which measures the degree to which respondents wished to seek the company and approval of peers. Scores were lower in the public sector for the middle manager group than for the senior executives, although the differences were marginal.

Public and Private: Perceptions about Each Other

There is a point of view in the public sector that a private sector approach to management is the best model for managing people in large organizations. This line of argument is predicated on the assumption that the methods and procedures of the private sector are easily transferred from one sector to the other. This section of the chapter further explains the degree to which managers in one sector have differing perceptions of the other's work place. This was done by asking respondents to judge the qualities of those who work in the other sector as well as the general characteristics of the public or private sector. In so doing, we were interested in determining, to the extent possible, whether there is enough of a consensus as to the characteristics of the other sector to allow for a transfer of methods. In Tables 2-5 and 2-6, respondents were asked to judge the qualities of the other sector in a number of dimensions. These were grouped under two general factors. The first contains items that describe people-oriented attributes. This includes attributes of employees such as their innovativeness, propensity to take risks, and honesty. The second factor includes institutional attributes, such as job stress, pay and work satisfaction.

Respondents were asked to rate a range of people-oriented and institutional attributes on a five-point scale, according to whether they thought an attribute was significantly more, somewhat more, neither more nor less, somewhat less, or significantly less prevalent in one sector than in the other. The results were collapsed into three response categories for ease of interpretation and presentation. Table 2-5 contains the responses of public sector managers, Table 2-6 the private sector response. One column shows the percentage of respondents who felt that a given attribute was found less often than in their own particular sector; a second column shows those who believed the attribute was present equally in both sectors; a third shows those who found the attribute more often in the other than in their own sector.

The public sector results in Table 2-5 suggest that, on average, public servants did not perceive large differences between the two sectors with regard to people-oriented attributes. For example, 24 per cent of public sector respondents felt that the private sector was more innovative, 18 per cent indicated that it was less innovative, and 58 per cent suggested that there was no essential difference. As further examples, leadership and work effort were also perceived by public servants to be similar in both sectors. Only risk-taking and motivation were thought to be significantly more prevalent in the private sector. Aside from the perceived risk-taking characteristics of private sector managers, most public sector managers felt that they were not necessarily different from their private sector counterparts. For example, public servants thought that leadership, efficiency, management skills and work effort were equally prevalent in both sectors.

Table 2-5
Public Sector Senior Managers' Perceptions
of the Private Sector

	Less or much less than in the public sector	Same as in the public sector	More or much more than in the public sector
People-Oriented Attributes			
Innovativeness	17.5[1]	58.0	24.4
Risk-taking	5.7	28.6	65.8
Work effort	13.7	74.2	12.1
Motivation	7.7	67.1	25.2
Leadership	13.3	69.3	17.4
Efficiency	10.2	71.4	18.5
Getting things done	8.0	55.0	37.0
Commitment to excellence	19.1	71.5	9.4
Management skills	16.2	73.1	10.8
Honesty	22.4	76.4	1.3
Institutional Attributes			
Job stress	22.4	52.8	24.8
Pay	7.4	36.0	56.5
Fringe benefits	14.5	27.2	58.4
Work satisfaction	11.3	54.8	33.9
Incentive awards (e.g., bonuses)	1.1	5.2	93.7
Opportunities for advancement at present level	2.8	37.2	60.0
Autonomy	9.8	35.7	54.5

[1] per cent

However, when it came to institutional attributes, such as incentive awards, pay, work satisfaction, opportunity for advancement and job autonomy, we found that public sector managers consistently perceived the private sector to be much more heavily endowed with these attributes. As an example, almost 34 per cent of public servants saw private sector managers as being more satisfied at work, while only 11 per cent saw them as less satisfied.

The single attribute thought to be less prevalent in the private sector was employee honesty. Twenty-two per cent of public servants

Table 2-6
Private Sector Senior Managers' Perceptions
of the Public Sector

	Less or much less than in the private sector	Same as in the private sector	More or much more than in the private sector
People-Oriented Attributes			
Innovativeness	69.1[1]	29.4	1.5
Risk-taking	79.6	17.7	2.7
Work effort	76.6	22.6	0.8
Motivation	72.5	25.5	1.9
Leadership	64.3	33.8	1.9
Efficiency	71.5	27.4	1.0
Getting things done	58.2	40.3	1.5
Commitment to excellence	67.6	31.5	0.8
Management skills	38.7	58.8	2.5
Honesty	13.0	85.7	1.3
Institutional Attributes			
Job stress	73.9	22.8	3.3
Pay	28.3	45.9	25.9
Fringe benefits	11.8	35.4	52.8
Work satisfaction	66.4	31.0	2.6
Incentive awards (e.g., bonuses)	50.0	34.1	15.9
Opportunities for advancement at present level	24.5	50.5	25.0
Autonomy	68.2	27.6	4.3

[1] per cent

saw employees in the private sector as less honest than public sector employees, while 76 per cent perceived the sectors to be essentially the same. In all other instances, public sector attributes were seen to be similar to those of the private sector or less prevalent.

Table 2-6 shows the public sector as evaluated by private sector respondents. Private sector managers were extremely harsh in their assessment of the public sector. With regard to the people-oriented attributes, in all but one instance, private sector respondents saw these as significantly more prevalent in the private sector. As an example of this lopsided weighting, 69 per cent of private sector managers thought the public sector was less innovative than their own sector, while 80 per cent held a similar view about risk-taking. In response to questions about the honesty of those working in each sector, private sector managers shed their feelings of superiority, indicating in large numbers (86 per cent) that public sector managers are as honest as private sector managers.

The private sector respondents were equally harsh in regards to the institutional attributes as they were with the people-oriented attributes. Private sector managers felt that public servants worked in a less stressful environment, had much less work satisfaction and much less autonomy. However, contrary to their public sector counterparts, they also thought that the public servants received better fringe benefits, had equal opportunities for advancement, and were better paid or equally well paid.

Analyzing differences in perceptions according to position in the hierarchy reveals additional insights. To simplify this complex issue, Table 2-7 shows public sector managers' perceptions of the private sector and private sector views of the public sector with regard to the prevalence of various attributes ("less" or "much less") in the other sector.

For example, 20 per cent of public sector respondents working one level below the DM thought that the private sector was less innovative than the public sector. This is in stark contrast to private sector respondents working one level below the CEO, where 62 per cent suggested that the public sector was less innovative. In this sense, the two groups of respondents held a similar view of the relative degree of innovativeness of their own sectors.

Public sector respondents, regardless of level, held similar views regarding the private sector on a number of scales. However, the "vertical solitude" pattern emerged in a number of instances. For example, 40 per cent of executives working one level below the DM indicated that the private sector exerted less "work effort" than the public sector, while only nine per cent of those working five levels below the DM felt the same way. A less dramatic spread was observed

Table 2-7
Public and Private Sector Managers' Perceptions of the Other Sector by Level of Respondent

Levels below DM/CEO	Public Sector View of Private Sector					Private Sector View of Public Sector				
	1	2	3	4	5	1	2	3	4	5
People-Oriented Attributes										
Innovativeness	20.4[1]	19.2	18.3	14.7	16.5	61.8	61.9	59.0	75.1	79.3
Risk-taking	13.3	5.9	6.5	4.9	4.1	82.6	80.2	80.7	78.4	77.0
Work effort	40.0	20.9	13.4	10.7	9.1	75.3	71.2	78.6	72.7	76.4
Motivation	11.1	9.8	8.6	6.3	6.4	73.9	72.3	78.7	77.5	74.2
Leadership	22.2	19.3	13.2	12.5	10.4	65.2	65.5	62.2	67.0	62.5
Efficiency	22.2	11.8	9.3	9.4	8.6	78.1	64.7	68.5	81.3	78.0
Getting things done	15.5	7.9	9.3	7.4	5.4	40.5	45.9	54.6	71.2	70.0
Commitment to excellence	31.1	17.9	19.2	17.4	18.7	63.8	65.0	56.2	69.9	70.7
Management skills	26.6	20.0	16.5	15.3	13.6	33.3	32.8	36.2	44.2	46.6
Honesty	22.2	21.7	23.5	19.7	24.5	10.3	10.2	13.0	15.3	19.5
Institutional Attributes										
Job stress	35.5	31.3	24.9	19.0	18.6	63.8	69.9	75.4	77.0	80.1
Pay	4.6	3.9	6.3	10.4	7.5	27.5	28.2	27.2	29.6	30.9
Fringe benefits	4.6	10.4	15.2	16.7	13.7	10.1	12.6	10.3	12.5	14.9
Work satisfaction	20.0	13.4	10.6	10.2	10.2	69.5	69.5	66.7	63.6	67.1
Incentive awards	2.3	1.3	1.0	1.2	0.8	53.6	53.1	57.3	47.6	39.0
Opportunities for advancement at present level	2.3	3.9	3.7	2.0	2.4	26.4	28.6	27.3	19.7	22.3
Autonomy	8.9	10.5	9.0	9.8	9.3	77.9	82.4	67.2	66.5	67.5

[1] (per cent who indicated "much less" or "less" than in sector of respondent)

in views on risk-taking, leadership, efficiency, commitment to excellence, getting things done, job stress and work satisfaction. The only case where the trend was reversed was fringe benefits, where a proportionately larger number of lower-ranking public servants (14 per cent) than those working one level below the DM saw fringe benefits as more generous in the public sector.

Values, Personality and Socio-Demographic Variables: Is There a Relationship?

To understand how values might have developed, we conducted a series of analyses to explain these findings. It seemed likely, given our understanding of how values are formed and of their relative permanence once they are part of an individual's value system, that a number of socio-demographic characteristics might determine work-related values. Accordingly, the data were looked at in terms of the possible impact of public sector respondents' ages, educational levels and work experience on the personality, importance in job choice and the "importance to you" items.[16, 17]

The results are summarized in Table 2-8, which indicates whether age, educational level and work experience are related to the value scores of public sector respondents. "Yes" indicates that a factor is statistically related. Overall, it does not appear that age, educational level and work experience are as powerful predictors of values as one might expect. Except for a few instances, discussed below, the impact of socio-economic factors on importance in job choice appears to be slight. But the age and level of education of respondents were important predictors of a number of the personality variables. For instance, both age and education were related to respondents' degree of acquisitiveness and level of competitiveness. Figures 2-1 and 2-2 demonstrate the extent of this relationship. In the case of acquisitiveness and educational level among the public sector respondents, those with higher levels of formal education, regardless of job level, were less interested in material gain. This relationship was most obvious in the case of the EX group.[18]

Competitiveness appeared to be related to the age of public sector respondents, even when controlling for job level. As seen in Figure 2-2, lower-level managers between 41 and 55 years of age[19] indicated a less competitive nature than younger respondents, although the overall level of competitiveness increased as one moved up the organizational hierarchy.

Table 2-8
Relationship Between Values and Socio-economic Factors
(public sector)

	Socio-economic Factors		
	Age	Education	Experience
Personality			
Acquisitiveness	Yes*	Yes	No
Concern for excellence	No	Yes	Yes
Status with peers	Yes	No	No
Achievement via independence	No	No	No
Competitiveness	Yes	Yes	No
Status with experts	No	No	No
Importance in job choice			
Salary	No	No	No
Job security	Yes	Yes	Yes
Opportunities for advancement at present level	No	No	No
Importance of:			
Satisfaction with organization	No	No	No
Independent thought	No	No	No
Pay	No	No	No
Job security	Yes	No	No

*   "Yes" indicates statistical significance while "No" indicates that the results are not statistically significant.

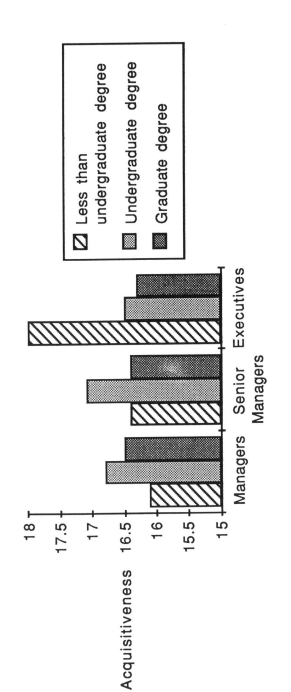

Figure 2-1
Acquisitiveness and Educational Level of Public Sector Respondents

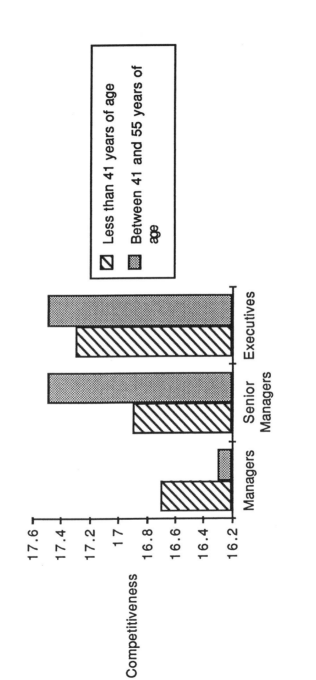

Figure 2-2
Competitiveness and Age of Public Sector Respondents

Relating Values to Outcome Measures: The Influence of Values and Personality on Work Satisfaction

Two of the more important factors in public sector respondents' choices of jobs, opportunities for promotion and challenging work responsibilities, were measured against the five work satisfaction indices to see to what extent personal values might be related to satisfaction. In the case of opportunities for promotion (Table 2-9), there did not appear to be much relationship to work satisfaction. Those who did not feel that opportunities for promotion were important in their decisions to work for their present employers were not appreciably more satisfied with their work, regardless of how satisfaction was measured.

Despite the restricted range (because of the small number of respondents who indicated that work responsibilities were unimportant to them in choosing their present employers), work responsibility had a significant impact on work satisfaction. In the case of intrinsic satisfaction, departmental satisfaction and job satisfaction, we observed a significant increase in work satisfaction when respondents placed a heavier emphasis on work responsibilities. Neither extrinsic satisfaction nor satisfaction with career progress was particularly affected by these variables.

This finding clearly suggests that managers, particularly those who said challenging work responsibilities were important, were also more likely to report higher levels of work satisfaction. This was especially the case for the intrinsic and job satisfaction components of work satisfaction.

We found a similar pattern of results when respondents were confident of the federal government's ability to solve the nation's problems (Table 2-10). Not surprisingly, those who indicated full confidence in the government's ability were relatively more satisfied with their work than those who expressed a great deal of scepticism.

Finally, the six personality factors were subjected to an analysis similar to that for previous variables. Acquisitiveness and competitiveness were chosen because they were revealed to be more prevalent in the private sector than in the public sector (Table 2-11), and might uncover some fundamental differences between the two sectors. Respondents who scored low in acquisitiveness, on average, were more satisfied with their work than were those who were particularly acquisitive. The most sensitive of the satisfaction indices was extrinsic satisfaction, which moved from 29 per cent to 43 per cent as a respondent scored higher on the scale of acquisitiveness. Competitiveness, on the other hand, had an opposite effect on the work satisfaction indices. For example, the level of job satisfaction was 49 per cent for those respondents who were low on the competitiveness scale, compared with 63 per cent for the highly competitive.

Table 2-9
Determinants of Job Choice and Work Satisfaction
(public sector)

Indices of Work Satisfaction	Importance of: Opportunities for promotion				
	Very Unimportant	Unimportant	Neither Important nor Unimportant	Important	Very Important
Intrinsic Satisfaction	50.9[1]	54.1	57.1	53.4	54.2
Extrinsic Satisfaction	29.4	37.3	33.1	34.7	33.5
Departmental Satisfaction	21.6	24.8	26.2	25.7	32.0
Job Satisfaction	54.7	62.7	58.5	59.1	58.8
Satisfaction with Career Progress	20.0	30.2	26.6	29.2	25.5

Indices of Work Satisfaction	Importance of: Challenging work responsibilities				
	Very Unimportant	Unimportant	Neither Important nor Unimportant	Important	Very Important
Intrinsic Satisfaction	*	*	31.1	48.8	61.5
Extrinsic Satisfaction	*	*	32.9	34.8	33.7
Departmental Satisfaction	*	*	10.8	22.3	31.8
Job Satisfaction	*	*	31.1	51.5	68.3
Satisfaction with Career Progress	*	*	23.3	26.0	30.1

*   small sample size

1   per cent who are "satisfied" or "very satisfied"

Table 2-10
Relationship between the Perceived Ability of the
Federal Government to Solve the Nation's Problems
and Work Satisfaction
(public sector)

Ability of the Federal Government to Solve the Nation's Problems

	Strongly Disagree	Disagree	Neither Agree Nor disagree	Agree	Strongly Agree
Intrinsic Satisfaction	32.5[1]	49.0	56.9	68.1	*
Extrinsic Satisfaction	26.8	34.2	33.1	42.0	*
Departmental Satisfaction	11.5	20.7	27.6	42.2	*
Job Satisfaction	34.2	53.0	63.2	70.2	*
Satisfaction with Career Progress	13.5	23.6	29.3	42.2	*

* small sample size
[1] per cent who are "satisfied" or "very satisfied"

Job Level, Values and Satisfaction

Turning our attention to the effect of job level on the interaction between personality and respondents' job satisfaction, we found that personality did not appear to exercise much influence on job satisfaction as a function of job level (Table 2-12). In both groups of managers, those scoring high and medium on a three-point scale measuring their concern for excellence and their competitiveness were found to be most satisfied with their jobs when they worked at higher levels in the hierarchy. While differences in levels of job satisfaction were greatest among those with the greatest concern for excellence (72 per cent one level below the DM versus 51 per cent five levels below), or for those who exhibited only medium levels of competitiveness (71 per cent one level below versus 49 per cent five levels below), the vertical solitude appeared, albeit in a diminished form, in the other categories as well.

Table 2-11
Relationship between Personality and Work Satisfaction
(public sector)

	Low[1]	Medium	High
Acquisitiveness			
Intrinsic Satisfaction	63.0[2]	54.0	53.2
Extrinsic Satisfaction	43.4	36.1	28.6
Departmental Satisfaction	30.0	25.5	28.2
Job Satisfaction	70.0	58.2	58.5
Satisfaction with Career Progress	40.4	27.3	27.2
Competitiveness			
Intrinsic Satisfaction	51.7	51.7	59.5
Extrinsic Satisfaction	39.0	36.7	28.9
Departmental Satisfaction	13.6	25.8	29.3
Job Satisfaction	49.2	57.4	62.7
Satisfaction with Career Progress	22.4	27.2	29.8

[1]   The respondents were divided into three groups (Low, Medium, High) according to their responses on the two personality measures

[2]   per cent who are "satisfied" or "very satisfied"

Table 2-13 contains a somewhat more complex analysis of the potential impact of job level and personal values on job satisfaction. Two measures of personal values are included as an example of how this class of factors performed under this mode of scrutiny. For example, in the case of the importance public sector managers placed on promotion opportunities in their decision to work for their present departments, we found that job level had only a minor impact on job satisfaction. That is, in instances where employees said opportunities for promotion were important to them, the vertical solitude essentially disappeared, except for executives working one level below the DM, who were generally more satisfied with their jobs. The effect of the vertical solitude was also less prominent for those respondents who indicated that opportunities for promotion were important in their decision to work for their present employer.

Looking at managers' confidence in the ability of the federal government to solve the nation's problems, we found a similar pattern.

Table 2-12
Personality and Job Satisfaction Controlling for Job Level
(public sector)

Levels below DM	Low	Medium	High
Concern for Excellence			
1	*	66.7[1]	71.9
2	*	53.6	59.1
3	*	40.3	57.1
4	*	50.0	58.4
5	*	60.9	50.9
Competitiveness			
1	*	71.0	71.9
2	*	58.5	61.6
3	*	52.3	60.5
4	*	55.6	58.9
5	*	49.2	57.6

* Small sample sizes
[1] per cent who are "satisfied" or "very satisfied"

For those who thought the federal government could solve the nation's problems, job satisfaction varied from 83 per cent at one working level below the DM, to 64 per cent at three levels below the DM. As in the earlier case, the vertical solitude—usually a steady downward trend line as one moves down the hierarchy—was not as clearly defined. Even among optimists who felt that governments could solve problems, only the executives one level below the DM remained relatively satisfied with their jobs; everyone in the remaining four groupings expressed essentially the same levels of job satisfaction.

Values and Personality: Little Difference Between Private and Public Sector Managers

In terms of their motives in choosing a job, there appeared to be little that distinguishes managers in the private and public sectors. Job challenge appeared to be the principal source of motivation for managers, regardless of sector or level in the hierarchy. We found greater variation among the private sector respondents with regard to the importance of job challenge, indicating that private sector

Table 2-13
**The Effect of Factors in Decision to Work for Present Employer,
and Confidence in Government's Perceived Ability to Solve
Problems on Job Satisfaction Controlling for Job Level**
(public sector)

Levels below DM	Unimportant	Neither	Important
Opportunities for promotion advancement at present level			
1	80.8[1]	81.7	66.5
2	64.1	54.9	59.7
3	57.7	56.3	53.4
4	*	51.6	59.3
5	*	43.9	53.9
Confidence in the Ability of the Federal Government to Solve the Nation's Problems			
1	66.1	73.7	83.1
2	54.3	61.9	69.7
3	45.9	61.3	63.6
4	50.4	62.5	66.0
5	51.1	53.6	66.7

* Small sample sizes
[1] per cent who are "satisfied" or "very satisfied"

managers are likely to be more heterogeneous than those in the public sector.

On general measures of values, such as personal responsibility and confidence in the government's ability to solve problems, we found few significant differences between the two sectors, although some interesting findings did emerge. For example, public servants were less interested in the opportunity to influence strategic decisions, less interested in furthering organizational goals, and less interested in the opportunity to be involved in important decisions.

As for personality differences, private sector respondents rated significantly higher on scales of acquisitiveness and competitiveness. These findings were subsequently confirmed through analyses of the perceptions of respondents with regard to managers in the other sector. Private sector respondents proved unkind in their assessment of the public sector and the people who work there. Except for one factor, honesty, the private sector saw itself as being far superior on a range of attributes, both institutional and personal. On the other hand, public sector respondents saw themselves as essentially the same as the private sector with regard to the institutional factors, but far behind on the people-oriented attributes.

By linking job satisfaction to the various work value factors, we found that high levels of commitment to work responsibilities and confidence in the federal government's ability to solve problems were associated with higher levels of work satisfaction. As well, two aspects of personality—acquisitiveness and competitiveness—produced different levels of work satisfaction, depending on how significant they were for each manager. Typically, public sector managers low in acquisitiveness and high in competitiveness expressed higher levels of work satisfaction, particularly job and intrinsic satisfaction.

Notes

1. G.W. Allport, *Personality: A Psychological Interpretation*, (New York: Henry Holt, 1937), p. 48.

2. H. Gough, "Personality Assessment," in *Handbook of Industrial and Organizational Psychology"*, M.D. Dunnette, ed., (New York: Rand McNally, 1974), p. 573.

3. In the field of social psychology, there are many different value systems. See D. Katz and R. Kahn, *The Social Psychology of Organization* (New York: John Wiley and Sons, 1978), p. 361. Given the nature of this study, we have limited our investigation to those values which are directly related to the work place.

4. S. Maddi, *Personality Theories: A Comparative Analysis* (Homewood, Ill.: Dorsey Press, 1980), p. 41.

5. F. Fiedler, *A Theory of Leadership Effectiveness* (New York: McGraw Hill, 1967), p. 310.

6. G.W. England, *The Manager and His Values: An International Perspective from the United States, Japan, Korea, India, and Australia*, (Cambridge: Mass.: Ballinger, 1975), p. 177.

7. E. Spranger, *Types of Men* (Halle, Germany: Max Niemeyer Verlag, 1928), as quoted in V.S. Flowers *et al.*, *Managerial Values for Working*, (New York: American Management Association, 1975), p. 11.

8. A. Sikula, "Values, Value Systems, and Their Relationship to Organizational Effectiveness," Proceedings of the Thirty-First Annual Meeting of the Academy of Management, 1971, pp. 271-272.

9. See R. Tagiuri, "Value orientations and relationships of managers and scientists," *Administrative Science Quarterly*, vol. 10, no. 2, (June, 1965), pp. 39-51.

10. Maddi, p. 41.

11. K.A. Kovach, "What motivates employees? Workers and supervisors give different answers," *Business Horizons*, vol. 30, no. 5, (September-October, 1987), pp. 58-65.

12. Kovach, pp. 58-65.

13. D.C. McClelland, *The Role of Money in Managing Motivation, Managerial Motivation and Compensation*, (Ann Arbor: University of Michigan, 1972), p. 527.

14. Despite the apparent small difference between the averages, the large sample size and relatively low variability of the results yielded statistically very significant results.

15. See N. Islam and S. Ahmed, "Business Influence of Government: A Comparison of Public and Private Sector Perceptions," *Canadian Public Administration*, 1984, vol. 27, no. 1, pp. 87-101, for a more detailed description of the personality scales. As in this study, the authors, who used a more restricted sample, found acquisitiveness to be higher among business people than among public servants.

16. An analysis of variance (ANOVA) was carried out on the data.

17. Sex was not included because only seven per cent of the sample were women.

18. No private sector data have been presented in this figure or any of the following tables in this chapter since our primary concern is public sector management.

19. There were too few public servants above 55 years of age who are SMs or above to warrant a separate analysis.

Chapter 3

Leadership

Introduction

Both observers and experts in management issues concur that leadership, particularly the level of leadership provided by those at the top, is one of the key elements in explaining the success of those organizations which have prospered during this decade. Many of North America's most established and historically profitable organizations have been criticized for their lack of competitiveness, and some of the critics' frustrations stem from what they see as poor leadership. Lack of innovation, an aversion to risk-taking and an inability to motivate the work force are among the leadership issues central to discussions about the state of management in North America today.

This chapter examines the degree to which perceptions of managerial leadership manifest themselves in the public and private sectors and the extent to which this is linked to work satisfaction.[1] We are also concerned with the possible impact of intervening factors such as job level. As with all analyses in this study, the basic unit of measurement is the perception of the individual respondent.

Whatever differences might exist between the two sectors would be of limited value if we could not establish a strong link between leadership and work satisfaction in both sectors. Consequently, a large part of this chapter is devoted to analyzing the extent to which leadership is related to work satisfaction to present a stronger case for the need for greater managerial leadership in the workplace. This should help to answer the question of whether employees who perceive a high incidence of leadership among managers are more satisfied with their work than those who report low levels of leadership.

In particular, we tested the hypothesis that "high flyers", or managers who have been promoted relatively quickly in their organizations, might be less influenced by the level of leadership in their organization, since they have received the "lion's share" of the rewards. We also chose this series of analyses because we felt that high flyers might have a greater propensity to see the management system in a more favourable light because of their relative success in the system.

The Meaning of Leadership

Most discussions of leadership start with definitions, to give the reader an appreciation of the range of uses of the term and to convey the lack of consensus among academics and practitioners regarding its meaning.

Our interest is in managerial leadership in large organizations, as opposed to the leadership observed in other types of organizations, such as small groups, sports teams or the military. Most psychological and sociological definitions of leadership do not distinguish between the different forms of leadership; nevertheless, we are concerned with its essentials in hierarchical, service-oriented bureaucratic organizations. In this limited context, we have found a fair degree of concord among commentators.

Consider the following definitions:

- Leadership may be considered as the process of influencing the activities of an organized group in its efforts toward goal-setting and goal achievement.[2]

- Leadership is a process of influence between a leader and those who are followers.[3]

- The statement, "a leader tries to influence other people in a given direction", is relatively simple, but it seems to capture the meaning of what we mean by leadership....[4]

- The new leader is one who commits people to action, who converts followers into leaders, and who may convert leaders into agents of change.[5]

The consensus appears to be that leaders, through various forms of activity and action, attempt to influence by communicating and, in the process, set an example and create an environment for actions by subordinates. Although there are several theoretical models which aim to explain leadership behaviour, there is clearly no one correct way of leading.

Leadership Theories

Early research on leadership espoused the trait approach, a left-over from the study of the psychology of instincts. It was believed that leaders were born with traits that produced leadership qualities. The demise of this theory resulted from a tautological and useless list of traits on the one hand, and the inability to demonstrate which, if any, of these traits differentiated leaders from non-leaders.

After the 1930's, theorists began suggesting that leadership effectiveness was more complicated than the use of a set of qualities by an individual. They postulated that specific leadership traits were related to a given situation and should be viewed as outputs, rather than inputs. The rationale was that the nature of any situation would determine which traits were necessary for success, and the person within a group who possessed these traits would emerge as the leader. When the situation acts as a theoretical base to show which traits are important, the idea of considering them in the selection of leaders becomes more palatable.

An alternative is to fit the leader's style to the situation, rather than attempt to change the style. In this respect, widespread recognition has been given to a number of situational or contingency models. For example, Fiedler holds that the effectiveness of a group depends on the personality of the leader and the degree to which the situation gives the leader power, control over sanctions, and influence over the task structure.[6] Under this theory, a leadership style is made more effective by altering various situational factors, such as subordinate relations, the routinization of tasks, participation in decision-making, and the power to reward and punish. Fiedler believes that this approach is much better than leadership training intended to change personality/leadership.

One of the key factors of leadership is not simply to effect changes in others' behaviour, but to ensure that this behaviour becomes routine. This notion relates to the leader's ability to motivate, an ingredient often considered the *sine qua non* of leadership. The notion linking motivation with leadership is reinforced by Mintzberg's classic study delineating ten managerial roles. One of these is described as the "leader role", the key purpose of which

> . . . is to effect an integration between individual needs and organizational goals. The manager must concentrate his efforts so as to bring subordinate and organizational needs into common accord in order to promote efficient operations.[7]

The typical manager has three major functions in an organizational setting, all of which require a form of leadership. One function, managing interpersonal relationships, involves building and maintaining relationships with a variety of individuals inside and outside the organization. A second, managing information, involves gathering and disseminating information that originates both inside and outside the organization. The third function, decision-making, involves making a range of decisions about internal operating practices and exchanges with other units of the organization and the outside world.

The most recent leadership theory, known as the attribution theory of leadership, suggests that understanding and predicting how people will react to events are enhanced by knowing what their causal explanations for these events are. Attribution theory is mainly concerned with the cognitive processes by which a person interprets behaviour as being caused by (or attributed to) certain cues in the relevant environment. The emphasis of attribution leadership theory is on why a behaviour has occurred, and since most causes of subordinate or follower behaviours are not directly observable, determining causes requires reliance on perceptions.

The attributional approach starts with the position that the leader is essentially an information processor.[8] The leader is searching for information or cues from the work environment that explain why something is happening. From these cues, the leader attempts to construct causal explanations that guide the leadership behaviour. In turn, this assessment leads to some form of leadership behaviour based on the way the leader attributes the original behaviour. Much of our analysis in the latter part of the chapter searches for the appropriate cues which would trigger the types of leadership behaviour we are studying.

Leadership literature underscores how important the degree to which managers can influence behaviour is in determining their effectiveness as leaders. The ability to influence is itself the product of being able to set an example through action, communicating what is intended and creating the right environment for subordinate action. The behaviours which characterize the activities associated with this kind of leadership are: "encouragement", "commitment", "involvement" and "example-setting." Accordingly, a series of six questions were developed to measure leadership in the public and private sectors. The items which are described in Table 3-1 measure these four aspects of leadership.

Leadership Attributes Surveyed

Perceived Degrees of Leadership

Comparing perceived leadership behaviour in the private and public sectors, we were struck by differences in perceived instances of leadership in the two sectors (see Table 3-1). With regard to DM/CEO leadership, more than 80 per cent of private sector respondents reported that their most senior officer demonstrated leadership to a great or very great extent. The comparable figure for public sector managers was 51 per cent.

Table 3-1
Leadership in the Public and Private Sectors

		Levels below DM/CEO					
		1	2	3	4	5	Av.
DM/CEO gives	Public	70.8[1]	55.8	46.1	41.8	28.3	50.7
leadership	Private	84.5	78.2	83.0	77.0	78.0	80.8
Subordinates are	Public	77.5[2]	66.5	61.4	53.1	46.9	62.6
encouraged to participate in important decision	Private	77.5	77.2	79.3	67.3	73.6	76.0
Senior management	Public	63.7[1]	43.3	34.5	34.6	26.5	41.4
encourages surbordin-ates to be innovative	Private	72.5	63.7	73.9	65.1	62.9	68.5
Senior management	Public	75.1[2]	61.1	51.0	46.9	41.5	56.2
committed to develop-ment of department/company	Private	80.5	88.6	87.4	92.8	87.1	88.8
Senior management	Public	46.0[1]	46.8	37.4	35.1	30.4	40.3
involved in daily operations	Private	56.5	52.5	54.5	56.0	59.0	55.4
Senior management	Public	74.4[1]	67.1	57.9	62.5	55.3	63.9
involved in long-term planning	Private	87.4	88.0	86.8	89.1	91.3	88.1

[1]   per cent who responded "to a great" or "very great extent"

[2]   per cent who responded "agree" and "strongly agree"

This gap between the two sectors was reinforced by similar findings on two questions about perceptions of senior management's commitment to the development of the organization and the degree to which subordinates are encouraged to participate in important decisions. Seventy-six per cent of the private sector respondents from all five levels suggested that subordinates were encouraged to participate in important decisions, compared to 63 per cent of public sector respondents. Similarly, 89 per cent of private sector respondents indicated that senior management was committed to the development of the company, whereas only 56 per cent in the public sector saw the same level of commitment to departmental development. With respect to the involvement of senior managers in day-to-day operations, the gap between the private and public sectors was only 15 percentage points (55 versus 40); the gap was 27 percentage points on questions about long-term planning.

In considering the impact of job level on perceptions of leadership, Table 3-1 shows the decline in perceptions of leadership as one moves down the organizational hierarchy in the public sector. In each of the six leadership measures, it was clear that the lower a respondent was in the management structure in the public sector, the less favourable were the perceptions of leadership. The table also shows that the public sector numbers indicating perceptions of leadership were lower at each level below the DM than the figures for private sector managers working at the comparable level. Among public sector respondents, the question with the narrowest range of responses was the one asking managers to rate the extent to which senior managers were involved in the day-to-day operations of their organizations. The greatest variation, and hence the greatest difference in perceptions between those working one level below the DM and those working five levels below, was with regard to encouragement to participate in decisions. A gap of more than 31 percentage points (78 per cent at the higher level versus 47 per cent), displayed in Figure 3-1, provides dramatic evidence of the differences in perceptions among executives, senior managers and managers in the public service.

The second most dramatic difference between the two sectors was in responses to the question regarding the degree of DM/CEO leadership. Only 51 per cent of public sector respondents suggested that their deputy minister demonstrated leadership "to a great extent" or "to a very great extent", while 81 per cent of private sector managers expressed this view of their CEO.

Regardless of position in the hierarchy, private sector responses on the leadership items were more positive than those from public sector managers, with one notable exception: the perception of the degree to which subordinates were encouraged to participate in important decisions at the assistant deputy minister level (i.e., those working one level below the DM). This group saw itself as equally committed to encouraging subordinates to participate as their counterparts in the private sector. In other words, except in this one instance, private sector managers perceived higher levels of leadership in their own organizations than public sector managers saw in theirs.

Figure 3-1

Degree to which Superior Encourages Subordinates to Participate in Important Decisions by Job Level

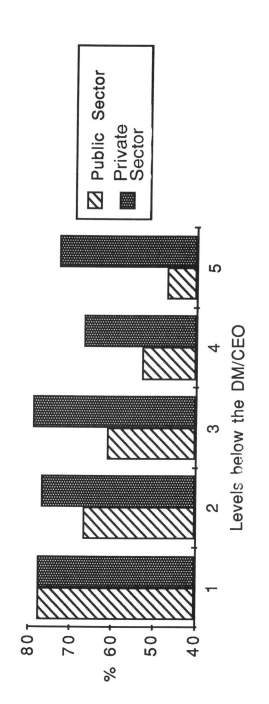

Note: Per cent "to a great" and "very great extent"

In the private sector, managers working at all levels saw leadership as fairly constant, despite the increasing distance between many managers and the CEO. As well, leadership was thought to be present to a greater extent in almost all instances in the private sector, compared to public sector managers' perceptions. As a corollary, the gap between the two sectors in perceptions about leadership is at its largest among managers four and five levels below the DM/CEO.

Whom Do Managers Try to Satisfy?

Another way of examining the type of leadership in terms of commitment is to consider how managers are seen to allocate their time among competing interest groups. Table 3-2 contains the responses to questions asking respondents to rate the importance placed by senior management to ensure the satisfaction of various client groups.

In the public sector, the senior management cadre is perceived to be almost equally preoccupied with satisfying the needs of politicians and those of their clients and more concerned about satisfying these groups than any other group about which answers were elicited. More than 87 per cent of public service respondents suggested that satisfying the needs of politicians was important or very important to them, while 84 per cent thought that the satisfaction of their clients was either important or very important. By contrast, satisfying unions, in general, was seen to be a matter of relatively less concern to public sector senior managers, as only 38 per cent of the managers cited it as important.

Private sector response patterns were somewhat similar to those in the public sector. The major preoccupations of private sector managers were: keeping the board of directors (91 per cent) and the company's clients (94 per cent) satisfied.[9] Of least interest to private sector managers were interest groups, with only 47 per cent of respondents suggesting that they felt importance in keeping them satisfied.

Given the general view that the public service is a service-oriented institution, it was intriguing to find that respondents felt differently about how much importance senior management attaches to satisfying the general public. It came as a surprise to find that the general public, as a target of senior management's attention, was thought to be significantly different in importance by managers in the two sectors. For example, 91 per cent of private sector respondents felt that their senior management placed considerable importance on ensuring the satisfaction of the general public, where only 67 per cent of public sector respondents had similar views. This finding did not vary much by job level of the respondent.

Table 3-2
Importance placed by Senior Management
on the Satisfaction of Various Groups

Satisfaction of:		Levels below DM/CEO					
		1	2	3	4	5	Av.
Respondents' Clients	Public	91.9[1]	83.8	82.7	81.0	75.9	83.7
	Private	95.1	95.3	92.5	93.1	90.4	94.1
General public	Public	72.3	68.4	65.7	65.1	61.3	67.0
	Private	94.5	87.7	87.6	88.1	90.6	90.5
Interest groups	Public	69.0	66.1	62.5	63.0	61.9	64.7
	Private	53.5	45.1	45.1	35.7	149.6	47.2
Media	Public	58.1	59.5	57.5	56.3	58.3	58.0
	Private	55.0	47.1	50.9	43.1	57.9	51.1
Politicians/Board of Directors	Public	90.7	90.2	85.8	88.4	78.2	87.6
	Private	92.2	90.0	88.9	91.8	92.1	91.0
Central agencies/ Auditors	Public	70.0	72.9	76.2	78.7	69.5	74.1
	Private	58.2	72.6	64.3	73.5	74.1	62.8
Unions	Public	45.2	40.6	36.6	32.4	30.4	37.8
	Private	54.1	53.9	55.5	61.8	70.5	57.1

[1] per cent who responded "important" and "very important".

According to the data, senior managers in both sectors attach importance to satisfying essentially the same two crucial audiences: those to whom they are ultimately accountable (politicians and the board of directors), and their client groups. This basic similarity between the orientations of managers in the two sectors is strong evidence suggesting that despite large differences in the perceived levels of leadership in the two sectors, there is a considerable degree of consistency in the importance placed by senior management on satisfying their client groups. That is, while senior managers in both sectors may be heading in a similar direction, private sector managers appear to demonstrate higher levels of leadership skills.

Managerial activity at the top of the management hierarchy in both sectors appears to be complicated and somewhat schizophrenic. Senior managers are preoccupied simultaneously with satisfying those at the pinnacle of their organizational structure (i.e., ministers and members of the board of directors) and those at the other end of the structure (their clients). We argued, in Chapter 1, that public sector managers operate in a high-pressure environment, but there is no reason to believe, on the basis of this study, that a principal difference between the two sectors is that public sector managers are preoccupied with their political masters at the expense of other constituencies.

The data show clearly that private sector managers think they are as busy satisfying the needs of their boards of directors as public servants are with those of politicians.[10] Given that the principal orientation of the public service has traditionally been toward satisfying the needs of the client base, it is worrisome that, overall, public sector respondents perceive that their senior management cadre do not place the same emphasis on ensuring the satisfaction of the general public and clients as do those who work in the private sector.

Looking at the issue of perceptions of leadership according to respondents' place in the organizational hierarchy (Table 3-2), two significant differences in perception emerge. First, higher-level public sector managers perceive the senior management group to be more interested in satisfying the department's clients and satisfying politicians than do those who work at lower levels in the organization. Second, in contrast to the public sector, the perceptions of private sector managers about this issue do not change much as one moves down the organizational structure.

Figure 3-2 displays two of the variables from Table 3-2. Data concerning the importance attributed to satisfying clients and politicians/members of the board of directors are displayed graphically to underscore the importance of the vertical solitude and the gap in perceptions between the public and private sectors. The figure demonstrates how the perceived importance to the public sector senior management cadre of satisfying clients falls off as one moves down the hierarchy. By contrast, the private sector data highlight the consistency in the private sector's view of the importance of maintaining high levels of client satisfaction, especially at lower levels. These data provide important evidence as to the extent to which the views of public sector executives differ from those of the SMs and SM-1s. The responses of senior managers and those one level below them in the hierarchy represent a serious breakdown in communication between the executive and managerial groupings. The SMs and the SM-1s, whose jobs require more regular contact with the public than executive jobs, are relatively less persuaded that the senior management cadre is committed to satisfying the groups with which they work.

In terms of satisfying the demands of politicians or boards of directors, we found that the private sector pays much the same level of attention to the concerns of its corporate masters as the public sector

Figure 3-2
Importance of Satisfying Clients and Politicians or Members
of the Board of Directors

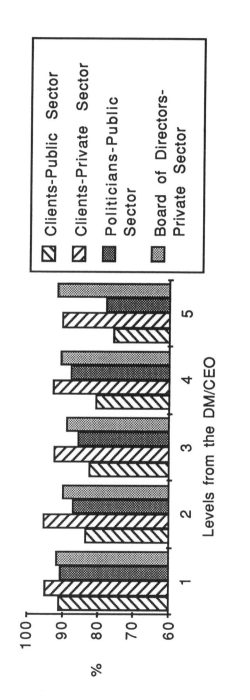

(91 per cent versus 88 per cent). While we have no intention of equating the intensity of the relationship between politicians and senior public servants with that of private sector managers and their boards of directors, this finding does demonstrate that the private sector, much like the public sector, is accountable to a governing body.

Relating Leadership to Outcome Measures: The Influence of Leadership on Work Satisfaction

We have, so far, demonstrated that as one moves down the public sector hierarchy, managers believe that there is less leadership at more senior levels than do private sector executives. This section establishes the importance of leadership by showing how perceptions of leadership are related to work satisfaction.[11]

Leadership and Satisfaction

Three measures of leadership in the public sector—leadership provided by deputy ministers, the commitment of senior management to the future development of their respective departments, and the degree of participation in decision-making—were all analyzed by linking them to work satisfaction.[12] The data for the three leadership measures are shown in Tables 3-3, 3-4 and 3-5. In each table, the degree of perceived leadership is arrayed across the page, while the five work satisfaction measures have been listed vertically. In Table 3-3, for example, the numbers in the body of the table represent the percentage of public service respondents who were "satisfied" or "very satisfied" with the various work satisfaction indices and who indicated to what degree the DM provided leadership.[13]

Table 3-3 indicates that DM leadership is strongly correlated with all but one of the satisfaction indices. Satisfaction with intrinsic work factors, with the department in which the respondent works, and with respondents' perceptions of their jobs and career progress were all significantly related to the degree to which respondents perceived their DMs as providing leadership. Only the degree of extrinsic satisfaction was unaffected by the amount of leadership perceived to be provided by a DM. Given the nature of extrinsic rewards in the public sector (pay and benefits), factors over which deputy ministers have virtually no control, this finding is not unexpected. Since compensation is centrally controlled and administered by the Treasury Board, respondents would not expect their extrinsic satisfaction to be related to the leadership provided by the deputy minister. It is, therefore, not surprising that there is little relation between pay satisfaction and leadership.

Table 3-3
Relationship Between Deputy Minister as Leader
and Work Satisfaction
(public sector)

Indices of Work Satisfaction	To a very Little Extent	To a Little Extent	To Some Extent	To a Great Extent	To a Very Great Extent
Intrinsic Satisfaction	38.2[1]	43.2	47.6	58.7	73.8
Extrinsic Satisfaction	28.4	31.2	31.8	37.0	34.2
Departmental Satisfaction	11.9	14.8	22.2	29.3	44.7
Job Satisfaction	42.8	49.2	53.1	64.3	74.1
Satisfaction with Career Progress	9.3	18.7	23.0	33.8	41.7

[1]   per cent of respondents who are "satisfied" or "very satisfied" on the five work satisfaction indices

Of the five work satisfaction measures, the one most affected by variations in perceptions of DM leadership was intrinsic satisfaction. At one end of the scale, where respondents indicated that they perceived leadership by their deputy minister "to a very little extent", we found 38 per cent indicating that they were satisfied or very satisfied with the elements that make up the intrinsic job satisfaction index. At the other extreme, of those who indicated that their deputy minister demonstrated leadership "to a very great extent", more than 73 per cent were also satisfied with the degree of challenge and independence in their jobs (i.e., the intrinsic work satisfaction factors). This dramatic difference of more than 35 percentage points confirms that the leadership provided by the deputy minister is very strongly related to managers' perceptions of their level of work satisfaction.

The two remaining tables in this series contain similar findings. Table 3-4, for example, shows that perceptions of the degree to which senior management is committed to the future development of the department have an impressive impact on all five work satisfaction indices. In fact, the level of respondents' perceptions of the commitment of senior managers to the future development of their departments produced an even wider spread in work satisfaction than was found in the question on deputy minister leadership. In this instance, for example, there was a difference of more than 50 percentage points in the respondents' levels of intrinsic satisfaction between those who strongly disagreed that there was commitment on the part of senior management to the future development of their departments and those who strongly agreed.

Table 3-4
Relationship Between Commitment of Senior Management to Future Development of Department and Work Satisfaction
(public sector)

Indices of Work Satisfaction	Strongly Disagree	Disagree	Neither Agree Nor Disagree	Agree	Strongly Agree
Intrinsic Satisfaction	21.9[1]	28.6	42.8	65.6	73.2
Extrinsic Satisfaction	28.6	30.2	30.0	36.3	43.5
Departmental Satisfaction	4.7	6.2	16.5	33.2	55.6
Job Satisfaction	33.9	38.1	47.8	67.6	81.5
Satisfaction with Career Progress	6.3	16.1	19.1	33.1	49.3

[1] per cent of respondents who are "satisfied" and "very satisfied" on the five work satisfaction indices

Equally dramatic findings are evident in Table 3-5, relating to the question of the degree to which employees perceive that they are encouraged to participate in decision-making. For example, in the case of intrinsic satisfaction, the range of satisfaction scores varies considerably. Twenty-two per cent agree or strongly agree that they are "intrinsically" satisfied when they "strongly disagreed" that their superiors encourage subordinates to participate in decision-making, while 78 per cent are intrinsically satisfied when they strongly agree that they are encouraged to participate in decision-making. As was found in the previous two tables, extrinsic satisfaction was less affected by the leadership measures than by any of the other work satisfaction indices. The other index significantly affected by the level of perceived encouragement to participate in decision-making was job satisfaction, which varied from a low of 30 per cent in the situation of little encouragement, to a job satisfaction score of 80 per cent in those instances where employees perceived they were encouraged by their superiors to participate in decision-making. The other two indices, departmental satisfaction and satisfaction with career progress, provided less dramatic but similar patterns of response.[14]

Table 3-5
Relationship Between the Degree to which Subordinates are Encouraged to Participate in Decision-Making and Work Satisfaction
(public sector)

	Superior encourages subordinates to participate in decision-making				
			Neither		
Indices of Work	Strongly		Agree Nor		Strongly
Satisfaction	Disagree	Disagree	Disagree	Agree	Agree
Intrinsic Satisfaction	21.9[1]	32.0	40.9	62.9	77.5
Extrinsic Satisfaction	25.8	32.7	29.8	36.7	35.6
Departmental Satisfaction	5.4	12.9	17.3	31.6	44.8
Job Satisfaction	29.8	36.5	44.6	68.6	80.4
Satisfaction with Career					
Progress	9.8	13.1	17.9	32.5	47.1

[1] per cent of respondents who are "satisfied" and "very satisfied" on the five work satisfaction indices

Given the consistency of these findings, we can draw a number of conclusions about public sector leadership. Among three leadership measures (perception of leadership by the DM, commitment of senior management and participation in decision-making), the least influential in predicting intrinsic satisfaction was the leadership provided by the DM. This assertion is supported by noting that the difference in intrinsic satisfaction between those who reported high levels of DM leadership and those who reported low levels was the smallest of the three leadership variables.[15] Conversely, the degree to which subordinates perceive that they are encouraged to participate in decision-making was the variable that most strongly affected the items which comprised the intrinsic satisfaction index. Finally, active involvement in decision-making yielded the highest level of intrinsic satisfaction (78 per cent), although this was only marginally higher than the other two leadership items.

Figure 3-3 provides graphic proof that leadership, as measured by these three variables, has a profound impact on the levels of intrinsic satisfaction that managers derive from their work. The nature of this relationship is essentially linear in that each increment in level of

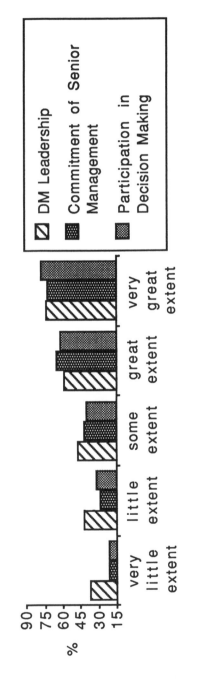

Figure 3-3
Relationship Between DM Leadership, Commitment
of Senior Management, and Encouragement to Participate
in Decision-Making and Intrinsic Satisfaction
(Public Sector)

leadership is matched by increases in levels of work satisfaction. While there is obviously an upper boundary to this phenomenon, there is no denying that managers who perceive more leadership in their organization are more satisfied while at work.[16] On the basis of these findings, which are consistent across all five satisfaction indices, we conclude that leadership is one activity that must be stressed at the executive level.[17]

Managerial Level, Leadership and Satisfaction: Leadership Matters Irrespective of Job Level

We know, from the organizational design literature, that the position held in an organization can have a considerable effect on the way an employee perceives the organization.[18] While there is ample evidence in this study to indicate the importance of job level, the next series of tables and charts provides further evidence of the relevance of job level in the public sector in interpreting the survey findings.

To test the strength of the relationship between perceptions of leadership and work satisfaction by building on the attributional theory of leadership, an additional question was added to the analysis. In considering job level and leadership variables, at the same time we sought to identify a way of determining which of these two general factors (leadership or job level) was the more important in influencing work satisfaction in the public sector.

A separate analysis was done for each of the six leadership questions, controlling for job level on the five satisfaction indices. The data presented here are representative of the general findings. In In Table 3-6 and Figures 3-4 and 3-5, two elements of work satisfaction (departmental and job satisfaction) are presented alongside the leadership measures (DM leadership and encouragement by superiors to participate in decision-making), and job level (executive, senior manager and manager). The figures demonstrate two essential findings. Those who perceive high levels of DM leadership or are encouraged to participate in decision-making are more satisfied with their jobs than those who do not. As well, the results underscore the earlier observation that the relationship between work satisfaction and perceived levels of leadership is a fundamental one, no matter what the job level of the respondent.

Thus, job level alone is not responsible for the low satisfaction scores found among SM-1s. Perceptions of low encouragement to participate in decision-making and perceptions of low DM leadership, not job level, are the principal predictors of satisfaction. This finding is critical in our understanding of managing in the public sector because it demonstrates that many of the structural solutions often used to

Table 3-6
The Effect of Job Level on Perceived Leadership and Two Indices of Work Satisfaction
(public sector)

		Degree to which subordinates are encouraged to participate in decision-making		
		Disagree or strongly disagree*	Neither agree nor disagree	Agree or strongly agree
Departmental Satisfaction				
Job Level	Executives (EXs)	31.9[1]	45.9	76.8
	Senior Managers(SMs)	35.4	47.4	66.6
	Managers(SM-1s)	27.9	47.8	64.6
Job Satisfaction				
Job Level	Executives	51.8[2]	65.8	89.1
	Senior Managers	53.2	61.9	84.5
	Managers	49.5	69.1	86.2

		Perceived level of deputy minister leadership		
		To a little extent	To some extent	To a great extent
Departmental Satisfaction				
Job Level	Executives	31.6[1]	54.3	77.5
	Senior Managers	28.7	58.4	69.2
	Managers	31.8	44.8	67.8
Job Satisfaction				
Job Level	Executives	53.1[2]	60.4	79.6
	Senior Managers	46.0	53.3	65.3
	Managers	45.8	48.7	59.5

*   The data for this and the following table have been combined into three groups for simplicity. The results of this analysis using five groups based on degree of agreement were essentially the same as those presented above.

[1]   per cent of respondents who are "satisfied" or "very satisfied" with their department

[2]   per cent of respondents who "agree" or "strongly agree" that they are satisfied with their job

Figure 3-4
Perceived Levels of Leadership Provided by the Deputy Minister and Job Satisfaction, Controlling for Job Level
(Public Sector)

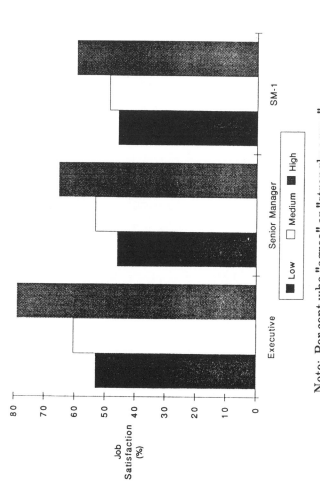

Note: Per cent who "agree" or "strongly agree"

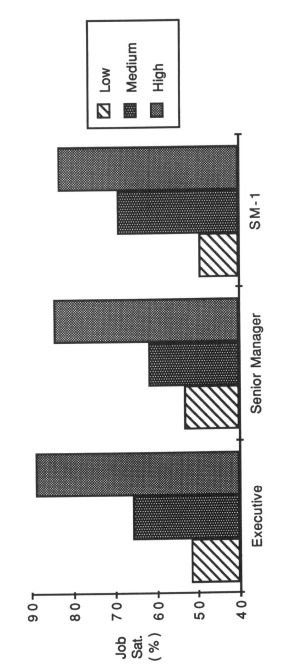

Figure 3-5
Level of Encouragement to Participate in Decision-Making and
Job Satisfaction, Controlling for Job Level
(Public Sector)

Note: Per cent who "agree" or "strongly agree"

remedy management problems, such as minimizing a department's span of control or increasing the frequency of communication, do not necessarily directly address the relevant issues.

To test this finding, the data were subjected to one further analysis. Public sector data were divided into three groups according to the way respondents evaluated their own rate of progress through the ranks of the public service. The question was whether the high flyers were more generous than others in their assessment of the leadership provided by senior management and whether the rate of progress they reported was related to job satisfaction.

Table 3-7 shows that this was not the case. After separating those reporting a faster rate of progress, there was virtually no difference between high flyers and others, in terms of their assessment of job satisfaction. This finding is important because it effectively eliminates a popular hypothesis that malcontents (i.e., those who are not moving rapidly up the bureaucracy) might have more negative attitudes to senior management and might be more likely to disparage their leadership skills. In summary, while satisfaction declines as one moves down the hierarchy, we now have evidence that the origin of this problem is not necessarily one's place in the corporate hierarchy. The public sector data in this chapter lead us to suggest that a lack of demonstrated leadership at the executive levels might be one of the principal reasons for these results.

Table 3-7
Job Satisfaction and Encouragement to Participate in Decision-Making, Job Level and Rate of Progress through the Ranks

			Degree to which subordinates are encouraged to participate in decision-making		
		Rate of Progress**	Low	Medium	High
	Executives	Neither Fast nor Slow	*	59.51	93.9
		Fast	*	62.9	92.1
Job Level	Senior Managers	Neither Fast nor Slow	35.1	57.5	82.1
		Fast	61.9	63.1	87.9
	Managers	Neither Fast nor Slow	33.3	61.1	87.1
		Fast	36.8	68.5	89.5

* = small sample size

** = represents respondents' rate of advancement in the public service as reported by them.

1 per cent of respondents who "agree" or "strongly agree" that they are satisfied with their jobs

Is Leadership Important?

Table 3-8 shows the relative value of the six leadership items in predicting the five work satisfaction indices. Except for extrinsic satisfaction, which is generally poorly predicted by the leadership items, the remaining four work satisfaction indices were predicted relatively well, especially intrinsic and departmental satisfaction. (The multiple correlations were 0.60 and 0.61 respectively.) Among the leadership measures, "senior management encourages you to be innovative in your job" was the single best predictor of work satisfaction. In three of the five cases, participation in decision-making was the second best predictor, while senior management commitment to the development of the department was the second best in two cases.

While we are satisfied that the linkage between perceptions of leadership and work satisfaction has been well established in this analysis, we realize that several other factors, such as rewards, corporate culture and work environment, might influence this relationship. On balance, however, job level may be a deceptively simple and erroneous explanation of work satisfaction because, when we control for the effect of level of participation in decision-making, the effect of job level almost disappears. This is a problem of collinearity: those working at high job levels are also, by virtue of their tasks, being encouraged to participate in decision-making. Therefore, it is most probable that the level of involvement, not job level, is the crucial factor.

Two major findings emerge from our analysis of leadership. First, the evidence clearly supports the conventional wisdom that leadership matters in both sectors. In the context of the public sector, we tested the results by examining the possible impact that slow career progress might have on perceptions of leadership. Even under this condition, those who perceive a greater degree of leadership are more likely to be satisfied at work.

The second major finding suggests that while the vertical solitude exists to a considerable degree, job level is not necessarily the cause of discontent among the lower ranking senior managers. The consistent evidence in Figures 3-4 and 3-5 shows that leadership, such as the behaviour of the deputy minister, is a more powerful predictor of work satisfaction than job level. Those encouraged to become involved in decision-making or those who perceive a great deal of leadership from the DM are usually more satisfied with their jobs, regardless of their level. Being senior managers does not necessarily mean that they belong to a group of dissatisfied managers. However, failure to experience strong leadership or to be encouraged to participate in important decisions will almost certainly produce dissatisfied managers.

Table 3-8
Predicting Work Satisfaction on the Basis of Leadership Indices
(public sector)

	Intrinsic Satisfaction	Extrinsic Satisfaction	Job Satisfaction	Departmental Satisfaction	Satisfaction with Career Progress
Subordinates are encouraged to participate in decision-making	2*		2	3	2
Senior management encourages you to be innovative in your job	1	1	1	1	1
Senior management committed to development of department/company	3	2	3	2	3
Senior management involved in daily operations	4		4	5	
Senior management involved in long-term planning			6	6	
Deputy minister gives leadership			5	4	
Multiple Correlation	0.60	0.16	0.55	0.61	0.46

* = The integer represents the ranking of the most important predictor of the work satisfaction indices, where 1 is the best predictor and 5 is the least effective predictor of each index of work satisfaction.

The results of this analysis are obviously discouraging, but solutions are possible if managers are prepared to assume responsibility for managing their subordinates. The public sector management system needs to promote greater leadership among its executive cadre through more participative decision-making and greater demonstrated commitment to the organization. Above all, deputy ministers must be encouraged to become leaders and to practice leadership so that this behaviour is emulated by those lower down the hierarchy. As noted earlier, leadership is an idiosyncratic characteristic which must be developed and encouraged. The federal program of increased ministerial authority and accountability (IMAA) initiated in 1987, is a step in the right direction. Unfortunately, it has tended to concentrate on the elimination of restrictive rules and regulations, and not on developing more innovative managers.

Notes

1. Some of the findings in this chapter were presented at the annual meeting of the Royal Institute of Public Administration. The reference is D. Zussman and J. Jabes, "Perceptions of Leadership: A Comparison Between Government and Business Organizations", Canterbury, September, 1988.

2. R.M. Stogdill, "Personal factors associated with leadership: a survey of the literature," *Journal of Psychology*, vol. 25, no. 2, (1950), p. 3.

3. E.P. Hollander and J. Julian, "A Further Look at Leader Legitimacy, Influence and Innovation", in L. Berkowitz (ed.), *Group Processes*, (New York: Academic Press, 1978), p. 1.

4. A.K. Korman, "The predictors of managerial performance: a review," *Personnel Psychology*, vol. 21, (1971), p. 115.

5. W. Bennis and B. Nanus, *Leaders: The Strategies for Taking Charge*, (New York: Harper and Row, 1985), p. 3.

6. F. Fiedler, *A Theory of Leadership Effectiveness*, (New York: McGraw Hill, 1967).

7. H. Mintzberg, *The Nature of Managerial Work*, (New York: Harper and Row, 1973), p. 62.

8. S.G. Green and T.R. Mitchell, "Attributional processes of leaders in leader-member interactions," *Organizational Behavior and Human Performance*, vol. 23, no. 3, (June 1979), pp. 429-58.

9. In this question, "Board of Directors" serves as the private sector counterpart to the question on politicians which was used in the public sector questionnaire. Although one may argue that comparability of the two is limited, it was felt that this was the best approximation one could obtain.

10. This does not prove that their actual behaviours with respect to the board of directors and politicians are the same. We are dealing with perceptions, not actual time spent.

11. Since the data represent information gathered at one time (the summer of 1986), the information cannot show conclusively that having a better leader will lead to higher levels of work satisfaction among subordinates. However, despite our inability to prove causality, the survey findings support the general notion that higher levels of leadership are inextricably linked to higher levels of satisfaction.

12. See Chapter 1 for a description of the work satisfaction measures. The other three leadership scales produced similar findings.

13. The other three leadership measures (encouragement in innovativeness, involvement in daily operations, and involvement in long-term planning) were not presented in this chapter in order to keep the chapter to a reasonable length. An analysis of the remaining leadership questions provides a similar pattern of results, although the actual percentages were somewhat different.

14. Although the private sector data have not been presented in this series of tables, it should be noted that the private sector pattern of responses was similar to that reported for the public sector data.

15. The range was 36 per cent for DM leadership, 51 per cent for commitment of senior management, and 55 per cent for encouragement in decision-making.

16. Note that the job satisfaction question used a different stem (agree, disagree) than the one used for the other work satisfaction measures (satisfied, dissatisfied). The five-point scale was used in all cases.

17. A similar pattern was found in the private sector data.

18. E.F. House, *Management,* 2nd ed. (St. Paul, Minn.: West Publishing Co., 1982); R.L. Trewatha and M.G. Newport, *Management,* 3rd ed. (Plano, Texas: Business Publications Inc., 1982).

Chapter 4

Organizational Culture

Introduction

This chapter is about organizational culture.[1] Anthropologists have defined culture in numerous ways, but the diverse definitions have some common characteristics.[2] From a social or anthropological standpoint, culture refers to the pattern of beliefs and behaviour within a society. Culture reflects the learned behavioural traits shared by a society's members and stems from tradition and heritage. Yet cultures do not depend on heritage alone and are constantly changing. In this chapter we apply the concept of culture to government and private sector organizations by analyzing the values and attitudes of respondents. We introduce the concept of corporate culture, and then look at the survey data pertaining to organizational goals, attitudes towards loyalty, organizational orientation and organizational values. After comparing the public and private sector cultures, we relate cultural dimensions to work satisfaction to determine the importance and role that culture plays in public and private sector organizations.

Corporate Culture: A New Trend in Studying Organizations

The management literature of the early 1980s introduced the concept of corporate culture to describe values shared by members of an organization. The idea that culture is a useful way to explain why an organization functions the way it does has been around for a long time, though the term "culture" was rarely used. In a series of books for the mass market, consultants and academics alike popularized the idea that organizations have an internal culture.[3] Their writings suggested that an organization's culture can be studied by learning about the rituals, legends and stories that circulate around an organization and by surveying the attitudes and beliefs of the organization's members. Organizational culture, often referred to also as corporate culture, is viewed as a system of values and beliefs that is influenced by the organization's structure, environment and technology to produce norms. Defining organizational culture as a system of shared values and viewing it as the social glue that holds the organization together comes close to an anthropological definition of culture.

It has also become fashionable to view corporate culture as an asset on the road to economic and managerial effectiveness and efficiency. Inappropriate corporate cultures have been blamed for acting as roadblocks to the adaptation of organizations to their environments. There is now a desire not only to understand what corporate culture is but to prescribe what it ought to be. This concern is justified if the goal is to ensure that the culture is in harmony with the mission of becoming more productive.[4] In our view, although the concept of culture has been overemphasized in the management literature, we believe the idea has considerable merit.[5]

Given recent preoccupation with private sector management success stories, one aim of this research was to identify similarities and differences between public and private sector management cultures in Canada. Although the management literature is somewhat arid in comparisons of public and private sector cultures, there is enough anecdotal evidence, in Canada and around the world, to produce some stereotypes. One is that public bureaucracies are inefficient, slow and indifferent to citizens' needs.[6]

Making fun of public bureaucracies is common in many countries: one rarely sees plays or humorous vignettes about inefficiencies or piles of paperwork in the private sector. Gogol's "The Inspector General" is still performed in many countries because it continues to fit the stereotype in its characterization of government bureaucracies. Particularly in countries where public administrators are considered lazy and self-serving, a play like this provides catharsis for the spectator. Studies of organizational culture may provide some answers where such perceptions might match reality.

Information on values is important in understanding culture. The survey tapped respondents' opinions, attitudes and values related to their organizations and the sector in which they work. The cultural categories we discuss were arrived at by analyzing a host of concepts associated with the study of corporate culture. We discuss the differences between the public and private sectors, acknowledging that their cultures are themselves the composite of a number of different organizational cultures.[7]

We believe that the middle and lower levels of the senior management cadre are crucial links in the administrative, communication and the cultural chain. They are often responsible for large numbers of employees and have the important task of socializing them to the culture and mores of the organization. We focus on this group to understand to what degree they know, understand and transmit the culture of their organizations. In a later section we discuss how well these matters are communicated within the management cadre.

Cultural Dimensions and Attributes Surveyed

Organizational Goals: Better Known at the Top

Goals provide an organization with a road map[8] and a standard for assessing efficiency and effectiveness.[9] Most readers will agree that effectiveness is "the degree to which an organization realizes its goals."[10]

In most work organizations, mission statements have been developed to state goals explicitly and publicly. In some cases, all employees contribute to the development of goals, which then reflect the collective will. By contributing to the realization of organizational objectives individuals also satisfy their personal goals. However, conflict may occur when objectives developed by different units are not in harmony, making their attainment difficult. Furthermore, stress may emerge to compound the problem when employees expect that they will be evaluated on how well the organization's goals have been accomplished. As well, an organization's objectives may be at odds with those of the larger system of which it is part, or with its environment. For this reason it is important to establish goals that are clear to the organization's members and not in conflict.

Most respondents in both sectors reported knowing the goals of their organizations (Table 4-1). As elsewhere, there was a significant tendency, however, for the level of knowledge to decrease as respondents worked further from the CEO/DM. Over 50 per cent of the respondents one level from the CEO/DM indicated that a mission statement incorporating goals and philosophy had been developed in their organization, but this percentage fell to 29 per cent in the public and 36 per cent in the private sector at the fifth level from the CEO/DM.

These findings are surprising because mission statements are public documents within an organization and should be known at all managerial levels. The data suggest that the higher a manager is in the organization, the more likely he or she is to be aware of objectives, whether official, as the mission statement, or operational.[11] Respondents working higher up in the hierarchy were probably involved in the development or modification of the mission statement and objectives, but a serious communication problem exists when such information does not reach all managerial levels.

Table 4-1
Organizational Goals

Characteristics		Levels below DM/CEO					
		1	2	3	4	5	Av.
Organization accom-	Public	60.2[1]	53.7	53.2	51.2	43.3	53.3
plishes its objectives	Private	78.7	71.3	74.8	78.9	79.1	76.2
I know organizational	Public	87.9	79.7	70.8	65.6	57.7	74.0
goals	Private	85.1	76.7	76.9	72.7	72.1	78.8
Organizational goals	Public	53.1	43.0	41.7	42.0	37.1	43.6
are realistic	Private	79.1	76.5	76.7	78.5	70.8	77.0
Mission statement	Public	52.4	45.3	41.4	36.3	29.0	42.5
developed	Private	58.9	53.5	53.0	41.0	36.4	51.8

[1]   per cent who responded "agree" and "strongly agree" or "to a great" or "very great extent"

Similarities between the two sectors regarding goals end here. One important measure of the appropriateness of goals is the degree to which they are seen as realistic. Seventy-seven per cent of the private sector respondents felt that their company's goals were realistic; in the public sector, there was greater variation and a generally lower level of agreement than in the private sector. Only 44 per cent of the respondents perceived their department's goals as realistic (Table 4-1), with significant fall-off at lower managerial levels.

There were also differences between the two sectors with respect to the accomplishment of objectives. Significantly fewer respondents in the public sector felt that their departments were accomplishing their objectives. Given that they also felt that departmental goals were not very realistic this did not come as a surprise! The diminishing rate of agreement that we observed in most of the public sector data when going from higher to lower levels of management was evident in responses on this issue.

Organizational objectives exist so that members can work toward a common purpose. Goals give an organization its identity. Thus, official and operational goals, and mission statements should facilitate the management of organizations. Since goals are critical in measuring effectiveness, those working in an organization should have a solid understanding of official and operational goals. In both sectors in Canada, the highest levels of senior management to some extent know and understand their organizations' goals. However, this success is not repeated at the lower levels of top management. As we shall see in Chapter 6 (Table 6-2), in both sectors goals were not perceived to be in conflict with other organizational objectives.

Orientation to People: From Platitudes to Reality, or Does Anyone Care?

Corporate culture research puts great emphasis on the way people are perceived as part of the organization. Peters and Waterman describe in detail the success of organizations which share the basic belief that organizations should have respect for the individual.[12] They emphasize that respect for individuals does not mean simply paying lip service — these companies really care. Perhaps the most widely cited example is IBM's philosophy, where respect for the individual is cited as the most important organizational belief.[13] Another company that traces its success to a people-oriented philosophy is Hewlett-Packard, where the approach has been called "the HP Way".[14]

The respect of employees for co-workers, superiors and subordinates is an important indicator of culture in the workplace. Many organizations incorporate this ideal into their mission statements. Survey participants were asked: "To what extent does your department have a real interest in the welfare and overall satisfaction of those who work there?"

The differences in response between the two sectors (Table 4-2) are revealing. Public sector senior managers did not view their organizations as caring institutions. Only 23 per cent described their departments as caring about people to a great or very great extent. This percentage varied from 37 per cent, for those working one level away from the DM, to 18 per cent to those five levels away.

As a whole the public sector data point out that managers hold the strong perception that their departments show a lack of interest toward the welfare of their employees. The public service of Canada has put in place some processes for managing human resources. Some of these efforts involve the application of the merit principle to ensure that the most deserving get hired and promoted, others are to provide equal opportunities for visible minorities at work, and others revolve around legal, conventional and industrial-relations statutes to ensure fairness. To this, one should add training of managers in human relations skills aimed at enlightening them about the importance of people and their treatment in the workplace. However, these practices have not led to a perception of "caring." As a consequence, serious efforts will be required at genuinely nurturing human resources— efforts that will go beyond ensuring that an equitable process is in place.

Table 4-2
Caring for the Welfare of Employees

| | Levels below DM/CEO | | | | | |
	1	2	3	4	5	Av.
Public Sector	36.8[1]	22.7	18.2	17.9	17.5	22.7
Private Sector	58.7	56.3	47.8	52.7	47.1	54.1

[1] per cent who responded "to a great" or "very great extent"

In their popular book on corporate culture, Deal and Kennedy emphasize the importance of internal cultural elements, of which values, the "bedrock of corporate culture", are one.[15] An important function of values is that they are known and shared by employees throughout a company. Caring about people was not perceived to be a value shared by all managers when they described the public service culture.

Organizational Orientation: Ask for Service, but Don't Expect Creativity

How managers perceive the orientation of an organization provides another perspective on culture. Public and private sector respondents drew very different pictures of the orientation of their organizations. As can be seen in Table 4-3, with the exception of service to clients, which we argued previously was the *modus operandi* of public sector organizations, we found significant differences in every other dimension. One example is the degree to which respondents saw their organizations as oriented towards innovation and creative management.[16]

Anecdotes about differences between the private and public sectors emphasize greater creativity and risk-taking in the private sector. There is a related perception that large organizations do not typically provide environments that encourage innovation and creativity. Notwithstanding beliefs about the private sector as a creative environment, many large private companies function like bureaucracies. Traditional organizations in the private sector can stifle the creative spirit and the intra-organizational entrepreneur very easily.

Table 4-3
Organizational Orientation

Organizational Orientation		Levels below DM/CEO					
		1	2	3	4	5	Av.
Toward service to	Public	82.0[1]	77.3	86.2	70.2	67.7	75.5
clients	Private	84.8	82.3	73.8	79.9	76.0	80.6
Toward employees	Public	17.7	8.6	7.5	4.5	5.7	8.9
	Private	41.0	38.5	35.6	33.7	33.6	37.7
Toward innovation	Public	29.7	19.7	19.9	21.1	12.6	21.1
	Private	55.3	52.4	56.6	60.0	53.6	55.2
Toward creative	Public	27.9	18.4	13.1	11.3	12.5	16.8
management	Private	50.2	42.1	45.3	42.1	40.1	45.2
Toward efficient	Public	50.6	42.0	35.0	26.8	27.8	37.3
management	Private	68.2	63.2	65.3	73.5	66.2	67.0
Toward quality of	Public	68.7	64.0	58.9	53.0	47.9	59.8
service	Private	79.9	76.7	69.8	70.5	67.4	74.7

[1] per cent who responded "to a great" or "very great extent"

Respondents have perceptions that conform with the stereotype about the relative degree of creativity and innovation in the two sectors. In describing their companies, private sector managers reported that their organizations were oriented toward innovation and creative management. Some 55 per cent and 45 per cent of private sector managers described their companies as being oriented to a great extent toward innovation and creative management respectively. This was in contrast with the public sector, where only 21 per cent and 17 per cent shared these perceptions. Table 4-3 shows there was virtually no difference in responses related to innovation across the private sector, whereas 17 points separated the high score from the low score in the public sector. We saw similar differences across managerial levels in the public sector in responses regarding the orientation toward creative management.

The perception of a lack of innovation and creative management is strengthened by a perception that management is much less efficient in the public sector. As we shall see, many public sector managers believe that the values espoused by their departments revolve around efficiency. Yet only 37 per cent said efficient management existed to a "great" or "very great extent" in describing the orientation of their departments. Another surprising finding was the degree to which managers perceived their departments or companies as employee-oriented. Only 9 per cent and 38 per cent of managers in the public and private sectors respectively described their organizations as being to a great extent employee-oriented. As can be seen in Table 4-3, even the most senior managers in the public sector did not think of their departments as being particularly employee-oriented. However, these results are consistent with the data presented in the previous section on caring about people.[17]

Innovation and creativity, two of the most highly prized attributes of successful organizations, are often fostered by organizational forces. Korman cites studies showing that highly hierarchical environments that control behaviour, routinize and specialize activities also tend to produce non-creative problem-solving behaviour. In contrast, environments with low hierarchical control of behaviour and low routinization and specialization lead to creative and innovative behaviour.[18]

Our data suggest that, in relative terms, public sector departments are perceived by their senior managers as being more highly routinized and programmed than private sector companies. Thus, the challenge for public sector managers is to transform the hierarchical system and values that prevail from an earlier era of scientific management into values that nurture an environment characterized by a less hierarchical orientation.

Loyalty: To Canadians Above All

Where do employees' allegiances lie? Over the years, significant shifts in attitudes have occurred. In particular one sentiment, loyalty, has shifted dramatically away from the employees' place of work and toward loyalty to a profession.[19] However, since the vast majority of these studies which document such shifts in allegiance are based on private sector data, we expect that working in the public sector may entail different loyalties. Also, given that being a public servant means serving the public, we wanted to verify the extent to which respondents felt loyal to the Canadian public.

To improve our understanding of the notion of organizational loyalty, participants in the study were asked to indicate the extent of loyalty they felt to

- the Canadian public

- the person to whom they reported

- their DM/CEO

- their organization

- the industry/policy area in which they worked

- the local community.

The responses demonstrated several differences between the two sectors and variability across levels in each sector. Table 4-4 shows the percentage of respondents who indicated loyalty "to a great" or "very great extent" to various individuals or organizations. In general, private sector managers felt the greatest loyalty to the person to whom they reported, to their CEO, and to their organization. In turn, public sector managers were more loyal to the Canadian public, the person to whom they reported, and the policy area of their work.

Overall, 90 per cent of the respondents in the private sector and 69 per cent of those in the public sector felt loyal to their organizations to a "great" or "very great extent". However, respondents' degree of loyalty to the Canadian public produced a more variable pattern of responses between the public and private sectors. Forty-five per cent of respondents in the private sector and 84 per cent of those in the public sector felt a high degree of loyalty to the Canadian public. In looking at the data in relation to job level, it is worth noting that loyalty to the organization declined across levels in both sectors, while the degree of loyalty to the Canadian public showed very little variation across levels in both sectors.

The data suggest that public sector managers are directing their loyalty to the public rather than to individuals or departments. The data also hint that managers may share more of a public sector-wide culture rather than a departmental culture when stating their most important loyalty is to Canadians. The data on loyalty may be viewed to be slightly contradictory to what was reported in the previous chapter in Table 3.2 about who senior managers try to satisfy. In that discussion, public sector managers were seen to place more importance on satisfying their clients than the general public. If we keep in mind that clients are the Canadian public, and that we did not query whether or not managers felt loyalty to their clients, it becomes easier to reconcile that difference.

Table 4-4
Loyalty in the Public and Private Sector

Loyalty to		Levels below DM/CEO					
		1	2	3	4	5	Av.
Canadian public	Public	87.8	84.0	81.2	84.1	86.8	84.2
	Private	46.7	44.1	45.2	41.2	48.2	45.2
Person to whom you report	Public	81.3	77.4	72.4	65.2	73.0	74.0
	Private	83.4	77.8	79.2	73.9	83.5	80.1
DM/CEO	Public	82.4	65.7	48.0	39.7	39.5	56.4
	Private	83.3	65.9	67.2	56.9	58.2	70.0
Department/Company	Public	80.5	73.5	65.0	61.1	60.6	69.1
	Private	93.4	89.2	88.7	82.6	87.9	89.6
Policy/industry area of work	Public	79.0	77.4	67.9	63.4	63.8	71.2
	Private	61.1	53.7	51.8	52.4	61.9	56.8
Local community	Public	52.3	58.0	54.6	59.9	59.4	56.5
	Private	54.0	44.7	51.6	43.0	57.9	50.2

1   per cent who responded "to a great" or "very great extent"

Organizational Values: Efficiency versus Excellence, and a Foundation to Build on

To measure organizational values, participants answered open-ended questions designed to elicit their unprompted views of corporate culture.[20] Respondents were asked to list the values encouraged in their organizations, the mechanisms used to inculcate these values and how outstanding accomplishments were rewarded.[21] The statements in Table 4-5 summarize the responses to the open-ended questions. We tried to capture the values expressed by doing a content analysis of the results for the purposes of managing the data set.[22]

The table demonstrates the degree to which private sector values are different from those espoused by public sector managers. The public sector values are based largely on efficiency and value for money, while the private sector values reflect a commitment to excellence in management. In terms of rankings, efficiency and value for money prove to be the most important values in the public sector, followed by respect for clients and good management. Another significant outcome is that nearly 12 per cent of public sector respondents were not aware of the values encouraged by their departments, making the "don't know" category the third most important in the public sector responses.[23] In the private sector, excellence is the most important value, followed by creativity, productivity, the importance placed on human resources and good management.

Table 4-5
Rankings of Values Encouraged
in the Public and Private Sectors
(first response only)

Public Sector	%	Private Sector	%
1. Efficiency/Effectiveness	16	1. Excellence/Competence	16.4
2. Value for Money	11.6	2. Creativity	9.8
3. Don't Know/No Value	11.6	3. Productivity	9.0
4. Respect for Clients	9.9	4. Importance of Human Resources	8.1
5. Good Management/Planning	8.5	5. Good Management/Planning	7.5

Public sector managers, especially in the last decade, have become very cost conscious and, as a result, have developed elaborate financial control mechanisms. This bottom-line approach (which one would stereotypically expect to find in the private sector) constitutes the "value for money" category. On the other hand, respect for clients is a marketing-oriented value. It combines statements related to quality of service and knowledge of client needs. Finally, good management and planning in both sectors reflects a systematic and structured approach to managing which is goal-oriented. It is a value which at times reflects the notions of objective-setting, vision, priority-setting and participatory management.

Unlike the values described by private sector managers, the public sector responses were oriented toward financial or control systems. By contrast, the private sector responses focussed on managing people and providing or creating excellent products and services. Notions of excellence were the most important values expressed by private sector managers. Under "creativity" we grouped respondents' statements related to innovation, identifying initiative, use of new technologies, self-reliance and flexibility. Simple hard work and improvements in quality and quantity were assimilated under the "productivity" value. Finally, anything to do with people was included under the value "importance of human resources". Some examples include statements on team spirit, co-operation, respect for the individual, development of subordinates, and workplace health and safety. Good management and planning, implying a systematic, structured goal-oriented approach, is the fifth value cited by managers in both sectors.

The data on values reinforce two points. First, there are significant differences between the two sectors; second, there are differences in the values perceived by managers at the very high and middle and lower levels of senior management in the public sector.

Table 4-6 shows the three values cited most often by respondents at each management level in each sector. It provides further evidence of the vertical solitude by demonstrating the differences in the value systems of EXs, SMs and SM-1s. The mix of values and their order for each sector showed little variation. However, in the public sector 12 per cent of managers three levels from the DM cited "don't know" as an answer, and this percentage increased for the next two lower levels. In other words, those four or five levels down from the DM mentioned "don't know" more often than any other value. These levels correspond to the SM and SM-1 groups, whom we view as the managers who transmit culture between those higher up and those on the front lines.

We believe it is important that all senior managers have a set of common values; it should now be obvious, however, that there is a serious malaise in the public sector corporate culture. The problem, as we perceive it, is not the absence of values among senior managers but rather that managers at lower levels do not appear to share the values of their superiors. Having the benefit of a private sector sample, where values appear to be shared at all managerial levels in the companies surveyed, reinforces our perception that there is an immediate need to articulate the values of the federal public service. In this context, it is useful to recall that Canada has a strong public sector ethic. Improving communication and providing messages that reduce uncertainty and ambiguity around these values allows managers at the lower echelons of the senior ranks to deal more effectively with a difficult and complex environment and, in their role as culture carriers, to transmit the information to the operational levels.

There are lessons to be learned about inculcating and changing values in large organizations. Individuals internalize values and beliefs when they find them intrinsically rewarding and when they are consistent with their own values and beliefs. In a three-step process

Table 4-6
Values Encouraged in the Public and Private Sectors from the Perspective of Job Level

Public Sector

	Level 1		Level 2		Level 3		Level 4		Level 5
1. Efficiency	- 16.7%	1. Efficiency	- 19.5%	1. Efficiency	- 16.4%	1. Don't Know	- 19.8%	1. Don't Know	- 18.1%
2. Respect for Clients	- 14.2%	2. Value for Money	- 13.2%	2. Value for Money	- 12.1%	2. Efficiency	- 12.7%	2. Efficiency	- 13.9%
3. Good Management	- 11.7%	3. Respect for Clients	- 10.3%	3. Don't Know	- 11.7%	3. Value for Money	- 10.4%	3. Value for Money	- 13.9%

Private Sector

	Level 1		Level 2		Level 3		Level 4		Level 5
1. Excellence	- 18.9%	1. Excellence	- 17.1%	1. Excellence	- 15.8%	1. Excellence	- 15.2%	1. Creativity	- 13.6%
2. Creativity	- 10.1%	2. Productivity	- 10.0%	2. Creativity	- 13.3%	2. Productivity	- 11.9%	2. Productivity	- 12.8%
3. Accountability	- 9.6%	3. Good Management	- 9.7%	3. Human Resources	- 9.7%	3. Value for Money	- 9.3%	3. Human Resources	- 10.4%

described by Kelman, individuals usually comply with, identify with, or internalize new values.[24] Compliance occurs because people stand to gain by adopting new values, whereas identification results from a desire to remain associated with a group. But the true test of belonging to an organization comes when people internalize values, because then the values become intrinsically rewarding and difficult to distinguish from one's own. People also internalize values which are held by people they like or respect.

The data suggest that the most senior managers have internalized public sector cultural values, but for most managers at the SM and SM-1 level we observe a process of compliance or identification. For this reason, the values held may be very volatile. This situation may be advantageous if the aim is to change the culture. If most managers comply with organizational values in the public sector but do not believe in them, it may provide an opportunity to build a new foundation.

It is also important to note that any attempt to change values in a way that is inconsistent with the value system of an individual is usually doomed. We do not know the degree to which sectoral values in the public sector fit with the personal value systems of senior managers. Discrepancies between the two would make the process of internalization that much more difficult.

To Instill Values: Meetings, More Meetings and Training

Although values in the public and private sectors are quite different, there are similarities in the mechanisms used to inculcate values.[25] As Table 4-7 demonstrates, three of the five mechanisms used to inculcate values were the same, although ranked differently by respondents from each sector. Meetings, training and management techniques were cited most often by public sector managers; in the private sector, training was the most important mechanism, followed by meetings and management techniques. It is again important to point out that 13 per cent of public sector respondents did not know what mechanisms were used in their organizations.[26]

Under the heading "meetings", we grouped all statements referring to face-to-face, one-on-one, interpersonal and sometimes informal communication. "Training" refers to any activity involving learning new knowledge or skills. "Management techniques" is a broad category encompassing statements about work plans, management philosophy, techniques such as "Management by Objectives", and a good working environment. These were the most important mechanisms in both sectors. "Cost-related" techniques was the next most popular category, comprising steps to improve profitability by reducing costs, such as budget cuts, early retirement, downsizing, and cost recovery. Surprisingly, this turned out to be a mechanism invoked more often by public servants than by private sector managers. "Policies" as a mechanism includes processes and regulations but also traditions of the organization.

Table 4-7
Mechanisms Used to Inculcate Values
in the Public and Private Sectors
(first response only)

Public Sector	%	Private Sector	%
1. Meetings	14.1	1. Training	20.4
2. Don't know	13.3	2. Meetings	16.7
3. Training/Courses	10.3	3. Management techniques	11.2
4. Management techniques	8.4	4. Rewards	9.2
5. Cost-related	7.5	5. Policies	7.1

Looking at the data according to respondents' place in the hierarchy, we obtained results similar to previous analyses. As can be seen in Table 4-8, there is a gap in awareness on the part of public sector managers two levels and more below the DM. If 13 per cent of managers three levels below the DM do not know what mechanisms are used in their departments to inculcate values, we can surmise that the most senior managers either do not articulate their values well or are not committing the time and effort to communicate values to managers at lower levels.

Another striking difference between the sectors is that there were few references to reward systems in the public sector. Traditionally, reward systems are effective tools for reinforcing, inculcating and teaching values.

Rewarding Achievement: Words are not Enough

One way that organizational culture is transmitted is through myths and stories told in the organization. Stories of outstanding achievement serve the purpose of increasing loyalty, pointing out values and reinforcing culture. The manner in which outstanding achievement is rewarded reveals a great deal about an organization and the

Table 4-8
Mechanisms Used To Inculcate Values in the Public and Private Sectors from the Perspective of Job Level

Public Sector

Level 1		Level 2		Level 3		Level 4		Level 5	
1. Meetings	- 23.1%	1. Meetings	- 16.5%	1. Do not know	- 13.3%	1. Do not know	- 21.0%	1. Do not know	- 18.0%
2. Training	- 9.2%	2. Do not know	- 10.5%	2. Training	- 11.1%	2. Training	- 11.5%	2. Negative Comments	- 12.7%
3. Management Techniques	- 9.2%	3. Training	- 10.2%	3. Management Techniques	- 8.9%	3. Meetings	- 8.6%	3. Cost-related	- 10.0%

Private Sector

Level 1		Level 2		Level 3		Level 4		Level 5	
1. Training	- 21.9%	1. Training	- 24.0%	1. Meetings	- 19.0%	1. Training	- 19.2%	1. Training	- 16.7%
2. Meetings	- 19.7%	2. Meetings	- 14.9%	2. Training	- 15.2%	2. Meetings	- 13.7%	2. Meetings	- 11.7%
3. Management Techniques	- 12.9%	3. Management Techniques	- 9.4%	3. Reward Systems	- 10.9%	3. Reward Systems	- 11.6%	3. Management Techniques	- 10.8%
						4. Management Techniques	- 11.6%	4. Feedback	- 10.8%

philosophy under which it operates. When outstanding achievements are publicly recognized and amply rewarded, they tend to become part of the organization's mythology and culture.

After asking respondents about organizational values and the mechanisms used to instill them, we asked about the rewards offered in their organizations. Table 4-9, which summarizes the answers, suggests significant differences between the two sectors. First, whereas 42 per cent of managers in the private sector pointed to monetary rewards as the major means of rewarding outstanding achievement, few chose it in the public sector; it did not appear in the top three choices. Second, we see again the preponderance of the "do not know" response by the public sector respondents. Third, private sector managers, regardless of level, had a clearer view about the reward structure in their organizations.

Table 4-9
Rewards Given for Outstanding Achievement
in the Public and Private Sector
(first response only)

Public Sector	%	Private Sector	%
1. Recognition	23.0	1. Pay Rewards/Incentives	41.8
2. Promotion	18.2	2. Promotion	26.3
3. Do not know	15.9	3. Recognition	17.1

The lack of substantial monetary rewards for outstanding achievement in the public sector points to the importance of intrinsic rewards. We discuss the importance of intrinsic rewards such as recognition in later chapters. Suffice it to point out here that we detected a malaise resulting from the absence of significant rewards in the public sector. Praise does not seem to be enough; recognition is often perceived as empty rhetoric.

Relating Cultural Attributes to Outcome Measures: The Influence of Culture on Work Satisfaction

In looking at how culture affects work satisfaction, we conducted two kinds of analyses. First, we analyzed the degree to which the work satisfaction measures were influenced by the responses to survey questions about culture. Second, we examined how the relation between culture and satisfaction was influenced by the manager's job level. Here we report on only a few of the culture items, but these results are typical of the remaining items. Our choice of items was based on those that emerged as the most important predictors of work satisfaction.[27]

Of Cultural Halos: If They Care, I'm Satisfied

In this section, we looked at the degree to which respondents thought their organizations cared for the welfare of employees and whether this influenced work satisfaction. Table 4-10 shows a linear relationship between work satisfaction and the perception that the organization cares. The percentage of managers who were satisfied increased in tandem with the perception that the organization cared about its people. The slope of this linear relationship holds in both sectors. However, when we analyze the relationship between caring and satisfaction in the private sector, managers always reported greater satisfaction than their public sector counterparts. This comparison held whether the private sector managers perceived that the organization cared very little or a great deal.

Although the percentage of managers reporting that the organization cared to a "very great extent" was higher in the private sector, this difference was not very large, except in the case of extrinsic satisfaction, where the gap between the two sectors was extremely large. While it is difficult to pinpoint the reasons for this difference, we do know that private companies can exercise greater flexibility in their allocation of rewards. This would explain why the cultural variables may have a greater impact on extrinsic satisfaction in the private sector than in the public sector. Of greater significance, however, are the differences between the public and private sectors in the satisfaction measures when the perception of organizational caring is low. The scores in the first column of Table 4-10 do not augur well for the public sector, as they show that the morale of senior managers tends to be very low in all dimensions when they perceive that their departments do not care about employees' welfare.

Caring about people is especially important because of its enormous influence on all aspects of work satisfaction. While one would expect that caring about people would have a direct influence on intrinsic, departmental and job satisfaction, there is little reason to suspect that this behaviour would influence extrinsic satisfaction and the satisfaction derived from career progress.[28]

This pattern of results suggests that respondents may be failing to distinguish among the various satisfaction indices. This phenomenon, known as a halo effect, occurs when a specific perception is generalized to other perceptions of the same situation or object.[29]   In

Table 4-10
Relationship Between Perception that the Organization "Cares about People" and Work Satisfaction

Indices of Work Satisfaction		Organization "Cares about People"				
		To a very little extent	To a little extent	To some extent	To a great extent	To a very great extent
Intrinsic Satisfaction	Public	25.8[1]	36.5	55.9	78.1	84.5
	Private	45.1	48.5	67.1	83.8	91.3
Extrinsic Satisfaction	Public	21.9	26.2	34.1	46.5	36.7
	Private	32.3	39.4	45.3	66.5	85.6
Departmental Satisfaction	Public	5.0	8.3	25.6	52.0	84.5
	Private	22.6	29.6	44.5	76.2	90.5
Job Satisfaction	Public	9.0	15.1	20.5	39.4	66.7
	Private	23.3	15.3	22.1	41.3	63.8
Satisfaction with Career Progress	Public	11.8	14.6	26.3	50.3	53.7
	Private	30.0	17.4	34.9	53.7	61.8

1 per cent of respondents who are "satisfied" or "very satisfied" on the five satisfaction indices

this way managers may generalize their views that the organization cares by being satisfied with their career progress. Similarly, the halo effect may also affect levels of extrinsic satisfaction. It may of course be related to career progression. In other words, in organizations that are perceived to care, managers perceive that they progress, and progression always results in increased extrinsic satisfaction.

We noted at the beginning of this chapter that goals and objectives provide a road map for organization members. Knowledge of the organization's goals is akin to having been socialized to its culture and also influences work satisfaction, as can be observed in Table 4-11. In both sectors we found a strong linear relationship between work satisfaction and the degree to which respondents knew about their organization's goals. Looking at this result in cultural terms, we found people more satisfied when they understood the organization, its role, and the reasons for decisions. Regardless of the sector, respondents clearly indicated their dislike of being left in the dark about goals and objectives.

The relationship between the various cultural items and work satisfaction followed a distinct pattern. As in our earlier analysis of satisfaction and "caring", we found large inter-sectoral differences with respect to work satisfaction and knowledge of organizational goals. As an example, the percentage of private sector managers who were satisfied when they knew their organization's goals was consistently higher than that for public sector managers. Furthermore, in this case, the difference in the percentage who were satisfied when they knew the goals "to a very great extent" was marked. Many more private sector managers were satisfied because they knew the goals of their organization. Knowledge of goals turned out not to be as important as "caring" in the public sector. It did not produce a halo effect in all the satisfaction dimensions. In the public sector it was only the intrinsic aspects of work satisfaction that were satisfied by knowing goals and objectives.

In establishing the viability of this linkage, it is obviously important not only to look at the relationship between knowledge of goals and satisfaction but also to determine how much managers were satisfied when they perceived that goals were being accomplished. Once again, the pattern of results was the same (see Table 4-12). We found a linear relationship in both sectors between the perception that the organization was accomplishing its objectives and employee work satisfaction. We also found more private than public sector managers satisfied with their work when they thought that goals were being accomplished to a "great" or "very great extent".

In the public sector, managers showed higher levels of satisfaction when they thought organizational objectives were being

Table 4-11
Relationships Between Knowing Organizational Goals and Work Satisfaction

Indices of Work Satisfaction		Knowing Organizational Goals				
		To a very little extent	To a little extent	To some extent	To a great extent	To a very great extent
Intrinsic Satisfaction	Public	22.6	30.3	39.2	57.1	73.2
	Private	33.4	55.3	59.7	77.0	89.0
Extrinsic Satisfaction	Public	30.0	30.4	32.4	34.4	37.9
	Private	50.0	44.8	57.1	57.6	67.5
Departmental Satisfaction	Public	10.0	10.1	11.5	26.9	45.4
	Private	25.1	32.4	44.2	64.3	77.9
Job Satisfaction	Public	9.7	6.8	12.1	21.2	47.9
	Private	9.1	11.7	19.6	31.3	62.3
Satisfaction with Career Progress	Public	3.2	13.2	18.4	29.1	39.9
	Private	33.3	26.4	30.7	44.1	64.3

1   per cent of respondents who are "satisfied" or "very satisfied" on the five satisfaction indices

Table 4-12

**Relationships Between the Accomplishment of
Organizational Objectives and Work Satisfaction**

Indices of Work Satisfaction		Accomplishment of Organizational Objectives				
		To a very little extent	To a little extent	To some extent	To a great extent	To a very great extent
Intrinsic Satisfaction	Public	15.5	31.2	48.2	66.5	76.7
	Private	30.0	53.7	62.3	78.7	86.7
Extrinsic Satisfaction	Public	28.9	29.2	32.4	37.8	30.7
	Private	40.0	43.9	50.2	58.9	70.0
Departmental Satisfaction	Public	0.0	5.9	16.1	38.0	60.9
	Private	10.0	29.3	43.5	65.1	82.7
Job Satisfaction	Public	6.0	11.1	16.9	28.6	55.4
	Private	20.0	13.4	20.8	32.9	63.2
Satisfaction with Career Progress	Public	8.4	17.6	20.7	35.4	44.8
	Private	20.0	23.4	32.9	46.0	62.4

1   per cent of respondents who are "satisfied" or "very satisfied" on the five satisfaction indices

accomplished than when they knew the department's goals. However, when organizational objectives were seen to be accomplished "to a very great extent", public sector satisfaction remained lower than that in the private sector. It may be that public sector managers did not identify with objectives in whose elaboration they were not involved.

Managerial Job Level, Culture and Satisfaction: A Culture within a Culture

Further analysis of the data indicates that caring about people was one of the most important predictors of work satisfaction. To analyze this finding in more detail, the "caring about people" variable was linked to work satisfaction and job level in the public sector sample. These results have been displayed in Figures 4-1 to 4-3. Overall, these results show that the relation between culture and satisfaction, using three satisfaction indices (departmental, intrinsic and job satisfaction), is not as linear as our initial analysis suggested.

Figure 4-1 shows that, as far as satisfaction with a department was concerned, there was some linearity in work satisfaction among job levels when respondents perceived that the department cared about people "to a great extent". More than 50 per cent of respondents in each managerial category were "satisfied" or "very satisfied" with their departments when they perceived that "to a great extent" the department cared about the welfare of employees. The decline in the percentage of managers satisfied when this perception was less strong was also "somewhat" linear but was more dependent on job level. EXs were more satisfied than SMs and SM-1s when they perceived some or a small degree of caring. For example, when they perceived that the department cared little for employees' welfare, 17 per cent of EXs were satisfied or very satisfied while only 5 per cent of the SMs and SM-1s felt that way.

When we looked at how the job level of respondents influenced their responses about caring and intrinsic satisfaction, we observed (Figure 4-2) that the percentage of managers who were intrinsically satisfied declined as we moved down the managerial hierarchy. If 87 per cent of the EX category was intrinsically satisfied when the department cared about people, the percentage fell to 73 per cent for the SM-1 group. When little caring was perceived to exist, 45 per cent of the EXs were still satisfied intrinsically, whereas only 27 per cent of the SM-1 group claimed to be satisfied. These results were similar to our previous observation of the same factors when analyzed against departmental satisfaction.

In Figure 4-3, which displays the relationship between job satisfaction and caring about people across managerial levels, we

Figure 4-1
Relationship between the Perception that the Department Cares
about People, Managerial Level and Departmental Satisfaction
(Public Sector)

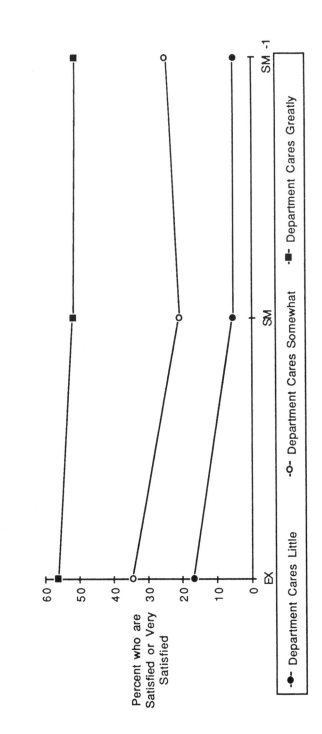

Figure 4-2
Relationship between the Perception that the Department Cares about People, Managerial Level and Intrinsic Satisfaction
(Public Sector)

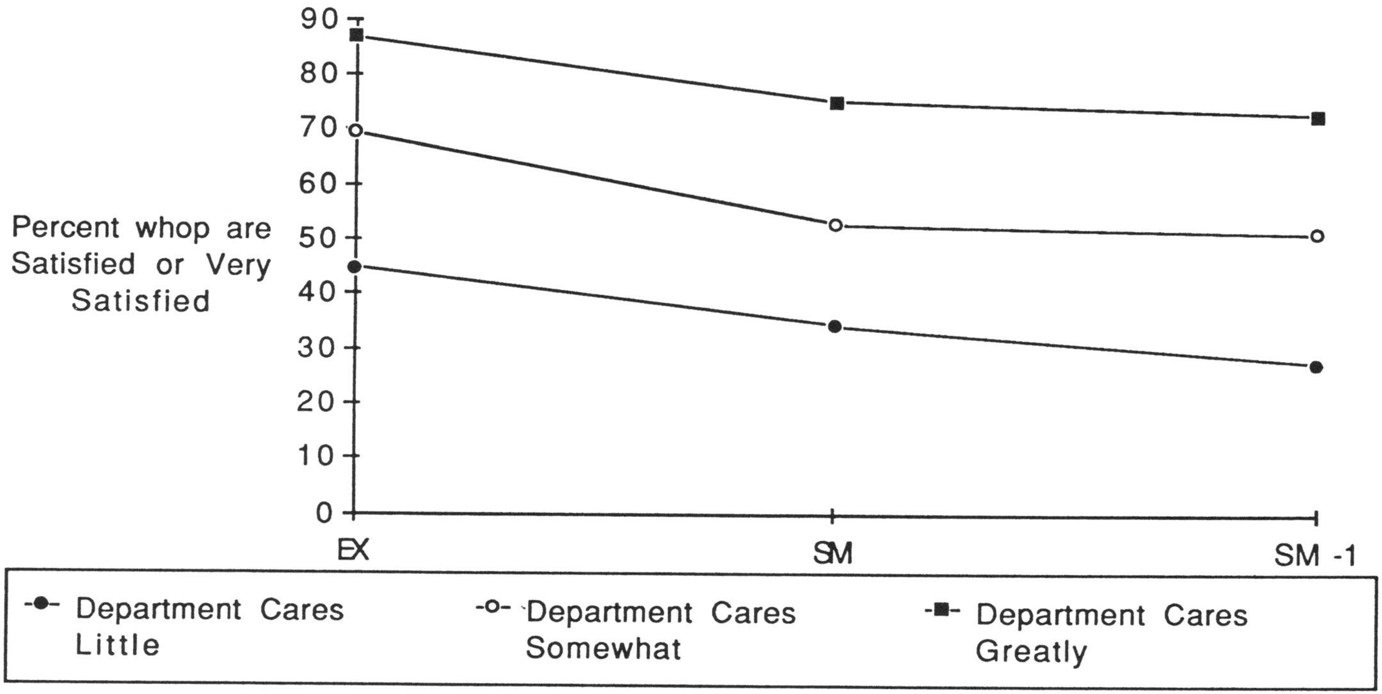

Percent whop are Satisfied or Very Satisfied

EX   SM   SM -1

-●- Department Cares Little

-○- Department Cares Somewhat

-■- Department Cares Greatly

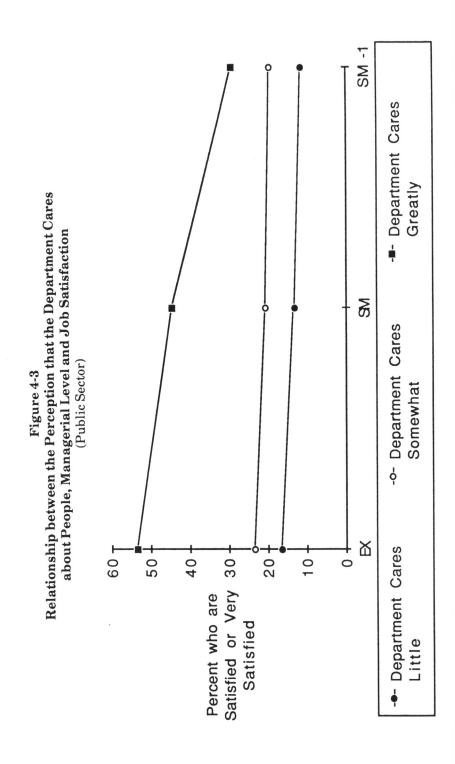

Figure 4-3
Relationship between the Perception that the Department Cares
about People, Managerial Level and Job Satisfaction
(Public Sector)

observed the results obtained for intrinsic motivation in yet more spectacular terms. While 54 per cent of the EX group was satisfied when they perceived that a department cared greatly, this number fell to a surprising low of 29 per cent for the SM-1 group. As they perceived some or little caring, all three groups of managers reported low levels of job satisfaction. Analysis of how job level influenced satisfaction, based on managers' perceptions of other cultural dimensions measured in this survey, yields very similar results.

Is Corporate Culture Important?

Culture is an important variable for a number of reasons. First, because of the concept's prominence in management theory, one cannot talk to managers today without discussing the importance of organizational culture for organizational performance. Second, we felt that it would be useful to define the borders of public and private sector cultures by observing those aspects of corporate culture that are common and those that are different. Third, it was important to provide an empirical link between cultural dimensions and work satisfaction.

How members describe their organizations is important because it gives us a sense of the culture and philosophy that guide the organization. Keeping in mind that we are looking at 20 departments and 13 companies and amalgamating data from each group to arrive at our cultural dimensions (a point to which we return at the end of the chapter) we have found that culture makes a difference in the degree of work satisfaction.

Public and private sector managers did not describe their culture in the same manner. In the private sector, managers talked of an environment in which they knew the goals of their companies, considered them realistic and felt that their companies were accomplishing their goals. They claimed to be familiar with their clients' needs, and the majority believed that their organizations cared about the welfare of their employees. By contrast, public sector managers characterized their organizations as caring little for their employees and described themselves as not fully knowledgeable about their departmental goals, which they viewed as unrealistic and not often achieved. Despite those serious problems, public sector managers felt they had a good handle on their clients' needs. By and large, private sector managers were more satisfied with those aspects of their workplace culture that had an impact on their jobs, organizations, and careers.

We also found that the differences between the sectors became more pronounced as one moved down the organizational hierarchy. As an example, the differences between managers working one level below the DM (e.g., an ADM) and a manager five levels down (such as an SM-1) tended to confirm our growing suspicion that, in the public sector, there are at least two distinct corporate cultures.

In general terms, the EX category was much more satisfied than the SM and SM-1 groups with all the aspects of organizational culture we studied. While we acknowledge the existence of many private sector examples where those at the top were happier and considered themselves different from those lower down, the significance of this finding is the existence of essentially two solitudes in the public sector.[30] The cost of such solitudes is especially high because it may lead to creating, within a similar system, classes of managers who have constructed for themselves different realities of their environment. Such discrepancies may give rise to neurotic tendencies such as the development of fears about uncertainty and risk, and attempts to rectify the situation by relying on numerous control mechanisms.[31]

One other reason to view these findings with alarm is that, as we argued earlier, the middle and lower levels of senior management play a crucial role as the culture carriers in the typical hierarchical organization. It is difficult to transmit cultural attributes within an organization when they are not well known or when there is a perception that doing so is of little concern to senior management. The data show that managers at different levels espouse different values and that satisfaction levels are strongly moderated by level in the organization. There is no direct evidence to suggest that there has been a conscious effort to keep middle and lower managers away from those at higher management levels. Instead, a separation seems to have evolved, probably as a result of the demands on senior managers to pay a disproportionate amount of attention to deputy ministers or ministers. As a consequence, perhaps insufficient time is spent in communicating about work-related issues with those working at lower levels of the organization.

The differences among levels are also significant because the cultural dimensions we measured were clearly related to satisfaction. One item from the survey, the degree to which organizations were thought to care about their employees, explained roughly 40 per cent of the variation in each analysis of the various work satisfaction indices. The consistency and strength of this relationship shows how important "caring" is in determining work satisfaction. It has been argued elsewhere that an organization's philosophy and orientation toward its employees are important and integral parts of its corporate culture.[32] Our data show the accuracy of this observation, regardless of sector. The addition of the other corporate culture survey items also improved our understanding of work satisfaction. On the basis of this analysis we conclude that culture is an important predictor of work satisfaction; that private and public sector cultures differ; and that in the public sector, the most senior managers have a different set of cultural values than those working at lower managerial levels.

Organizational Culture: From Uniqueness to Similarity

Studies of corporate culture often rely on descriptive analyses of single organizations, comparing them with the cultures of other organizations. Such studies usually concentrate on an organization's exceptional or noteworthy cultural strengths rather than attributes that might be considered routine.[33] In this way, organizational culture is said to be made up of values, beliefs, expectations and experiences that are different from those of other organizations. As a result, we expect Magna Corporation, for example, to possess a culture different from that of Canadian Pacific or Loblaw's.

Despite the cultural uniqueness of each organization, researchers have found many similarities in the cultures of "successful" organizations, leading them to question the value of preserving unique organizational cultures.[34] We also found through our analysis that there is a constellation of values that underlie the cultural make-up of private and public organizations.

Our data set includes 33 organizations and cultures. A large manufacturing company is different from a financial institution, which in turn is different from a retail and distribution conglomerate. What all these companies shared was that they were large in size, leaders in their field, and among the best examples of private sector firms in Canada. All but one were privately owned by Canadians. They considered themselves to be profit- and bottom-line oriented and had little interest in how the public sector is managed.

Similarly, one can argue that the Department of Supply and Services and the Department of Transport are two different entities, each with its particular culture. In our discussions with public servants we came across many departmental peculiarities, myths, and stories that made departments different. All public sector managers we met explained why their department was particular. In general, however, these were large departments, all part of the federal administrative and financial system, ruled by similar procedures, and by the same guidelines and philosophy (such as the merit system) for personnel management.

By combining data from diverse companies and departments we have elevated the analysis from a department or company level to a private or public sector level. The analogy is that of the sector culture being akin to national culture, and of organizational cultures within the sector as ethnic subcultures. It is possible to show that ethnic subcultures are influenced by the dominant national culture while maintaining their identity. We believe that departments are different but alike within the public sector and that companies are different but alike within the private sector. Another way to view this is by invoking the psychological argument which states that while all individuals are different, they are also alike because of the many psychological characteristics and processes that they share. By aggregating such similarities, as we have in the survey, we can discuss sector-wide data.

Few Good Soldiers in the Public Service

Sathe has argued that organizations hire and socialize members who in some sense "fit in" with the culture. If employees deviate from accepted norms and behaviour, they are removed from the organization.[35] The data regarding culture in the public sector raises the issue of the degree to which senior managers "fit in" with the culture. Sathe used two dimensions to understand the degree of an individual's involvement in the organization.[36] One dimension is the extent to which the individual holds the culture's values. The other dimension is the extent to which the individual behaves in ways prescribed by the culture.

Based on the degree to which people conform with these two dimensions, Sathe identified four cultural caricatures. The person who conforms with both dimensions he calls the Good Soldier. Good Soldiers share the values of the organization and act in culturally expected ways. They both believe and behave as prescribed by the culture. The opposite caricature is the Rebel, the non-conformer. Rebels neither believe nor behave in ways prescribed by their culture. Between these extremes are two other types. Mavericks internalize cultural values but act out of role, in ways not prescribed by the culture. Those who act in prescribed ways but do not internalize the norms are the Adapters. Our data show that there are many Good Soldiers in the private sector in Canada. The few Good Soldiers in the public sector tend to be at the highest echelons. In the public service of Canada in all likelihood we have many types of Adapters, who stay on because they enjoy their jobs and value some of the organizational benefits – even if this may simply be the salary they receive.

In our view, the Adapters are senior managers who are probably working hard but who have, to some extent, lost faith in the system's ability to give them meaningful rewards and responsibilities. The number of such adapters may have grown in size over the years, and the reasons may be due to an inconsistent period of indoctrination during the first years of public sector employment and the misuse of critical management mechanisms at the disposition of senior managers (such as selection, promotion, and role modelling).

Schein defines organizational culture as the pattern of assumptions that is considered valid and therefore taught to new members as the correct way to deal with problems.[37] In this context, the federal public service is faced with some personnel management issues. First, the federal government is experiencing difficulties in recruiting "the best and the brightest" students into its entry level positions.[38] Second, the middle management groups (SM and down) have not internalized a consistent set of public sector values. Finally, EXs have not done a credible job of communicating a consistent view of public sector culture.

Schein also argued that an important way to reinforce culture is through role modelling, teaching, and coaching by senior managers and through the criteria used to allocate rewards and status.[39] Given the cultural dichotomy we observed in the public sector sample, there is an immediate need for top management to do more role modelling with middle level managers. As well, the Public Service Commission needs to reassess all its managerial training and development activities, since efforts to date have not resulted in the visible socialization process that is so important for value transmission. The Commission needs to address the issue of whether it wants to use training and development not only to educate but also to socialize managers in public sector values.

The lack of internalization of values by many senior managers suggests that new reward structures and criteria have to be built into the system. If the SM and SM-1 positions confer some status to their holders, as they invariably do, remaining in a given position for a long time should go hand in hand with mechanisms to strengthen culture. Acknowledging the seriousness of "plateauing", conditions must be created to ensure managers' awareness of the dominant cultural values of the public service. Otherwise, we run the risk of having too many discouraged employees occupying important positions in the organization who also sense that they have "nowhere to go".

Finally, the degree to which the organization cares for the welfare and development of its employees also requires attention. There is no quick solution to the perception that the organization does not care. We know from experience that quick-fix approaches are doomed to fail. While communications strategies designed to inculcate cultural values and improve organizational orientation are obviously part of the solution, they must be authoritative without sounding like propaganda. Statements such as "people are our most important asset" are not generally believed because they tend to be viewed as self-serving or patronizing. Managers are likely to remain sceptical if there are no visible signs that the senior management cadre subscribes to the espoused values. As well, the communication effort has to be implicit. Through stories, metaphors and other symbolic forms of communication, efforts need to be made to correct this perception of lack of interest in fellow employees.

In the End: Culture Matters

In the world of private perceptions, the world on which people build their assumptions and redefine reality, we see that the public sector is typically viewed by insiders occupying important positions as not "caring about people". It would be reassuring to ascribe some of the differences in organizational culture and work satisfaction which we found to socio-demographic factors such as age, sex, education level, linguistic group, or geographic location. Our overall analysis shows this not to be the case. The responses from female managers (although a small subset of our sample) were similar to those of male managers; francophone managers and anglophone managers responded similarly; older managers were no different than younger managers.

In the end two aspects stand out: the public sector culture versus the private and, especially in the public sector, the values held by the top echelons of management versus those at the middle and low echelons of management — two different cultures and a culture within a culture. What is perhaps most significant about this finding is its consistency. We expected to find differences between the public and private sector, but not to such degrees. As for the vertical solitude in the public sector, its consistency and pervasiveness has been shown in our analysis of organizational culture.

Notes

1. Some of the material in this chapter was presented at the Round Table of the International Institute of Administrative Sciences in Budapest, August 30-September 2, 1988, and published as an article entitled "Organizational Culture in Public Bureaucracies," *International Review of Administrative Sciences*, vol. 55, no. 1, March 1989, pp. 95-116.

2. See A.L. Kroeber and C. Kluckhohn, "Culture: a critical review of concepts and definitions," *Peabody Museum Papers*, vol. 47, no. 1, (Cambridge, Mass.: Harvard University, 1952), for a discussion of definitions.

3. T.E. Deal and A.A. Kennedy, *Corporate Cultures: The Rites and Rituals of Corporate Life*, (Reading, Mass.: Addison-Wesley, 1982); T.J. Peters and R.H. Waterman, *In Search of Excellence*,

(New York: Harper & Row, 1982); T.J. Peters and N. Austin, *A Passion for Excellence,* (New York: Harper & Row, 1985).

4. See K.L. Gregory, "Native-view paradigms: multiple cultures and culture conflicts in organizations", *Administrative Science Quarterly,* vol. 28, (1983), pp. 359-376.

5. J. Jabes and J.P. Gruère, "Organizations under siege: The onslaught of cultural explanations of organizational behavior" in C. Kagitcibasi, ed., *Growth and Progress in Cross-Cultural Psychology,* (The Hague: Swets and Zeitlinger, 1987), pp. 52-59.

6. D. Zussman, "The Image of the Public Service in Canada," *Canadian Public Administration,* vol. 25, no. 1, (1982) pp. 63-80.

7. We remind the reader that the sample included 13 private companies and 20 federal departments, each of which can be considered to have its own culture.

8. In this discussion "goals" and "objectives" have the same meaning.

9. A. Etzioni, *Modern Organizations,* (Englewood Cliffs, N.J.: Prentice-Hall, 1964).

10. A. Etzioni, *Modern Organizations,* p. 8.

11. See C. Perrow, "The analysis of goals in complex organizations," *American Sociological Review,* vol. 6, (1961), pp. 854-865, for a discussion of operational and official goals.

12. T.J. Peters and R.H. Waterman, *A Passion,* p. 238.

13. T.J. Watson, Jr., *A Business and Its Beliefs: The Ideas that Helped Build IBM,* (New York: McGraw-Hill, 1963).

14. W.R. Hewlett and D. Packard, *The HP Way,* (Palo Alto, Calif.: Hewlett-Packard, 1980).

15. T.E. Deal and A.A. Kennedy, *Corporate Cultures.*

16. "Innovation" refers to new ways of managing while "creative management" encompasses novel ways of managing with existing resources.

17. In fact, the responses to questions about organizational orientation provide a validity check on the issue of caring about people, confirming that this perception is stable and widespread.

18. A.K. Korman, *The Psychology of Motivation*, (Englewood Cliffs, N.J.: Prentice Hall, 1974).

19. W.G. Bennis, "The coming death of bureaucracy," *Think*, (November-December, 1966).

20. The questionnaire answered by participants was lengthy. It took on average a half-hour to fill out. Virtually all questions on this survey were closed, in that respondents chose from a number of fixed responses. The open-ended questions came at the end of the questionnaire; despite this, virtually all respondents provided some commentary.

21. Respondents were given the opportunity to list up to three values encouraged in their organizations, although most limited their responses to one statement. Since the first value written in by respondents provides their spontaneous reaction and can be taken as a reflection of the central tendency of their organizations, our analysis of values rests on it.

22. The open-ended responses were coded by two raters who partitioned the data into twenty dimensions. When there were difficulties in deciding where to assign a given response, a third rater was asked to resolve the impasse.

23. In most cases respondents used precisely those words, easing our task of categorizing values.

24. H.C. Kelman, "Compliance, identification and internalization: three processes of attitude change," *Journal of Conflict Resolution*, vol. 2, (1958), pp. 51-60.

25. All mechanism dimensions were generated through a process identical to the one used for values.

26. Let us emphasize here that a response was coded as "do not know" only when the respondent actually used those words. Negative comments or a blank were coded as a different response.

27. Culture items from the survey were entered into a multiple regression analysis aimed at predicting facets of work satisfaction. Important items are those with highest loadings, which best predict work satisfaction.

28. It might seem logical to assume that, in organizations where caring about people is important, career planning is taking place. It is difficult to sustain this view in light of contradictory evidence showing that little formal career planning is perceived

to take place in either the private or the public sector. This issue is discussed in more detail in Chapter 6.

29. W.H. Cooper, "Ubiquitous halo," *Psychological Bulletin* , vol. 90, (1981), pp. 218-244.

30. R. Blauner, *Alienation and Freedom*, (Chicago: University of Chicago Press, 1964); G.W. England and C. Stein, "The occupational reference group—a neglected concept in employee attitude studies", *Personnel Psychology*, vol. 14, (1961), pp. 299-304; V. Vroom, *Work and Motivation*, (New York: John Wiley, 1964); A.K. Korman, *The Psychology* . . .

31. M.F.R. Kets de Vries and D. Miller, *The Neurotic Organization*, (San Francisco: Jossey-Bass, 1984).

32. E.H. Schein, *Organizational Culture and Leadership*, (San Francisco: Jossey-Bass, 1985).

33. T.E. Deal and A.A.Kennedy, *Corporate Cultures* . . .

34. J. Martin, M.S. Feldman, M.J. Hatch and S.B. Sitkim, "The uniqueness paradox in organizational stories", *Administrative Science Quarterly*, vol. 28, no. 3, (1983), pp. 438-53.

35. V. Sathe, "Implications of corporate culture: a manager's guide to action", *Organizational Dynamics*, vol. 12, no. 1, (Autumn 1983), pp. 5-23.

36. V. Sathe, *Culture and Related Corporate Realities*, (Homewood, Illinois: Richard D. Irwin, Inc., 1985).

37. E.H. Schein, "Suppose we took culture seriously," *Academy of Management OD Newsletter*, (Summer, 1984).

38. J. Manion, From a speech given to a group of public administration professors for a meeting organized by the Public Service Commission, Ottawa, 1987.

39. E.H. Schein, *Organizational Culture*.

Chapter 5

Rewards

Introduction

The term rewards refers to material returns in exchange for work, such as salary and fringe benefits, but it also includes feelings of achievement and independence experienced on the job.[1] The former group is known as extrinsic rewards, to emphasize that they are generated and granted through sources external to the individual. The latter group is called intrinsic rewards to signify that they are generated internally by the employee.

We begin by briefly reviewing the literature of work motivation to understand how rewards are linked to satisfaction and work performance. In analyzing the data we also examined respondents' perceptions of equity, because individuals' views of fairness greatly influence the degree to which rewards are seen to be adequate.

We also examined whether respondents had different motivations for joining the public sector or the private sector. Finally, since all motivation theories establish a link between rewards and satisfaction, we also looked at the relationship between the perception of rewards and work satisfaction.

The Importance of Work Motivation

Many analysts believe that the key to creating a climate that fosters good work performance lies in understanding motivational processes.

Furthermore, the general view in motivation theory is that satisfaction, the end product of a motivational state, is linked to performance. In other words, many practising managers feel that there is a causal link between productivity and work satisfaction, resulting in high levels of productivity when workers are satisfied. Work satisfaction and motivation, as we shall see, are strongly influenced by rewards.

The basic motivational process starts with a need, which is defined as a state that involves any lack or deficit within a person. The need gives rise to a drive (often called a motive), which is actually the tension that energizes a person to fulfill the need. The drive, in turn, stimulates a search in the person's behaviour repertoire for the appropriate behaviour that will result in the attainment of the goal, thus fulfilling the need that set the process in motion. The reduction of tension at the end is referred to as a state of satisfaction. This complex process of establishing links among needs, motives, behaviour and satisfaction is the essence of motivation. In addition, it should be obvious that the arousal component may be generated from within the person or may be triggered by external events. In theory, once aroused, the person will direct behaviour toward a goal and, in general, will have to exert some effort to obtain that goal.

Theories of work motivation attempt to understand the arousal, direction and persistence of work-related behaviours while taking into consideration characteristics of workers and organizations in which they work. All theories posit that people go to work in response to psychological and social needs and persist in this type of behaviour because of the rewards they receive. The rewards lead to a level of satisfaction that is the key to sustaining the process. Therefore, an understanding of work motivation and any plan to enhance it must start with an analysis of the relationship among human needs, available rewards and perceived levels of satisfaction.

Although all aim to understand the process just outlined, motivation theories differ because of long-standing differences among the cognitive, behaviourist and humanist schools of psychology. A brief review of the literature points to parts of each theory that may be useful in understanding motivational issues in large bureaucracies such as the public service of Canada and providing some solutions to managerial problems. The review also highlights the role rewards play in motivation.

Work Motivation Theories: A Brief Review

Interest in workplace motivation was sparked by theories of motivation developed by Abraham Maslow. In advancing his need-hierarchy theory, Maslow argued that human needs are ordered along a hierarchy, starting with biological needs and moving up the ladder toward esteem and self-actualization needs.[2] Later, Herzberg applied the theory to work organizations through empirical research. His two-factor theory suggested that there were hygiene factors, which reduced work dissatisfaction, and motivation factors, which increased work satisfaction.[3] Herzberg's work was instrumental in job design strategies based on job enrichment.

More recent theorizing in the field of work motivation has looked at the role played by rewards and whether those receiving them believe them to be equitable. The expectancy theories of work motivation, for example, suggest that people make conscious decisions about the kind of organizations they want to work for and the degree to which they will persist in going to work every day. These theories are also predicated on the belief that individual needs and desires vary considerably and that they have a significant influence on actual work behaviour. Work productivity is based on the expectation that a certain performance level will be instrumental in bringing about desired outcomes for the individual. If individuals value the rewards available in the organization and perceive that good performance will lead to their attainment, then to the degree that their abilities, skills, or role perceptions do not interfere with or take away from perform-ance, the theory predicts that they will make the effort to produce. Their satisfaction is then based on receiving extrinsic and intrinsic rewards that they perceive to be fair and equitable.[4]

This brief discussion illustrates the complexities influencing satisfaction in the workplace while raising two issues related to rewards and motivation. First, the nature of the available rewards, be they extrinsic or intrinsic, is very important because rewards fulfill work related needs, act as an incentive toward performance and motivate people to choose certain organizations to work for.[5] Second, the perception of equitable distribution of rewards is a crucial determinant of motivation.

Extrinsic and Intrinsic Rewards

Since Herzberg's initial work, many have pointed out that individuals are differentially motivated by extrinsic and intrinsic rewards.[6] Extrinsic rewards are provided in all work situations and norms have evolved that indicate the appropriate reward to be offered for a given job. All employment has elements of both extrinsic and intrinsic rewards, although different combinations have been found to have a differential impact on individual motivation and job satisfaction.[7]

To complicate this issue, researchers have argued that the source of motivation itself, whether extrinsic or intrinsic, influences how a reward is received. Individuals who tend to be extrinsically motivated expect extrinsic rewards and choose work behaviours that facilitate obtaining them. On the other hand, individuals who are intrinsically motivated often become demotivated by large extrinsic rewards (amounts above and beyond the established norms) because they experience a sense of loss of control over their environment, partly because they feel an obligation to the person or the organization that rewards them. For these individuals, intrinsic rewards are important because they help maintain a self-image based on being the origin of their own behaviour and the perception of being in control of the situation.[8]

The important point is whether or not motivation varies as a function of the sum of the person's extrinsic and intrinsic rewards.[9] There are as many studies in which the introduction of extrinsic rewards to reinforce intrinsic motivation reduces satisfaction as there are those demonstrating the opposite.[10] Ultimately, whether rewards are intrinsic or extrinsic, people compare what they receive with what others obtain in similar situations, and the judgement they make about how well they are paid influences their degree of contentment. We turn now to a brief discussion of issues related to equity and fairness of rewards.

Equity and Fairness of Rewards

Equity theorists have suggested that individuals compare themselves to others, especially in work situations and more specifically regarding the rewards they receive.[11] This comparison is said to consider inputs, such as education, effort, and production rates, that a person brings to the work situation, and the outcomes received, such as feedback, benefits, time off, and so on. Workers compare their ratio of outcomes to inputs with those of co-workers and, if the comparison is perceived to be inequitable, they redress the situation by demanding greater outcomes, by reducing inputs, or by quitting the situation. The inability to redress the situation can lead to dissatisfaction unless the situation is rationalized by changing benchmarks or redefining the parameters. In a bureaucratic environment, where it is difficult to change financial rewards, the easiest way of coping is by lowering productivity.

Equity theory therefore makes a significant statement about the importance of equity and fairness in the allocation of rewards. It is not enough for a work organization to distribute rewards fairly; the social perception of fairness is paramount in determining whether the reward system is seen to be equitable. In this sense the administration of explicit guidelines and policies regarding hiring practices, for example, may not be at all useful if job applicants do not perceive the process as being fair.

Work Motivation Theories: An Evaluation

The Maslow and Herzberg need satisfaction theories have been tremendously popular, although rarely validated empirically. They have been moderately useful in guiding organizational change efforts to bring about more work satisfaction. Research has shown that basic needs and hygiene factors tend to be satisfied adequately in most work situations, but that greater effort must be spent in satisfying higher-order needs or motivators.[12] Furthermore, the evidence suggests that one's position in the organization is correlated with degrees of work satisfaction. The higher in the management hierarchy individuals are located, the higher in the needs hierarchy they find themselves. Interestingly, these findings seem to be universally valid, as shown in cross-cultural studies of work motivation.[13] In Canada, for example, Slivinski revealed similar relationships through a survey of public sector managers, albeit with a very small sample size.[14]

Expectancy theories, which have a behaviourist view of the world, seem to have gained a stronger foothold in the managerial literature, perhaps because they point out that motivational expectations can be managed by influencing employees in the workplace. This is accomplished by clarifying relationships between performance and reward, and feedback communication. Proponents of this theory emphasize asking employees, through interviews and surveys, about the rewards they value and providing an environment where performance leads to such rewards in a manner perceived to be equitable.

The great interest in work motivation rests on an important premise – that there is a significant relationship between productivity and work satisfaction. Although some classic studies have shown that a strong correlation cannot be established between performance and satisfaction,[15] this may be because the wrong questions were asked. Korman has argued that the research question should establish the conditions under which job dissatisfaction leads to decreased performance and conditions under which it does not.[16]

Those who adhere to need satisfaction theories of motivation argue that satisfaction leads to higher performance, while expectancy theorists contend that high performance leads to satisfaction. Attempts to resolve this controversy have led to more recent research on the link between satisfaction and productivity. The evidence, while supporting earlier work which shows consistently low positive correlations, also points out that productivity leads to satisfaction rather than the other way around.[17]

Both satisfaction and productivity can be seen as outcomes of performance, and personal growth and development can also be included as outcomes, thereby satisfying the self-actualization requirements suggested by Maslow. As pointed out, researchers have viewed performance as a function not only of motivation but also of ability and environment.[18]

In summary, current motivation theories suggest that individual needs dictate the degree to which rewards will be valued in an organization. Performance depends on the availability of these rewards and the expectation that a given level of performance will result in certain rewards being conferred. At the same time, rewards may satisfy both extrinsic and/or intrinsic outcomes, depending on the individual. Satisfaction results when these rewards are seen as equitable and fair.

Motivation in the Public Sector

Almost all organizational behaviour textbooks describe motivation theories in terms of private sector organizations. There has been very little systematic research into work motivation in public sector organizations in Canada, despite their importance in the economy.[19] There are many published accounts of public sector human resource management issues such as compensation, staffing, or industrial relations, but there is very little material on the behavioural aspects of motivation.

If the decision to work for a certain organization is a consciously motivated choice, based on the expectation that valued rewards will be obtained, then several critical questions can be asked about the public sector. For instance, why do people chose to work for the public sector when the extrinsic rewards are usually below those in the private sector?[20] We turn now to survey data about the factors influencing managers' decisions to work for their present employers in order to understand what motivates managers to work and stay in the public service.

Joining and Staying in the Public Sector: Choice or Circumstance?

The Canadian public service offers an open recruitment policy in support of its goal of a system based on merit. There are no elite feeder schools in Canada training people to become senior public servants. This is very different from France, for example, where top managerial jobs in the public sector are filled with graduates of l'École Nationale d'Administration Publique, the National School of Public Administration. The school admits two hundred students each year following a competitive entrance exam for which one or two years of preparation after obtaining a prestigious undergraduate degree are necessary. Graduates choose jobs according to their class ranking at the time of graduation, and they move quickly to the top echelons of the system, often before they are forty years old.

By contrast, public servants in Canada come from all walks of life and have diverse educational backgrounds.[21] While some efforts are made to inculcate public service values through executive level training seminars offered by the Public Service Commission, these courses are short in duration and do not accomplish the cultural socialization and vision sharing that the French system attempts in two years of graduate school.[22] Although the Government of Quebec does have a similar institution, l'École Nationale d'Administration Publique (ENAP), it is modeled more closely on a North American business school curriculum, and graduates are not guaranteed a fast-track managerial job in the federal or Quebec provincial bureaucracies.

Without the prestige of an elite school to train senior public service managers, the reasons public servants choose their type of employment may be less obvious. Many have argued that the intrinsic value of public sector work is a primary source of appeal to new government employees. For example, public service work is seen as challenging, and the fact that the most senior public servants are often able to see the impact of their work, which for some is considerable, makes up for the absence of significant material rewards. It has also been suggested that the "public interest", or dedication to serving the country, are strong sources of motivation for some employees. Finally, senior public sector managers exercise various degrees of power over their subordinates, and power has always been an important source of motivation.[23]

Our interest in understanding managerial motivation led us to ask senior managers why they chose to work for their present employers. Respondents were asked to rate the importance of certain factors in influencing their decisions to work for their present employers. The results to this question are shown in Table 2-1 and discussed in Chapter 2.

In general, public sector respondents attached significantly more importance to public recognition than the other choices, while private sector respondents indicated salary, fringe benefits, furthering company goals, and opportunities for promotion. There was no difference in the importance managers in both sectors placed on challenging work responsibilities, which received the highest score of all items.

As discussed in Chapter 2, these results reinforce our contention that public and private sector managers are motivated by different factors in choosing employment. Despite these fundamental differences, managers in both sectors placed a lot of importance on intrinsic job factors, but private sector managers also prized extrinsic factors. One might argue that differences between the two sectors reflect an attempt by respondents to rationalize their job choices; but we suggest there are real differences in values between public and private sector respondents that go beyond an attempt to explain career choice.

Looking at this issue in more detail, we considered whether respondents thought a career change was desirable. We examined whether public service managers saw the notion of "public service" as a lifelong decision or as a stepping stone to more rewarding work in the private sector. Although there has traditionally been some movement from the public service to the private sector, there is little evidence of movement in the opposite direction.

One way of discerning respondents' interest in movement between the sectors was to measure the degree to which senior managers were happy with their choice of career. We asked respondents to what extent they would be interested in working for the other sector if given the opportunity. As can be seen in Table 5-1, there were large disparities between the responses of public and private sector managers. Whereas, on average, fewer than 10 per cent of the private sector respondents said that they would "to a great" or "very great extent" be interested in working for the public sector, 40 per cent of those in the public sector were "to a great extent" interested in working in the private sector. These results were relatively stable across job levels, although managers at the highest echelons in the public sector and the lowest echelons in the private had the greatest interest in working for the other sector. The data are clear on at least one point. Few managers in the private sector are contemplating career moves out of the private sector, whereas close to one-half of the most senior managers in the public service of Canada show a keen interest in working for the private sector.

Table 5-1
Interest Shown by Respondents in Working in the Other Sector

| | Levels below DM/CEO | | | | | |
	1	2	3	4	5	Av.
Public Sector	45.3[1]	41.5	40.7	34.5	37.5	40.2
Private Sector	7.7	8.0	8.2	9.1	12.2	8.6

[1]   per cent who responded "to a great" or "very great extent"

Public sector managers have not decided to work for their current departments for financial reasons. They are clearly interested in the intrinsic aspects of their work. However, more managers in the public sector than in the private might contemplate career moves, possibly because many of their expectations are not met by their current jobs.

Reward Dimensions Surveyed

How do senior managers in the public sector perceive the rewards they receive? Are they thought to be fair and equitable? Do they think promotions are based on merit? Do they feel that there is a link between performance and rewards? How do they view their compensation package relative to others in the system and to those in the private sector? This section responds to these questions.

Are Performance Evaluations Fair?

In work organizations, rewards are designed to be contingent on performance. Employees receive their compensation at fixed times on the assumption that they have performed satisfactorily at predetermined levels. Other less tangible rewards, such as praise and recognition, also flow from employers to workers since managerial acknowledgement of achievement is a critical way of conferring status on employees. Of course, the degree to which acknowledgement is seen as important rests on employees' perceptions that recognition acts as a motivational force. One important way of providing this recognition is through annual performance evaluations.

Performance appraisals are an important managerial function in organizations. Normally, in organizations which are subject to collective agreements, performance appraisals are a part of the bargaining process. In the Canadian public sector, managers at all levels are regularly evaluated. Performance appraisals serve both judgmental and developmental purposes.[24] They are used to evaluate past performance with the goal of improving it through the subsequent use of rewards. In a developmental sense they are useful in assessing future performance needs of the organization and the employee's potential in meeting them. Performance appraisals take diverse forms; in most large-scale organizations in Canada the appraisal relies on an interview with the employee's supervisor and the use of some rating scale measuring the employee's behaviour and output.

Performance evaluations can be used to promote, transfer, or fire employees, to allocate salary increases and bonuses, to enlighten supervisors and subordinates of each other's problems, to identify training needs, and to improve formal human resource planning.

Some, if not all, of these aims would be part of the performance appraisals to which senior managers in our sample are subject.

An assessment of the reward environment must start with an appreciation of how the formal performance appraisal system is perceived. We asked senior managers in both sectors whether they felt that their performance ratings were a good indication of their actual job performance. The results are shown in Figure 5-1.

These results reveal that the majority of senior managers in both sectors saw the performance appraisal process as fair. In both sectors the average results tended to be similar. Sixty-eight per cent of public sector managers and 70 per cent of private sector managers felt that the process was fair. However, as with many other results, there was a fall-off between public sector managers one level from the DM and those five levels away. Seventy-three per cent of those closest to the DM perceived the performance appraisal process as fair, whereas five levels away this percentage fell to 59 per cent. An interesting reversal occurred in the private sector; those further away from the CEO were more satisfied with the performance appraisal system than those higher up. The differences were slight, however, moving from a low of 68 per cent for managers two levels from the CEO to a high of 74 per cent five levels down.

There are several explanations. At the lower senior management level in the private sector, the outputs of jobs are more easily quantified and can be measured against fixed bottom-line criteria such as sales, revenues or profits. Because of this, private sector managers working lower in the hierarchy can be evaluated on the basis of more explicit, mutually understandable, evaluation criteria.

In most public sector managerial jobs, performance goals are subject to change and may not be easily quantifiable. Because of changes in government priorities, managers in the public sector may be asked to work in ways or on projects not covered by their job descriptions. Thus, job ambiguity may be at the root of attitudes toward the performance appraisal system at lower levels of senior public sector management. As for the higher levels of the hierarchy, they hold positive views about performance appraisal. If we are going to find the causes of discontent in the reward environment in the public sector, they will have to come from somewhere other than the performance appraisal system.

Are Rewards Tied to Performance?

We asked senior managers to evaluate the degree to which performance was perceived to be instrumental in obtaining valued rewards. This perception was measured by asking a similar question

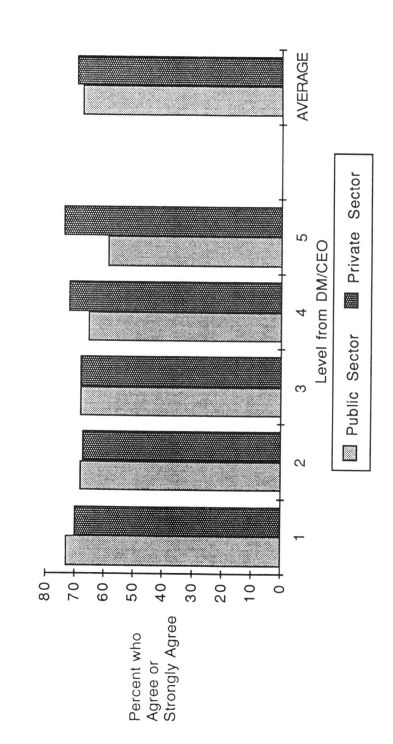

Figure 5-1
Performance Ratings are Fair

twice, once worded positively and once negatively, to ensure that the results were reliable. Respondents were asked first whether they agreed that financial rewards were seldom related to performance and then whether doing well on the job led to pay increases or advancement.

Table 5-2 shows significant differences between the perceptions of managers in the two sectors. One striking finding was that managers at all levels in the private sector had similar responses, whereas public sector responses varied considerably, confirming the existence of the vertical solitude. In the private sector, respondents felt that their rewards were tied to performance. Table 5-2 shows that on average 50 per cent of private sector respondents saw a strong linkage between performance and rewards leading to pay increases and advancement. By comparison, the percentage of public service managers with similar views was a dismal 15 per cent. Where only 20 per cent of private sector respondents indicated that financial rewards in their company were seldom related to performance, the percentage of disaffected public servants was significantly higher at 59 per cent.

Table 5-2
Relationship between Extrinsic Rewards and Performance

Indices Used in Survey		Levels below DM/CEO					
		1	2	3	4	5	Av.
Financial rewards	Public	44.9[1]	58.4	60.4	64.9	65.9	58.5
seldom related to	Private	15.2	21.5	20.8	24.3	23.8	19.8
performance							
Doing job well leads	Public	29.4	16.9	10.7	9.9	9.7	15.4
to pay increases or	Private	48.8	48.9	52.2	57.5	43.6	50.0
advancement							

[1]   per cent who responded "agree" and "strongly agree" or "to a great" or "very great extent"

At the most senior managerial level, 49 per cent of the respondents in the private sector and only 29 per cent of those in the public sector felt that performance was instrumental in obtaining rewards such as bonuses. While the figure remained stable among managers in the private sector, at three to five levels below the DM in the public sector only about 10 per cent of the respondents saw some connection between performance and rewards. To some extent this reflects the fact that bonuses are not available below the SM group. Let us also recall that many of our respondents in the public sector at four or five levels below the DM held SM-1 positions. By and large the data show that, in the public sector, respondents do not perceive managerial performance to be instrumental in obtaining additional rewards.

Are the Deserving Promoted?

Promotions are important extrinsic rewards at the discretion of management. Advancement in the organization confers status, increased pay, and sometimes the possibility of new rewards such as bonuses. Table 5-2 shows that only 15 per cent of senior managers in the public sector believed good performance was instrumental in providing advancement in their departments or in the federal government system. It was therefore important to find out more about their perceptions of the fairness of promotions. It was also important, for our public sector sample, to verify the degree to which the process was perceived to be one that rewarded deserving employees.

Respondents' perceptions about the way promotions are conferred was revealing. In judging the degree to which the promotion process is fair in the sense of rewarding deserving employees, 28 per cent of the respondents in the public sector felt that the system was fair, whereas 55 per cent of the managers in the private sector felt the same way (see Table 5-3).[25]

Analysis of the relationship between rewards and satisfaction showed that responses to questions about whether employees are given fair consideration for managerial openings was the best predictor of satisfaction. As Table 5-3 shows, only 25 per cent of public sector respondents felt that employees were given "to a great" or "very great extent" fair consideration for management level job openings. We argued earlier that there is evidence to suggest that perceptions of inequity can discourage employees. In this sense, unfavourable assessments of the fairness of the promotion system contribute to morale problems in the public service.

In the public service of Canada, the merit system provides for a selection and promotion process that rewards the most deserving candidate, regardless of sex, religion, politics or other considerations. The concept of merit is the cornerstone of public personnel management and constitutes a cultural pillar of the public administration system.[26] With the evolution of the public personnel system in Canada, the merit principle also evolved and often got examined. One of the most comprehensive reviews ever undertaken of personnel management in the public service of Canada pointed out that, among other problems, managers were ill-equipped to manage and were not accountable for the management of human resources.[27]

Table 5-3
Degree of Fairness Perceived in Promotions

Fairness in Rewards		Levels below DM/CEO					
		1	2	3	4	5	Av.
Hiring or promotions of senior managers based on merit	Public	48.8[1]	34.1	22.7	25.1	17.9	30.4
	Private	64.5	55.1	54.5	44.8	47.1	56.0
Employees fairly considered for management openings	Public	44.2	25.8	19.4	26.6	12.9	24.6
	Private	57.3	48.1	41.4	41.9	40.6	48.3
Promotions of all employees based on merit	Public	42.2	32.7	21.3	20.9	19.1	27.8
	Private	59.3	53.8	51.3	54.6	51.1	55.0
Generalists rewarded more than specialists	Public	25.7	29.9	38.9	33.9	41.8	33.5
	Private	23.2	25.3	27.2	32.5	25.8	25.9

[1] per cent who responded "agree" and "strongly agree" or "to a great" or "very great extent"

In judging whether public service promotions are based on merit, public servants were quite definite in their evaluation of the promotion system. As Table 5-3 shows, on average, no more than 30 per cent of respondents felt that the system rewards deserving employees; closer inspection of the data reveals that those at the lower levels of senior management are even less charitable toward the merit system's application. At the extreme, less than 20 per cent of public servants five levels below the DM indicated that promotions were based on merit. While even the most optimistic of these results is discouraging, the vertical solitude is once again a dramatic indicator of the problems associated with personnel management.

The private sector portion of Table 5-3 shows that managers perceived their process as much fairer. Despite this, we also observed an uncharacteristic fall-off in the percentage of private sector managers at the lower levels who saw the system as fair. While this result was interesting, it must be emphasized that the merit principle is not as important a principle in private sector organizations as it is in the public sector. As well, there are few ways by which managers in the private sector can protest an unobtained promotion, short of showing displeasure and quitting. There is no equivalent of the Public

Service Staff Relations Act or the Public Service Staff Relations Board in the private sector, where grievances related to appointments and promotions can be challenged.

The last question in Table 5-3 relates to the relative treatment of specialists and generalists. Participants were asked whether, through salary or promotions, their organizations rewarded generalists at the expense of specialists. Overall, the results suggest that most private sector respondents perceived a tendency to reward specialists over generalists, perhaps because many private sector managers are promoted to executive levels only after a successful career in a specialized area.

In the public sector, by contrast, those in the management group are viewed as generalists who, by virtue of their status, are readily transferable to other management positions as required, regardless of related experience. Hence, public sector managers can be seen to emphasize generalist over specialist skills. Interestingly, this sentiment was felt more strongly at lower levels of management. Those five levels below the DM indicated more often that the management system rewards generalists. As an example, since so many SM-1s are specialists, such as economists or engineers, they probably perceive that the system is unfair in its assessment of their skills. Regardless of whether or not there is a greater tendency to promote generalists, these SM-1s are obviously discouraged about their promotional prospects. While 42 per cent of those five levels below the DM thought generalists were rewarded more than specialists, the figure fell to 26 per cent for those working immediately below the DM.

Are Pay Schemes Comparable for Similar Work?

It is important that a compensation system be internally consistent so that employees with similar work responsibilities are rewarded in the same way. Through job evaluations and job classification, many public and private sector organizations have established elaborate compensation systems. However, in the private sector, which is less subject to the demands of a merit principle, senior management may be subject to a range of pay schemes. On the other hand, public sector managers, once appointed to a job level, receive the same pay across all federal departments, regardless of how stressful, demanding, or difficult the particular job may be.

We have noted that financial compensation was not the most important factor for managers in choosing their current employers. We turn now to consider whether public sector managers believe their compensation is equitable relative to others at the same level. Despite the comparability in pay scales at three to five levels below DM/CEO, respondents from both sectors were not fully aware of these similarities. Table 5-4 shows that 56 per cent of private sector managers felt their compensation was comparable to that of managers in the public sector. Of those one level from the CEO, 62 per cent held this view, while only about 50 per cent of respondents at lower levels felt the same way. On the other hand, in general, 41 per cent of public sector managers felt their compensation package was similar to that of private sector managers, supporting the public sector bias that the private sector is better paid. On a disaggregated basis, only 28 per cent of those one level from the DM felt their compensation was comparable to the private sector, whereas at four or five levels below the DM the percentage went up to 48 per cent, mirroring the objective data collected by the Advisory Group on Executive Compensation.[28]

Table 5-4
Perceptions about Comparable Worth and Value

Comparable Worth Indices		Levels below DM/CEO					
		1	2	3	4	5	Av.
Compensation similar to that of managers in public sector	Public	65.3[1]	62.2	67.2	68.6	63.5	65.5
	Private	61.8	55.9	50.9	49.7	53.3	55.9
Compensation similar to that of managers in private sector	Public	27.9	39.6	42.7	48.4	47.1	40.7
	Private	70.2	62.9	57.6	59.4	60.5	63.7
Salary reflects your value to your organization	Public	45.4	40.0	38.5	38.3	36.2	40.1
	Private	62.4	48.1	50.9	45.7	50.4	53.3

[1]   per cent who responded "agree" and "strongly agree" or "to a great" or "very great extent"

When private sector managers were asked whether they thought their compensation was similar to that of managers in the private sector with responsibilities similar to their own, 64 per cent agreed or strongly agreed. Despite the diversity of executive level jobs in the private sector and the various pay scales employed by different organizations and industrial sectors, private sector managers appeared more satisfied with their compensation packages than those in the public sector where compensation is more rigidly administered.

The last question about financial rewards was whether respondents thought their salary reflected their value to their organization. Table 5-4 shows that in the private sector 53 per cent of respondents felt their compensation reflected their value, ranging from a high of 62 per cent for those one level away from the CEO and hovering around 50 per cent for those at the other levels. In the public sector, a significantly lower number agreed with the statement. Only 40 per cent felt that their salary reflected their value to the federal public service; this question generated less variation among public sector respondents than previous ones. The results on the issue of compensation showed that the majority of senior public servants believed they were not relatively well paid and on average 41 per cent felt that their compensation package was not comparable to that received by their peers in the private sector.

Relating Perceived Rewards to Outcome Measures: The Influence of Rewards on Work Satisfaction

We have observed that rewards are perceived in different ways by senior managers in the public and private sectors and that the job level of public sector respondents influences this perception. As in other chapters, we turn now to the effect of the various reward questions on work satisfaction.

In looking at the relationship between rewards and satisfaction we report two kinds of results. First, we examine the relationship between selected reward attributes and the satisfaction indices. Second, we analyze how the degree of satisfaction is moderated by the reward attribute and the job level of respondents. The reward items analyzed in this chapter are those which our analysis shows to be the most influential.

Rewards and Satisfaction: The More the Merrier

The more respondents agreed that financial rewards were seldom related to performance, the more dissatisfied respondents in both sectors were (see Table 5-5). The level of satisfaction was higher in the private sector, since financial rewards are used more often and are often linked directly to performance in the private sector organizations.

It is interesting to note in Table 5-5 that, by and large, all the satisfaction dimensions show linear relationships with the degree to which respondents perceived that financial rewards were related to performance. While it was expected that extrinsic job satisfaction and satisfaction with career progress would be highly correlated with whether performance was instrumental in obtaining financial rewards, the surprising result in Table 5-5 was that intrinsic motivation was also influenced by perceptions of the relationship between financial rewards and performance. A halo effect may be at work in this instance, but it is more likely that financial rewards are a critical factor in influencing job satisfaction in both sectors.

Table 5-5
Relationship Between Work Satisfaction and the Perception that Financial Rewards are Seldom Related to Performance

Indices of Work Satisfaction		Strongly Disagree	Disagree	Neither	Agree	Strongly Agree
Intrinsic	Public	64.6[1]	70.4	51.1	49.8	42.1
Satisfaction	Private	86.7	81.0	68.2	65.8	52.5
Extrinsic	Public	46.0	47.3	36.1	30.5	27.2
Satisfaction	Private	72.5	68.5	42.1	50.0	41.0
Departmental	Public	41.6	43.3	28.1	20.2	21.1
Satisfaction	Private	78.1	67.2	52.5	49.7	46.6
Job	Public	49.0	30.3	24.3	19.4	19.6
Satisfaction	Private	51.7	37.6	27.0	27.3	26.7
Satisfaction with	Public	50.1	42.9	23.4	23.5	19.2
Career Progress	Private	56.9	51.2	34.3	35.6	31.7

[1] per cent of respondents who are "satisfied" or "very satisfied" on the five satisfaction indices

It is now evident that rewards moderate job satisfaction, but what about opportunities for promotion, which are a significant extrinsic reward in organizations? Table 5-6 shows the relationship between respondents' perceptions about fair access to managerial level promotions and satisfaction indices.

The perception of fairness in filling managerial positions influences satisfaction scores in the public and private sectors in virtually the same way it did in the earlier analysis. The relationship between satisfaction and fairness in being considered for openings (see Table 5-6) is linear for both sectors, although the private sector satisfaction scores tended to be slightly higher. All the work satisfaction indices were significantly related to the degree of perceived fairness in filling managerial positions. However, even in those cases where fairness in promotions was perceived to exist "to a very little extent", levels of extrinsic and intrinsic satisfaction remained higher than levels of job, departmental and career satisfaction.

Table 5-6
Relationship Between Work Satisfaction and the Perception that Employees are Considered Fairly for Managerial Openings

Indices of Work Satisfaction		To a very little extent	To a little extent	To some extent	To a great extent	To a very great extent
Intrinsic	Public	25.2[1]	37.4	58.3	74.0	84.5
Satisfaction	Private	28.9	45.0	74.9	83.5	90.6
Extrinsic	Public	23.4	25.8	37.9	40.9	37.3
Satisfaction	Private	35.5	36.9	52.1	68.8	76.8
Departmental	Public	7.2	21.2	26.7	43.7	59.7
Satisfaction	Private	24.5	33.3	53.9	74.9	82.0
Job	Public	9.4	13.6	21.8	37.5	59.3
Satisfaction	Private	15.9	16.2	24.2	46.2	62.5
Satisfaction with	Public	6.0	12.3	25.4	55.1	64.9
Career Progress	Private	8.9	14.0	35.1	59.7	71.1

[1] per cent of respondents who are "satisfied" or "very satisfied" on the five satisfaction indices

The data linking work satisfaction with perceptions about whether promotions are based on merit show the same pattern of results. Table 5-7 emphasizes the importance of the perception that the public sector personnel promotion system is based on merit. While we do not challenge the commitment of the public service to applying the merit system, we now know that only 28 per cent of respondents in the public sector believed that promotions are based on merit (Table 5-3). Juxtaposed against this view is a further perception that when the system is seen to be based on merit, it strongly influences satisfaction. For example, in both sectors, when the promotion process was believed to reward the deserving, there was an increase of about 60 per cent of respondents who were satisfied with their career progress (Table 5-7). Similar increases in satisfaction were apparent for the other work satisfaction indices.

The salary managers receive is both a measure of self-worth and an indication of how much the organization values their services. Table 5-8 shows the relationship between the extent to which respondents felt their salary reflected their value to the organization and their level of work satisfaction. Usually, in both sectors there was

Table 5-7
Relationship Between Work Satisfaction and the Perception
that Promotions are Based on Merit

Indices of Work Satisfaction		To a very little extent	To a little extent	To some extent	To a great extent	To a very great extent
Intrinsic	Public	29.4[1]	42	53.1	73.7	86.3
Satisfaction	Private	27.4	57.1	68.9	82	90.1
Extrinsic	Public	18.1	24	36.7	44.2	41.2
Satisfaction	Private	35.2	32.6	49.5	68.6	81
Departmental	Public	10.3	15.9	23.9	42.8	67.6
Satisfaction	Private	29.3	42.3	49.2	72.7	82
Job	Public	13.9	15.6	21	33.6	61.8
Satisfaction	Private	9.1	20.4	23.7	41	72.2
Satisfaction with	Public	6	12.5	25.2	50.7	68.8
Career Progress	Private	9.1	19.4	32.7	55.4	73.5

[1] per cent of respondents who are "satisfied" or "very satisfied" on the five satisfaction indices

a linear relationship between perceptions about salary reflecting one's value to the organization and work satisfaction. In all cases, extrinsic satisfaction was high when salary was believed to reflect one's value to the organization. This finding was expected, because salaries provide a measure of how much the job an employee does is valued by his or her organization. Career progress satisfaction was also related to respondents' views on the question of whether salary reflected worth to the organization.

Not every reward variable was a good predictor of satisfaction. Salary is usually fixed according to an employee's position in the hierarchy, and the low levels of satisfaction with career progress may simply reflect a feeling of not having been successful or having been passed over in favour of someone else. As an example, the public sector data suggest that, in those cases where respondents felt that their salary reflected their value to the organization "to a very great extent", only 55 per cent were very satisfied with their career progress; in the private sector 73 per cent were "very satisfied" under the same conditions. Salary plays a role but does not necessarily explain all the variation in career progression satisfaction, and it is therefore difficult to suggest that, for those who believed their salary did not reflect their worth to the organization, unhappiness about career progression was only sour grapes.

Table 5-8
Relationship Between Work Satisfaction and the Perception that Salary Reflects One's Value to the Organization

Indices of Work Satisfaction		To a very little extent	To a little extent	To some extent	To a great extent	To a very great extent
Intrinsic	Public	44.8[1]	49.9	49.5	63.9	71.0
Satisfaction	Private	48.5	57.2	68.4	84.2	88.1
Extrinsic	Public	15.5	13.1	28.3	47.8	69.8
Satisfaction	Private	12.1	31.4	44.4	72.1	90.0
Departmental	Public	17.5	18.3	22.7	32.7	52.0
Satisfaction	Private	30.3	42.3	55.1	70.0	82.0
Job	Public	18.3	17.8	18.2	27.6	57.9
Satisfaction	Private	24.2	17.1	28.1	38.8	74.2
Satisfaction with	Public	6.2	18.3	20.3	40.2	54.6
Career Progress	Private	12.1	30.5	30.1	56.7	73.1

[1] per cent of respondents who are "satisfied" or "very satisfied" on the five satisfaction indices

Managerial Job Level, Rewards, and Satisfaction: It is Better at the Top

The data on perceptions about the rewards system showed that the way rewards are thought to be allocated is significant in explaining work satisfaction in both sectors. In addition, the data suggest a strong linear relationship between rewards and work satisfaction, showing that managers who perceived the system as more equitable were also more satisfied. Finally, it was shown that the public sector vertical solitude exists in this case as it has in so many other instances.

Now we turn our attention to examining whether position in the managerial hierarchy influences satisfaction with regard to rewards. We look at the interrelationships among rewards, job level and satisfaction and compare rewards and job level with perceptions of actual or future progress to determine whether promotion expectations might affect work satisfaction. All analyses in this section have been done on the basis of job designations used in the federal public service.

The degree to which performance ratings were viewed as fair and the degree of intrinsic satisfaction were clearly related to managerial job level. As shown in Figure 5-2, the EX group was always more satisfied than the SM and SM-1 groups, irrespective of how they judged the fairness of performance ratings. Fairness ratings for the senior management category (SM) and for those immediately below (SM-1) were quite consistent, although they were significantly below those of EXs. While 50 per cent of managers at the EX level reported a high level of intrinsic satisfaction, even when they viewed performance ratings as unfair, only 25 per cent of the SM and SM-1 managers expressed equal satisfaction. Performance ratings certainly can influence extrinsic rewards and possible career movements, but in the immediate sense their effect is stronger on how one feels toward the intrinsic aspects of work, on departmental, and job satisfaction.

In examining the relationship amongst departmental satisfaction, managerial level and the degree to which the performance evaluation process was perceived to be fair, the same pattern was apparent. As can be seen in Figure 5-3, the EX group was the most satisfied of the three, while the satisfaction levels of the SM and SM-1 groups were virtually identical and significantly below that of EXs. While more than 25 per cent of managers in the EX category were satisfied with their departments, when they perceived the performance ratings as unfair this percentage fell to below 10 per cent in the lower public sector managerial levels.

A more significant issue with regard to the perceived fairness is the allocation of rewards. The intrinsic satisfaction of the EX group was quite a bit higher than that of other public sector managers when measured against the perceived degree of fairness in being considered for managerial job openings. Once again, the degree of intrinsic satisfaction of the SM and SM-1 groups was similar, and tended to be lower than that of the EX group. Although this set of data are not presented, they display the same trends observed in Figures 5-2 and 5-3.

Public sector managers might still have found the intrinsic aspects of their jobs motivating when they believed that promotion opportunities were not open fairly to all, but they tended to be less satisfied with their jobs in such cases. As Figure 5-4 shows, there were slight variations by level, but by and large the vertical solitude was not evident. It seems that the day-to-day personal satisfaction obtained from a job was strongly influenced by what managers perceived to be an unfair system. As a matter of fact, the equity theory of work motivation would predict that one way for respondents to reduce their feelings of unfairness about what they observe or experience in their work would be to see their jobs as being less attractive.

Figure 5-2
Relationship between the Perception that Performance Ratings are Fair,
Managerial Level and Intrinsic Satisfaction
(public sector)

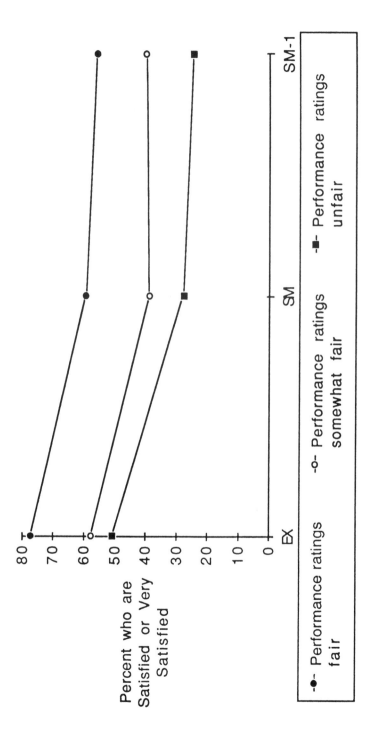

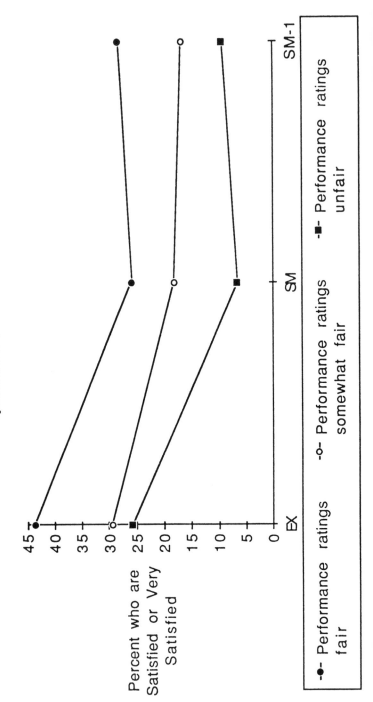

Figure 5-3
Relationship between the Perception that Performance Ratings are Fair,
Managerial Level and Departmental Satisfaction
(public sector)

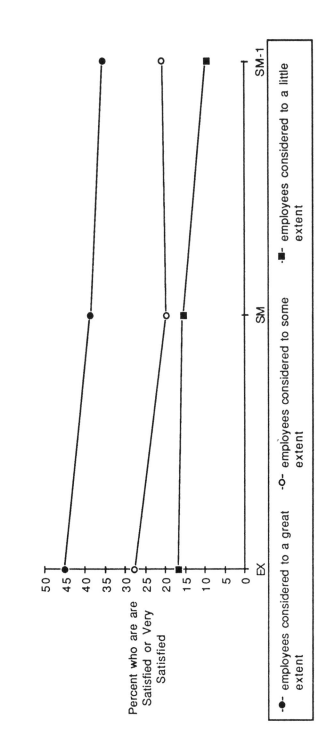

Figure 5-4
Relationship between the Perception that Employees are Considered Fairly for Management Job Openings, Managerial Level and Job Satisfaction
(public sector)

The degree to which managers felt their salaries reflected their value to the organization was also statistically related to the various satisfaction indices, and was moderated by job level. For example, although not shown graphically, when it came to intrinsic satisfaction, while 63 per cent of the EX category were satisfied even when they did not think their salary reflected their worth to their departments, this figure fell to 40 per cent at lower managerial levels. While this response pattern is the general rule, there was one satisfaction index where this relationship was inverted, as EXs were the least satisfied on the extrinsic satisfaction index (Figure 5-5). Even if they thought their salary represented an accurate assessment of their worth, only 38 per cent of the managers at the EX level were extrinsically satisfied, whereas on average 55 per cent of those at lower levels were satisfied. This finding is attributable, as we suggested, to the inverse level of satisfaction with financial compensation, reflecting the fact that in absolute terms higher-level EXs are poorly paid in comparatison to the private sector.[29] As a consequence, when SM-level managers (and those below them) indicated that their salary was not a good indication of their value to a department, their satisfaction with extrinsic rewards was higher than that of the executive group. This again may reflect the view that, compared with their private sector equivalents, SMs and SM-1s are paid at market rates.

While rewards strongly influenced different facets of work satisfaction, their effect was moderated considerably by a respondent's position in the organization. It can, of course, be argued that the higher one's place in an organization, the more rewarding the "rewards", and hence, the more one is satisfied. There is some truth to this statement, and managerial level may colour one's satisfaction because of that. However, we also saw that respondents perceived reward situations realistically when it came to salary differentials or similarities.

Experiences with the system and the working environment can colour perceptions and the degree of satisfaction related to one's career. In analyzing responses about satisfaction with career progression, we had to control for the sour grapes effect, i.e., where those who have not been promoted are dissatisfied with their failure to progress more quickly. For example, those who have not been promoted for a long time may view the system as unfair, their salary as not reflecting their value to the organization, and the whole process as inequitable. Teasing out this effect is difficult because a multiplicity of conditions may have generated it. It requires that we know more than the length of tenure in the last position; tenure in previous positions may also influence this view. In addition, many managers, given their skills and abilities, have reached the highest position to which they will ever

Figure 5-5
Relationship between the Perception that Salary Reflects One's Value to the
Department, Managerial Level and Extrinsic Satisfaction
(public sector)

Percent who are Satisfied or Very Satisfied

EX   SM   SM-1

-●- salary reflects   -o- salary reflects some   -■- salary reflects
    great value   value   little value

be promoted. It is difficult to determine how many are waiting to be promoted only because there is "nowhere to go", and for how many the wait is terminal because they have reached their level of competence.

To understand this issue we analyzed the relationship between the perception that senior promotions and hirings were based on merit and the respondent's perception about how quickly he or she had progressed in the system. The hypothesis was that high flyers might have a more positive outlook than those who progressed more slowly, since they were the obvious winners in the bureaucratic environment. Figure 5-6 indicates that, regardless of their rate of progress, the EXs perceptions of the merit principle are more favourable than those of the SMs and the SM-1s. Being an EX is a visible sign of success and, even if their rate of advancement was slow, the EXs did not denigrate the system. Fewer than a third of the SM and SM-1 respondents who felt their career progress was fast or normal indicated that the system "to a great" or "very great extent" promoted the most deserving to senior levels. Finally, it is worth noting that, in the EX category, slightly more than half the respondents (55 per cent) who progressed quickly through the system perceived it to be based on merit.

Public sector managers' perceptions concerning the existence of adequate career paths for themselves within their own departments provided another analysis. When we look at the relationship between perceptions about the availability of career paths and merit by job level as shown in Figure 5-7, we see that the EXs perceive career prospects to be more favourable than the SMs and SM-1s, who tend to be pessimistic about this issue. Even when they do not perceive that there are adequate career paths in their department, the EX group is more inclined to see the system as being based on merit.

The results in Figures 5-6 and 5-7 are very similar, showing that while the reward environment is important, the perception of merit to a great extent is moderated by job level. The fact of having succeeded in the public sector is demonstrated by access to the EX category. We were surprised by the number of EXs, especially in the higher echelons of the category, who believed that merit alone was responsible for their promotions. While not denying that merit plays a role, factors such as being in the right place at the right time, or the unwillingness of managers to search for the best candidates because of time constraints, clearly lead to problems in the application of the merit principle. But what is most surprising is that many executives harbour no pretensions about merit. They know that it is a vague, important but difficult to achieve, principle to be pursued when possible.

Figure 5-6
Relationship between Perceived Pace of Career Progress, Perceived Degree of Merit in Senior Promotions and Managerial Level
(public sector)

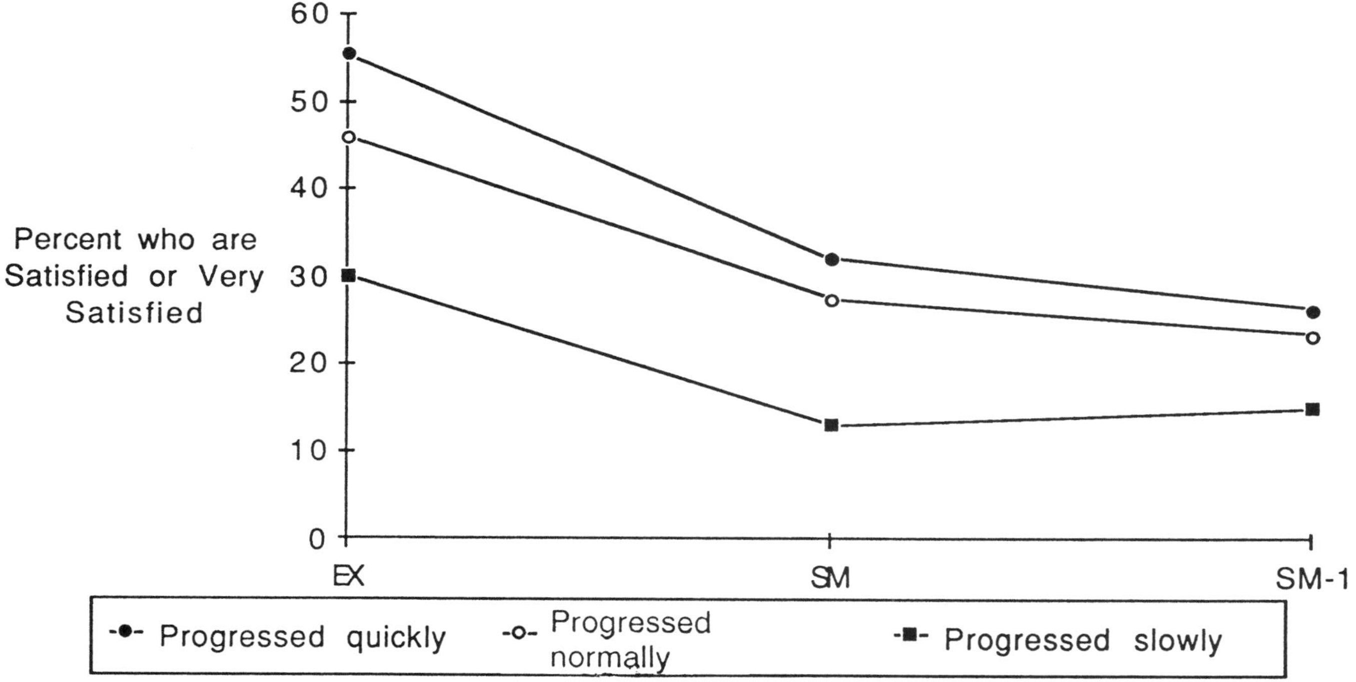

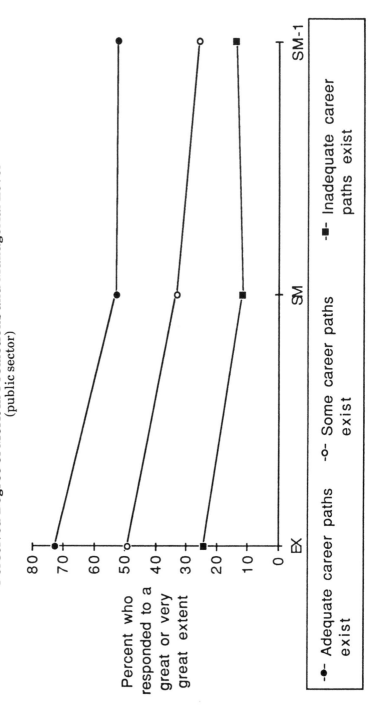

Figure 5-7

Relationship between the Perception that Adequate Career Paths Exist in the Department, Perceived Degree of Merit in Promotions and Managerial Level

(public sector)

Managing Rewards

The findings on rewards raise several questions about their management. First, would it be possible to manage a genuinely merit-based system? Second, given that public sector managers at the highest levels consider themselves relatively poorly paid, what would be the effect of offering a performance pay bonus system? Finally, in light of the above, what should be done about public sector executive compensation?

Merit and Personnel Policies

In issues related to personnel management in the federal public service, the Public Service Commission is the guardian of the merit principle. The application of this principle in terms of the personnel selection processes has resulted in a lengthy and unwieldy staffing process that managers consider slow and inflexible.[30] Data exist comparing staffing in the private and public sectors in Canada showing the public sector to be significantly slower in filling a position.[31] The process is not only slow, but managers believe it results in poor choices. In addressing these concerns, a former commissioner of the Public Service Commission questioned the selection criteria, criticized the interview method as the major selection tool, and admitted that many managers have a tendency to choose from among their immediate staff.[32]

One might expect that those who are successful in terms of their position in the hierarchy might be predisposed to believe that the personnel system is based on merit. However, less than half of the public sector respondents working one level below the deputy minister indicated that the promotion system was fair (see Table 5-3).

Despite these perceptions about the fairness of hiring and promotion systems, we have no objective information that the process is not based on merit. There is little evidence to suggest that any of the provisions in the Public Service Staff Relations Act are being disregarded although, given that the appointment process is slow, many managers circumvent the process by using replacement and acting positions.

If it is more expedient not to adhere to a very rigid interpretation of the merit principle, then attention should be directed to providing a public sector work environment which motivates managers and employees alike.[33] More attention should be given to the overall quality of working life and to providing intrinsic rewards, especially when public service managers cannot promote people or motivate them through other extrinsic means.

Performance Pay for Senior Managers in the Public Sector

Managers in the private sector think that performance should be the most important factor in determining their compensation, whether it is made up of salary, bonuses, time off from work or some combination of these.[34] As a consequence, performance pay is an integral part of private sector management in Canada. In 1981, the federal government introduced a bonus system for its senior managers which was designed, like other such systems, to link performance and rewards by recognizing outstanding achievement.

However, we know that many managers fail to perceive a link between performance and rewards, especially rewards in the form of pay. Hence, to the degree that perceptions are the critical basis for attitudes, the federal public service has not been able to demonstrate a clear link between rewards and performance. We also know that public servants do not believe that outstanding achievement is rewarded with pay rewards (or anything else for that matter). The current performance pay system awards bonuses equivalent to 10 per cent of basic annual salary for outstanding performers and up to 7 per cent for superior performers. Also, the system's guidelines suggest that no more than 5 per cent of senior managers are to be evaluated as "outstanding" and only 25 per cent as "superior" performers. While little has been written on bonus plans at the most senior levels, we can affirm that the amount offered to senior public servants in Canada is low in comparison with the private sector.[35] In the last few years, for example, the majority of public sector managers who were awarded bonuses received less than 10 per cent of salary. At similar managerial levels in private sector companies using a bonus system, we found that bonus pay could exceed 50 per cent of salary.

The major problems associated with this approach have been the small size of the bonus paid at the end of the year, along with the difficulties inherent in evaluating performance objectively. Lawler suggests that, in organizations where performance is at best subjectively evaluated and bonuses are small and work interdependencies are complex, efforts should be made to avoid linking performance with rewards.[36] Given that we have reported problems with the perceived fairness of the present reward system, it appears that the performance pay system has not worked well.

As a final point, it should be recalled that respondents were asked whether financial rewards in their organizations were tied to performance. While, as Table 5-2 shows, only 20 per cent of the respondents in the private sector agreed that financial rewards were seldom related to performance, this percentage went up to 59 per cent in the public sector, providing strong evidence of the lack of perceived instrumentality between performance and bonuses. Further evidence was provided by respondents' answers to the question about the extent to which good job performance led to pay increases or advancement. While 50 per cent of respondents in the private sector felt this to be the case "to a great extent", only 15 per cent of public sector respondents perceived this to the same degree. The reason why managers do not view performance to be instrumental in obtaining bonuses in the public sector is suggested by the intricacies of a complex work situation and the degree to which incentives become contingent on the overall performance of an organization rather than a manager.

Compensation Packages for Senior Managers in the Public and Private Sector

When it comes to extrinsic rewards, at its most senior levels the public sector fares much worse than the private sector. An important issue to be raised is whether this difference should be maintained.[37] Should the pay, benefits and responsibilities of public service jobs be competitive in all respects with comparable jobs in the private sector? Answers to this question have important budgetary ramifications and realistically rest in the political realm. Although bureaucrats often attempt to address the total compensation issue, this is never a popular theme with politicians or the public. Compensation at senior levels in the public sector will probably always lag behind that in the private sector.[38]

But our data suggest that it is not only compensation levels that are off track between the private and public sector. The public sector may not provide compensation similar to the private sector, but in other aspects of the work—those related to creating an inherently rewarding environment—we see differences too. Furthermore, differences are emphasized not only across sectors but also within the public sector. The vertical solitude of the SM and the SM-1 group has been evident in most of the reward dimensions examined in this survey. The important issue is not comparable salary but having a reasonable pay level and a work environment with fair advancement possibilities and intrinsic rewards.

In the End: Motivation and Rewards are Important

We know from motivation theories that people will expend effort when they expect it to result in performance and when they expect performance to lead to consequences that they value. Many public sector managers believe that there is little relationship between job performance and rewards, while some believe the value of these rewards is inadequate. Performance pay based on small sums cannot be expected to act as a driving force to increase productivity or work satisfaction. Unless concrete changes are made in the reward environment, there is a distinct likelihood that the motivation of senior managers in the public sector will diminish even more.

In addition, there is the problem of managing the intrinsic reward structure. Our results show a deficiency in intrinsic rewards relative to the private sector, and this is worse at the lower levels of the senior hierarchy.

Creating a climate that is intrinsically satisfying is one of the most important challenges facing the public service. However, it is clear to us that it will take time to change a reward structure that managers now believe attaches insufficient value to the people working within it. Efforts will have to be made by central agencies, and not through the usual use of policy statements and manuals. Moreover, each department should be allowed to develop its own ways of promoting work challenge, independence and authority in managerial jobs, and of meeting the psychological needs of employees. A commitment is also necessary on the part of managers to study how their departments and units within their departments can accomplish these goals. Among the various means would be opportunities for public recognition, occurring frequently and immediately after appropriate performance, the opportunity to be assigned to important and powerful committees, and efforts to promote task variety through assignments requiring new knowledge and skills.

Notes

1. Some of the material in this chapter was presented at the 20th National Seminar of The Institute of Public Administration of Canada, October 1987, and published as an article. The reference is J. Jabes and D. Zussman, "Motivation, rewards and satisfaction in the Canadian federal public service," *Canadian Public Administration*, vol. 31, no. 2, (1988), pp. 204-225.

2. A. Maslow, "A Theory of Human Motivation," *Psychological Review*, vol. 80 (1943), pp. 370-396; Maslow, A. *Motivation and Personality*, (New York, Harper & Row, 1970). Alderfer has proposed ERG Theory which holds that individuals have three sets of basic needs. For a discussion see C. Alderfer, *Existence, Relatedness and Growth: Human Needs in Organizational Settings*, (New York: Free Press, 1972).

3. F. Herzberg, B. Mausner, and B. Snyderman, *The Motivation to Work*, (New York: John Wiley & Sons, 1959); F. Herzberg, *Work and the Nature of Man*, (Cleveland: World, 1966). F. Herzberg, and A. Zautra, "Orthodox Job Enrichment: Measuring True

Quality in Job Satisfaction," *Personnel*, vol. 53, no. 5, (1976), pp. 54-68.

4. V. Vroom, *Work and Motivation*, (New York: John Wiley & Sons, 1964); D. Nadler, and E. Lawler, "Motivation: A Diagnostic Approach," In J. Hackman, E. Lawler, and L. Porter (eds.) *Perspectives on Behavior in Organizations*, (New York: McGraw-Hill, 1977), pp. 26-38; J.R. Hackman, and G.R. Oldham, *Work Redesign*, (Reading, Mass.: Addison Wesley, 1980).

5. A.D. Szilagyi, Jr. and M.J. Wallace, Jr. *Organizational Behavior and Performance*, (2nd ed.; Santa Monica, Calif.: Goodyear, 1980).

6. J. Miner, *Theories of Organizational Behavior*, (Hinsdale, Ill.: Dryden, 1980).

7. E.L. Deci, *Intrinsic Motivation*, (New York: Plenum Press, 1975); J. Jabes, "Attention! Les récompenses peuvent nuire à la motivation au travail", *Revue Internationale de Gestion*, vol. 5, (février 1980), pp. 13-22.

8. R. DeCharms, *Personal Causation: The Internal Affective Determinants of Behavior*, (New York: Academic Press, 1968).

9. D.C.Feldman, and H.J. Arnold, *Managing Individual and Group Behavior in Organizations*, (New York: McGraw-Hill, 1983).

10. K.B. Boone, and L.L. Cummings, "Cognitive evaluation theory: an experimental test of processes and outcomes", *Organizational Behavior and Human Performance*, December 1981, pp. 289-310.

11. J.S. Adams, "Toward an Understanding of Inequity," *Journal of Abnormal and Social Psychology*, vol. 67, (1963), pp. 422-436; J.S. Adams, and S. Freeman, "Equity theory revisited: comments and annotated bibliography," in L. Berkowitz and E. Walster (eds.), *Advances in Experimental Social Psychology*, vol. 9, (New York: Academic Press, 1976), pp. 43-90; R. Vecchio, "Models of psychological inequity," *Organizational Behavior and Human Performance*, vol. 34, (1984), pp. 266-282; E. Walster, E. Berscheid, and G.W. Walster, "New Directions in Equity Research," *Journal of Personality and Social Psychology*, vol. 25, (1973), pp. 151-176.

12. M.A. Wahba, and L.G. Bridwell, "Maslow reconsidered: a review of research on the need hierarchy theory", *Organizational Behavior and Human Performance*, vol. 15, (1976), pp. 212-240; R.J. House, and L.A. Wigdor, "Herzberg's dual factor theory of job

satisfaction and motivation: a review of evidence and criticism", *Personnel Psychology*, vol. 20, (1967), pp. 369-389.

13. M. Haire, E.E. Ghiselli, and L.W. Porter, *Managerial Thinking: An International Study*, (New York: John Wiley & Sons, 1966); J. Slocum, P. Topicak, and D.A. Kuhn, "Cross-cultural study of need satisfaction and need importance of operative employees," *Personnel Psychology*, vol. 24, (1971), pp. 435-445; L.W. Porter, "A study of perceived need satisfactions in bottom and middle management jobs," *Journal of Applied Psychology*, 1961, vol. 45, pp. 1-10; L.W. Porter, *Organizational Patterns of Managerial Job Attitudes*, (New York: American Foundation for Management Research, 1964); L.W. Porter, and E. Lawler, *Managerial Attitudes and Performance*, (Homewood, Ill.: Irwin, 1968).

14. L.W. Slivinski, "Attitudes of managers in the Canadian public service," *Studies in Personnel Psychology*, vol. 1, (1969), pp. 71-92.

15. A. Brayfield, and W. Crockett, "Employee attitudes and employee performance," *Psychological Bulletin*, vol. 52, (1955), pp. 396-424.

16. A.K. Korman, *Organizational Behavior*, (Englewood Cliffs, N.J.: Prentice-Hall, 1977).

17. M.T. Iaffaldano and P.M. Muchinsky, "Job satisfaction and job performance: a meta-analysis," *Psychological Bulletin*, vol. 97 (1985), pp. 251-273; C.N. Greene, "The satisfaction-performance controversy," *Business Horizons*, vol. 15 (February 1972), pp. 31-41; M.M. Petty, G.W. McGee, and J.W. Cavender, "A meta-analysis of the relationship between individual job satisfaction and individual performance," *Academy of Management Review*, (October 1984), pp. 712-721.

18. L.L. Cummings, and D.P. Schwab, *Performance in Organizations: Determinants and Appraisal*, (Glenview, Ill.: Scott, Foresman, 1973).

19. L.W. Slivinski, "Attitudes of managers" for example, has shown that managers working in federal departments have a need structure which follows Maslow's model.

20. Canada, Advisory Group on Executive Compensation in the Public Service, (Chairman: J.W. Burns), *12th Report*, (Montreal: The Group, 1987).

21. R.J. Van Loon, and M.S. Whittington, *The Canadian Political System*, 4th ed., (Toronto: McGraw-Hill Ryerson, 1987).

22. In April 1988, the Deputy Prime Minister announced the creation of the Canadian Centre for Management Studies, a new training institution for senior public servants. At the time of writing this book, the Centre is preparing to launch its first programs.

23. D.C. McClelland, *Power: The Inner Experience*, (New York: Irvington, 1975); D.C. McClelland, and D.H. Burnham, "Power is the Great Motivator," *Harvard Business Review*, vol. 54, (March-April 1976), pp. 100-110.

24. L.L. Cummings, and D.P. Schwab, *Performance in Organizations*.

25. Correlation coefficients for these three items in Table 5-3 varied between 0.46 to 0.64, which for the size of sample turned out to be statistically highly significant.

26. See K. Kernaghan, and D. Seigel, *Public Administration in Canada*, (Toronto: Methuen, 1987) for a discussion of the evolution of the public personnel system in Canada and its relationship to the concept of merit.

27. Report of the Special Committee on the Review of Personnel Management and the Merit Principle (the D'Avignon Committee) (Ottawa: Supply and Services, 1979).

28. Advisory Group on Executive Compensation in the Public Service.

29. R.J. Van Loon, and M.S. Whittington, *Canadian Political System*, p.547.

30. Report, The D'Avignon Committee, p. 183.

31. Public Service Commission, Annual Report: 1981, p. 4.

32. J. Edwards, "Equal opportunity in the public service," *Dialogue*, vol. 6, (February 1982), pp. 4-5.

33. K. Kernaghan, and D. Siegel, *Public Administration*, p. 101.

34. E.E. Lawler, "Managers' attitudes toward how their pay is and should be determined," *Journal of Applied Psychology*, vol. 50, (1966), pp. 273-279.

35. E.E. Lawler, *Pay and Organization Development*, (Reading, Mass.: Addison-Wesley, 1981).

36. E.E. Lawler, "Reward Systems", in J.R. Hackman and J.L. Suttle (eds.), *Improving Life at Work*, (Santa Monica, Calif.: Goodyear, 1977), pp. 163-226. Expectancy theorists always suggest that when reward outcomes are being changed, that the change should be significant enough in order to make a difference; see also D. Zussman, "Bonuses and Performance in the Public Sector," *Canadian Psychology*, vol. 23, no. 4, (1982), pp. 248-255.

37. It is important to note that we are less concerned with the magnitude of the difference than with the fact that it exists.

38. Although this is typical in most countries, Japan is an exception. In 1987 the difference in average pay rate between the private and public sectors was only 1.47 per cent. This was established through a survey, commissioned by the Japanese government, of half a million employees in each sector, taking into consideration salary and allowances.

Chapter 6

Work Environment

Introduction

This chapter describes the working environment of senior managers. At the outset we discuss the notion of work environment and job characteristics to set the stage for a later section on how senior managers in the public and private sectors are constrained, the amount of authority they have to carry out their work, the degree of conflict they perceive among organizational goals, the nature of their work, the processes available to respondents at work, the extent of participation they perceive in their organizations, and the propensity for change in their organizations. Later we consider how some of these perceptions influence work satisfaction. As in other chapters, we relate the job level of public sector respondents to these measures. We conclude with a discussion of the importance of managing the work environment.

Concern for the Work Environment

If we trace the beginning of management literature to the work of Taylor and *The Principles of Scientific Management,* we discover that early in the twentieth century working conditions were an important area of study.[1] Industrial psychologists concentrated their efforts on modifying physical working conditions to maximize worker productivity. To this end, experiments were conducted manipulating heating and lighting conditions in factories to optimize production levels. The philosophy of scientific management was simple: workers toil for financial rewards, and the greater the material incentives provided, the higher the productivity.

Changes in this philosophy first emerged with the Hawthorne studies and the discovery that other factors, such as workers' involvement in work-related issues, made them more satisfied and more willing to produce.[2] The human relations school of management and the recent literature on open systems and socio-technical design emphasize the importance of the work environment and job characteristics in influencing work satisfaction and productivity. As well, most researchers now acknowledge that work satisfaction is contingent on situational factors, especially the work environment, in influencing work behaviours.[3] Put simply, contingency theory argues that a single set of organizational rules cannot cope with all work situations; there is more than one best way to manage work situations—a position that is at odds with scientific management and early motivation theorists.

The work environment defined and manipulated by management can have an immediate influence on work-related behaviours. For example, constraints, whether real or imagined, influence how employees act. If, for example, managers view auditors as constraints, they will spend a lot of time ensuring that audit constraints are met. The extent to which the work environment is described as conflict-prone, hierarchical, constraining and non-participative, as opposed to conflict-free, flat, unconstraining and participative, will result in employees having different perceptions of themselves and of their organizations.[4]

Similarly, job characteristics influence employees' perceptions of the work environment. Routinized, mechanical jobs that minimize ambiguity often produce a situation where employees feel less in control, less responsible, and less accountable for their work. Stress is another factor affecting work satisfaction. The nature of their work and the perception of the organization are also influenced by how employees view work constraints and workplace democracy, as exemplified by concepts of participation and the ability to influence change. Degrees of formal authority that they think they possess also colour work satisfaction and the overall image of the organization.

Work processes usually provide guidance about the work behaviours that tend to be rewarded. Performance appraisals, training and development and career planning provide an indication of the degree to which employees believe an organization is working for their well-being.

Work environments tend to be hierarchical. Authority increases as one ascends the organizational pyramid and, even in relatively flat organizations, degrees of authority increase higher up the managerial ladder. For this reason, we expected to observe the vertical solitude in both the private and public sectors. Therefore, we hypothesized that job level would be an important moderator of perceptions about the work environment and job characteristics in both sectors.

To understand the environment in which survey respondents worked, we looked first at constraints managers face in their work. In doing so, we tested for the incidence of goal conflicts and the amount of authority managers exercise in accomplishing their goals. We went on to examine the nature of managerial work and the systems in place to monitor progress. Finally, we examined the notion of workplace democracy as an example of a desirable work environment by looking at work participation and the ability of employees to influence change.

Work Environment Attributes Surveyed
Perceived Constraints on the Organization

The degree of complexity inherent in the environment surrounding an organization is often discussed in introductory management texts. This characterization is often framed in open systems theory, showing how an organization is constrained by its immediate environment. Interest groups, such as clients and unions, are often described as constraints because they limit what an organization can achieve. Through the various feedback mechanisms that exist in any organization of some size, an organization can influence these interest groups by its actions. These organizational actions tend to be the result of transformations of inputs into finished products or behaviours of top managers.

Survey participants were asked to rate the extent to which certain external forces placed constraints on their organizations (Table 6-1). The list of possible constraints was worded slightly differently for each sector to take into account their different external environments and included the following: politicians/board of directors; general public/shareholders; central agencies or auditors; special interest groups; unions; and the media.

The results point to two very different sets of pressures. Politicians, auditors and special interest groups were the principal constraints identified by the public sector respondents. In contrast, private sector managers viewed unions as their most significant constraint. While shareholders/general public and the media were perceived as fairly important constraints, there was not a great deal of difference between the two sectors.

Thirty-three per cent of the private sector respondents viewed unions as a serious constraint on their companies' activities. This contrasts with the much lower figure of 12 per cent in the public sector. This difference in perception between the two sectors should not be a great surprise, given the imbalance in union activities between the two sectors in Canada. While most senior public sector managers have, at one time, been members of a public service union, we speculate that many of our private sector respondents, in their role of professional managers, have not been part of an organized worker movement or belonged to professional unions.

Table 6-1
Constraints that Curtail Organizational Achievement in the Public and Private Sectors

		Levels below DM/CEO					
Constraints		1	2	3	4	5	Av.
Politicians/Board	Public	54.2[1]	62.8	60.3	62.8	65.3	60.8
of directors	Private	31.5	27.0	31.1	32.0	33.0	30.6
General public/	Public	20.0	22.5	19.9	18.2	17.9	20.0
shareholders	Private	21.3	16.9	18.8	17.9	13.6	18.5
Central agencies/	Public	47.4	44.7	44.5	37.8	41.8	43.7
auditors	Private	5.7	4.0	12.2	7.6	12.7	7.3
Interest groups	Public	34.3	36.5	32.7	28.4	28.7	32.7
	Private	28.2	17.1	26.1	23.9	20.9	20.3
Unions	Public	11.1	13.4	11.3	12.0	12.8	12.1
	Private	33.2	28.8	32.2	34.8	36.4	32.5
Media	Public	23.6	26.2	22.3	18.8	20.4	22.7
	Private	16.4	13.7	24.4	15.5	24.8	19.2

[1]   per cent who responded "to a great" or "very great extent"

Overall, public sector respondents felt that politicians were the most important constraint on their organizations. While 61 per cent of senior managers in the public sector saw politicians as a constraint, only 31 per cent of senior managers in the private sector felt the same way about their boards of directors. As in earlier cases, the results were not distributed evenly among management levels. In this instance the lower levels of senior management in the federal public service felt constrained by politicians more strongly than those higher up. This finding may result from the fact that directions from politicians are often routed through the highest levels to the lower levels for immediate action; routines are disturbed, often without any explanation of why such demands are being made. It may also be possible that managers at higher levels who lack managerial skills or are constantly changing work procedures, objectives or job content may blame the politicians for their own inappropriate behaviour.

An even more significant difference in perceptions relates to auditors or central agencies. In general, private sector managers do not view auditors as significant constraints in achieving their goals, whereas public sector managers believe quite strongly that central agencies represent constraints. This is not surprising, given that several agencies exercise control over departmental activities. Table 6-1 shows that on average 44 per cent of public sector respondents saw central agencies as important constraints on their behaviour, while only about 7 per cent had the same view in the private sector. The Treasury Board and the Comptroller General are two examples of central agencies whose mandates strongly affect the way senior managers are permitted to perform. Although, every "good" manager in Ottawa can provide copious anecdotal evidence of creativity in beating the rules, the view that emerges from this survey is that central agency constraints are a serious impediment.

Interest groups make numerous demands on an organization, and organizational effectiveness is usually related to how well these demands are met.[5] Although the interest groups identified in the survey may not believe they have the constraining power claimed by our respondents, it is important to understand how respondents construct perceptions of reality; in Canadian public and private sector organizations these differ significantly—politicians constrain the public sector and unions the private sector.

Conflicting Organizational Goals

A work environment that encourages accomplishment should minimize conflicts. While the literature on conflict management argues that some conflict in the workplace is useful, leading to new work arrangements and creative work solutions, intense conflict among subgroups and individuals can be dysfunctional and harmful to performance.[6]

One of the many factors producing conflict among employees is conflicting organizational goals. Conflict may also occur when limited resources have to be allocated among competing interests, competitive reward structures are present, individuals have different personal goals, and there are no clearly stated organizational goals.[7]

We considered it important to ask respondents whether they believed their departments' goals were in conflict with broader governmental goals, and similarly whether the goals of a given company were seen to conflict with the goals of the industrial sector to which the company belonged. The expectation was that a government would have an overall set of goals with which departmental goals were aligned or to which they were subjugated. In the private sector, one might expect industrial sector goals to be well-articulated and known by all companies belonging to the sector. It is doubtful, for example that the service industries get together to determine goals, objectives and direction for their sector and that each major company aligns itself to such goals, especially with the absence of a central economic planning agency in Canada. It could well be that major companies, like those in our sample, privately and informally articulate their sense of sector-wide direction and how their goals fit into this larger picture. However, we do not know whether they are involved in such exercises. The results of the two questions on this issue are shown in Table 6-2.

Nineteen per cent of the public sector respondents and 9 per cent of those in the private sector believed that their organizations' various goals were in conflict. Furthermore, these perceptions showed little differentiation across levels; when they did, they did not follow a pattern. Even fewer managers in both sectors felt that organizational goals were in conflict with sectoral goals. In the public sector 13 per cent of the managers felt that their departments' goals were in conflict with those of the federal government. In the private sector only 8 per cent of the respondents perceived conflicts between company goals and the goals of the industrial sector to which the company belonged.

Table 6-2
Organizational Goal Conflicts in the Public and Private Sectors

Perception of Goals		Levels from DM/CEO					
		1	2	3	4	5	Av.
Goals of organization in conflict	Public	16.2	19.2	20.1	18.6	18.1	18.7
	Private	7.2	9.8	13.5	6.1	7.3	8.8
Goals of organization and sector in conflict	Public	9.2	13.7	12.4	14.8	16.1	13.0
	Private	10.0	5.7	9.5	6.2	8.2	8.1

1   per cent who responded "to a great" or "very great extent"

Authority

In the chapter on leadership we reviewed senior managers' perceptions of their leaders. We found that public sector managers were more critical of leadership in their organizations than were their private sector counterparts (as is shown in Table 3-1). The ability to manage and to lead is influenced by the amount of formal authority at a leader's disposal. Being able to provide meaningful leadership, therefore, depends on the nature of the work environment. Of course, managers at the top of organizations have greater formal authority than managers below them by virtue of the nature and structure of a bureaucracy. Furthermore, in many organizations authority differs among positions of equal status because certain activities are more important to the organization. The authority vested in a managerial position normally allows the individual to direct subordinates, make decisions and allocate resources. The formal authority attached to a position thus has many facets. Managing, influencing, and developing human resources through hiring, and promoting or firing personnel are part of a manager's responsibilities.

We tried to discover how managers were constrained by asking them about the degree of authority they had for various tasks. Table 6-3 summarizes the results. The authority questions were posed both positively and negatively, to take into account the possibility of response bias. In the questions, we attempted to consider the manager's authority to influence human resource management issues and then to get on with the job of meeting work goals.

As can be seen in Table 6-3, public sector managers said they had little authority for promoting, hiring, firing or determining salaries of employees. While 54 per cent felt they had little authority to hire, the number increased to 79 per cent who felt they had little authority in determining salary. In all aspects of authority related to human resource management issues, we found instances of the vertical solitude.

Managers in both sectors who were lower down the hierarchy felt they did not have enough authority to hire, promote, determine salary, accomplish work goals, or carry out decisions which fell within the realm of established policy without consulting superiors, compared to those higher up in the hierarchy. With the sole exception of the authority to determine salary (where 35 per cent said they did not have it), no more than 25 per cent of the private sector managers felt constrained by a similar lack of authority to promote, hire or fire.

While the findings show that the private sector is subject to some of the same constraints as the public sector, the public sector is severely restricted in the way it conducts personnel matters. For example, 14 per cent of private sector managers one level below the CEO agreed or strongly agreed that they did not have enough authority to hire people. At the comparable public sector level, 35 per cent of the managers expressed similar sentiments. As one might expect, the lack of authority to hire increased as one moved down the organizational structure, to the point where, at five levels below the DM/CEO, 66 per cent and 46 per cent of the public and private sector managers, respectively, felt they did not have enough authority. A similar distribution of findings can be observed in Table 6-3 regarding managers' lack of authority to determine salaries and to fire employees who are performing poorly.

Table 6-3
Perceived Authority of Managers
in the Public and Private Sectors

| | | \multicolumn{6}{c}{Levels below DM/CEO} | | | | |
Perceived Authority		1	2	3	4	5	Av.
Not enough authority to	Public	14.0[1]	29.2	36.8	42.2	44.3	32.5
decide within policies	Private	17.0	22.2	22.1	28.3	27.1	21.7
Authority to accom-	Public	80.0	68.9	60.6	60.3	58.6	66.0
plish work goals	Private	88.4	80.9	81.1	81.4	77.8	83.2
Not enough auth-	Public	39.7	55.6	62.6	71.6	86.4	59.6
ority to promote	Private	13.1	25.5	30.9	36.9	39.7	25.2
Not enough authority	Public	34.7	50.3	58.5	64.4	65.8	53.8
to hire	Private	13.7	19.3	31.2	35.2	45.5	24.2
Not enough authority	Public	58.5	63.5	72.3	74.2	74.6	68.0
to fire for poor	Private	13.6	23.8	30.8	31.1	39.0	24.1
performance							
Not enough authority	Public	73.0	78.6	81.3	79.0	82.2	78.7
to determine salary	Private	26.2	35.9	36.8	44.0	44.1	34.7

[1] per cent who responded "agree" or "strongly agree"

We detected significant differences in the pattern of responses to the question about authority to promote, where 13 per cent of private sector managers one level below the CEO expressed agreement or strong agreement that they did not have enough authority to promote. This number compares with 40 per cent of public sector managers at the comparable level. Five levels down the bureaucratic structure, 40 per cent of the private sector managers expressed similar views, while

86 per cent of respondents in the public sector felt they had no authority to promote.

About two-thirds of public sector managers said they had the authority to accomplish their work goals. In Table 6-3 we see that 33 per cent in the public sector, and 22 per cent in the private sector, felt they had no authority to decide within existing policies, while 66 per cent and 83 per cent of public and private sector managers respectively felt they had the authority to accomplish their work goals. These two items, one worded positively and the other negatively, show how consistent respondents were in answering the questions relating to authority, adding to the validity of the findings. Moving down the hierarchy, there was more of a decline in the level of authority perceived by public sector managers.

Of course, the public sector responses reflected personnel management practices derived from an interpretation of the Public Service Employment Act. Without negating the need for some form of centralized control over public sector managers, it is important to ensure the managers have enough authority to create an environment that encourages good management. It will be interesting to see whether and how Increased Ministerial Authority and Accountability (IMAA), the initiative Treasury Board implemented in 1987, will allow managers more authority.

Nature of Work

In the previous chapter we reviewed the major motivation theories to show how rewards are important in motivating employees. Recent work in this field has taken a specific interest in how job design can encourage motivation within an organization. Thinking in this area has moved from a narrow view of work specialization and work simplification to include ideas such as job rotation and job enlargement as a way of varying routines to reduce boredom and stress.[8] More recent strategies have attempted to offer job enrichment by increasing the number of motivators on the job.[9] These approaches to giving employees more responsibility and autonomy have interested many private sector organizations. The most notable example in North America is General Foods, in Topeka, Kansas, which incorporated some of these ideas along with socio-technical job design notions of semi-autonomous work groups.[10]

Given the difficulties of applying job enrichment to solve many job design problems, other motivational theorists have suggested a more encompassing view known as the job characteristics model.[11] According to this approach, different job characteristics such as autonomy, feedback, task identity and task significance influence critical psychological states, rendering the job meaningful and the employees satisfied. Job characteristics can be given meaning in several ways, such as allowing employees to have greater contact with clients, increasing the number and variety of tasks they do, and asking the employees to do whole tasks as opposed to isolated components. This approach comes with the caveat that job design is not for everyone. Some employees with strong needs for achievement and growth would appreciate such efforts. On the other hand, employees with lower needs might not seek responsibility or autonomy.

We can surmise that managers in both the private and public sectors have strong needs for growth and try to avoid jobs that are routine and boring. By definition, these individuals are ambitious and are interested in working in a challenging environment. Table 6-4 presents results of questions that enable us to analyze job characteristics related to feedback, variety, accountability, and stress to see to what degree the work environment of respondents is enriched.

Table 6-4
Perceived Nature of Work in the Public and Private Sectors

Job Characteristics		Levels below DM/CEO					
		1	2	3	4	5	Av.
Know what I have	Public	96.1[1]	90.9	90.8	89.9	89.8	91.6
to do	Private	95.1	91.9	92.3	94.0	93.3	93.8
Opportunity for	Public	47.0	37.2	35.0	34.9	30.7	37.3
feedback on performance	Private	57.0	49.3	50.0	51.2	49.2	52.3
Work routine	Public	15.4	23.8	26.6	32.0	34.7	25.6
predictable	Private	36.9	21.2	21.2	28.9	17.2	27.0
Have control over	Public	49.8	51.8	50.4	56.3	55.1	52.3
pace of work	Private	73.7	65.5	68.9	62.7	69.3	68.9
Accountable for	Public	88.4	83.4	81.1	77.7	76.5	81.9
quality of own work	Private	90.0	93.3	90.0	87.2	89.3	90.6
Extent of job stress	Public	68.8	61.6	58.2	61.9	50.5	61.0
	Private	66.0	65.7	62.4	57.9	58.6	63.5

[1]   per cent who responded "agree" or "strongly agree" or "to a great" or "very great extent"

Feedback

By feedback we mean all the information employees receive about how well they are performing. Feedback can be obtained through comments from supervisors and co-workers or through the job itself. In other words, building feedback mechanisms into a job usually enriches it. For example, allowing workers to execute their own quality control provides immediate feedback.

Managers receive feedback during annual performance reviews but, depending on the job and relationship between managers and their superiors, they may receive it more often. In addition, managers may create their own means to obtain feedback by instituting various sensing mechanisms. For example, in an operational unit a manager may rotate along with the employees staffing an information desk to find out how clients are reacting to the unit's product or service.

In both sectors, and at every level, an overwhelming number of managers felt that they knew what they had to do on their jobs, as can be seen from Table 6-4. Ninety-two per cent of the public sector and 94 per cent of private sector managers endorsed this view. However, when it came to receiving feedback on how well they were doing, the results were different. In the private sector over half the managers felt they had a good opportunity to find out how well they were doing in their jobs, whereas only 37 per cent in the public sector felt the same way. While there was little variation among levels in the private sector, in the public sector 47 per cent of managers one level from the DM felt their jobs provided feedback, while only 31 per cent of those five levels below the DM felt the same way.

Although there are many possible sources of feedback, we were interested in the performance feedback obtained from doing the job itself. When a repairman finds that the tool he was fixing works, or when a clinician learns that his patient is feeling better, they have obtained direct feedback through their jobs. This kind of feedback tells employees about the actual results of their work activities, which produces a critical psychological state that strongly influences internal motivation.[12] Feedback from supervisors and co-workers can also enhance knowledge, but direct feedback from the job itself is immediate and can lead more easily and immediately to performance improvements.

The differences between the two sectors in terms of the amount of feedback obtained may well relate to the nature of jobs. In policy-related public sector work it may be some time before one obtains feedback on work accomplished, because it is only later that the effects of policies become clear. However, all things being equal, the data may also be pointing out that fewer managers in the public sector take time to provide this feedback. We say more about this issue when we discuss perceptions related to participation.

Variety

In both sectors, three-quarters of respondents felt that their daily work routine was not predictable. Work was less routine as one moved down the managerial levels in the private sector, whereas "routineness" increased at lower levels in the public sector. The numbers at the first and fifth levels are mirror images. Fifteen per cent of those one level below the DM in the public sector felt their work routines to be predictable; at five levels below, the number went up to 35 per cent (Table 6-4). In the private sector 37 per cent of those one level below the CEO felt their routine was predictable, whereas only 17 per cent shared this view five levels below.

Related to work routine is a manager's control over the pace of work. With virtually no fluctuation across levels, 69 per cent of the managers in the private sector felt they controlled the pace of their work, while in the public sector only 52 per cent shared the same sentiment. These results were similar to those found in the earlier analysis of work routine, suggesting that public sector senior managers live in a less predictable work environment.

Responsibility/Accountability

Accountability is one of the most heavily researched areas of public sector management. The research often revolves around the theme of administrative and managerial accountability, which concerns how public servants can be held accountable for their actions through giving them enough authority and clarifying the lines of responsibility.[13] Almost without exception, most of these discussions conclude by identifying the deputy minister as the pivotal player.[14] Our concern in comparing feelings of responsibility between private and public sector managers is not related to this concept of public administration, but rather to more psychological notions of being in control and feeling autonomous.

In his discussion of how to enrich a job to make it more motivating, Herzberg argued that, among other factors, jobs should give people an opportunity to be accountable and increase their feelings of responsibility by allowing them control over resources.[15] It is in this sense of job enrichment and psychological growth needs that we examined managers' feelings of responsibility.

Table 6-4 shows that 82 per cent of public sector and 91 per cent of private sector managers felt personally accountable for the quality of their own work. This perception was affected by the vertical solitude in the public sector, while remaining virtually identical across the five levels in the private sector.

Stress

At any moment many stressors, some organizationally based, impinge on the individual.[16] Stress generated because of organizational structure, although rarely studied, has been shown to influence satisfaction and performance. One study found that salespersons working in flat organizations felt less stress than those working in a hierarchical, bureaucratic structure.[17] Job level can be another source of stress, with those higher up in the organization usually experiencing more stress than those at lower levels.[18] Other sources of stress are related to role conflicts experienced by managers, personal characteristics, task characteristics, and lack of career progress.

We wanted to find out, in general, how stressful managers considered their jobs to be. The expectation, based on the literature, was that as one moved up the managerial ladder the stress level would increase. The data, as displayed in Table 6-4, support our contention although, on average, we found no differences across sectors. In the public sector 61 per cent of the managers felt their jobs were stressful. There was little difference in the private sector where 64 per cent of managers felt the same way. In both sectors stress diminished at lower managerial levels. However, this vertical solitude, which we expected to find in both sectors, was much more pronounced in the public sector. Whereas 69 per cent of the managers one level from the DM felt their jobs to be stressful, only 51 per cent five levels below the DM felt that way. In the private sector the variation was much less, with 66 per cent of managers one level from the CEO feeling their jobs to be stressful and 59 per cent five levels below experiencing the same feelings.

The differences across levels in the public sector may be explained by the fact that the higher managers rise in public sector departments the greater the various demands made on them by different actors. Many experience role conflict and overload, as well as multiple leaders whose attention and leadership quality vary. Furthermore, the demands from the political side of the organization tend to be immediate and disrupt the flow of work, creating tension and providing another avenue for building stress.

Work Systems and Processes

One other dimension of work is the various systems and processes used to control behaviour and to ensure the development of the organization. Performance appraisal systems, training models and methods, and career planning are examples. Most large private and public sector organizations in Canada have a range of these systems. The data in Table 6-5 show managers' views in relation to work systems and processes.

Table 6-5
Systems and Processes in the Public and Private Sectors

Systems and Processes		Levels below DM/CEO					
		1	2	3	4	5	Av.
Use of performance	Public	76.8[1]	71.0	66.8	65.7	58.2	68.7
appraisals important	Private	69.7	75.0	70.0	76.3	75.3	72.6
Superior sets clear	Public	50.6	39.7	39.6	34.4	33.2	40.0
goals for me	Private	40.3	46.9	49.1	46.1	58.5	46.2
Adequate training	Public	47.7	41.2	37.7	28.4	29.6	37.8
opportunities offered	Private	47.5	40.5	50.0	45.2	39.3	45.0
Organization uses	Public	15.6	7.5	5.3	4.2	1.5	7.2
formal career planning	Private	15.8	10.2	11.3	10.4	6.5	11.9
Discuss career planning	Public	19.4	11.9	9.7	7.3	7.1	11.3
with superior	Private	23.4	20.6	18.9	12.8	12.8	19.4
Adequate career paths	Public	22.6	14.7	12.6	12.4	10.7	14.7
in organization	Private	43.3	33.9	29.1	27.8	23.9	34.4

[1]   per cent who responded "agree" or "strongly agree" or "to a great" or "very great extent"

Performance Appraisal

In both sectors the use of performance appraisals is perceived as an important duty of a manager, with 69 per cent of the managers in the public sector and 73 per cent of those in the private sector endorsing this view (Table 6-5). Probably because lower-level managers in the private sector are more likely required to do performance evaluations more often than senior managers, they attach greater importance to the function than those one level below the CEO. In the federal public sector, the performance appraisal system has been part of the formal personnel system for many years and, given the frequency of its use, we are surprised to find yet another instance of the vertical solitude.

We can recall from Chapter 5 on rewards that most managers in both sectors view the performance appraisal process as fair, although not instrumental in providing additional rewards. Some senior managers may, of course, be somewhat lax in their approach to performance evaluation, letting their subordinates fill out their own forms. The wide variation in application may partially explain the differences in perceptions of public sector managers obtained here.

Goal-Setting

The management literature shows that, when superiors set clear, specific, attainable goals considered legitimate by subordinates, it is usually possible to improve performance and to create a highly motivating climate within the organization.[19] Most importantly, involving subordinates in setting their own goals enhances work satisfaction. As a result, the goal-setting literature produced a cottage industry known as "Management by Objectives".[20]

Managers in our sample did not agree overwhelmingly that their superiors set clear goals. Only 40 per cent of respondents in the public sector and 46 per cent in the private sector said their superiors had done so (Table 6-5). Interestingly, in this case we found a perception that there is less goal-setting by superiors among public sector managers. In contrast, in the private sector as we moved down the hierarchy there was a perception of increased goal-setting. This finding supports a general tendency in this study for public sector managers to feel that there is not enough direction given from the top. This may result from the greater involvement of senior public sector managers in strategic work and less in operational work. In the private sector, by contrast, we may have more managers at all levels concentrating on operational work and fewer working on strategic directions. The duties of an operational manager include all the traditional duties of appraisal and goal-setting because such a manager typically oversees many employees. Strategic managers may have less goal-setting and other similar duties as they may be working directly with and supervising significantly fewer people.

Training and Development

The extent of training and development is yet another illustration of the importance management attaches to people in an organization. Significantly fewer than half the managers in both sectors felt that they had adequate training opportunities in their organizations. Although there were few differences in this view across levels in the private sector, the vertical solitude appeared strongly in the public sector. For example, 48 per cent of respondents in the public sector one level from the DM felt that there were enough training opportunities while that number fell to 28 per cent four levels below (Table 6-5).

The consistency of this is surprising in view of the federal government's commitment to the training of its senior managers. For example, all SMs are obliged to follow a three-week residential course, while new EXs follow a two-week course. EXs who move to become assistant deputy ministers also follow a one-week special course. As well, many training opportunities of shorter duration exist within the federal public service.

Career Planning

Career or succession planning is closely related to the promotion process.[21] Career planning typically involves counselling and communicating with employees about job prospects and developing career paths. Career planning can be an important human resource management tool, especially if it is designed not only to move people up the organization, but also to provide interesting lateral movement opportunities for those whose careers have reached a plateau.

Neither sector is perceived to be good at career planning. Whether the issue is feedback from superiors or the organization's use of career planning, respondents from both sectors did not rate the situation positively. Eleven per cent of public sector respondents, and 19 per cent of those in the private sector, felt that their superior discussed career planning with them. While 12 per cent of those in the private sector perceived that their organizations used formal career planning, only seven per cent of those in the public sector felt that way. As can be seen from Table 6-5, in both sectors perceptions differed lower on the managerial ladder—managers five levels below the DM/CEO rarely agreed with either of these statements.

It seems easier to progress in a career sense in the private sector, where 34 per cent of respondents on average said there are adequate career paths in their companies; only 15 per cent of the respondents in the public sector agreed. In both sectors, managers at the top perceived greater possibilities for career advancement. This is important because it may mean that it is relatively less common in Canada to establish and maintain a career in a single department (with the exception of External Affairs and to a lesser extent National Defence), as is the case, for example, in the public service of Britain, Norway or Japan. Contrary to the Canadian experience, many countries nurture departmental allegiance by providing career opportunities within the department.

The fact that so many respondents are sceptical about the career planning process requires some explanation. It may be that we should think of career planning as being divided into components, such as recruitment and selection, mobility and retention, lay-offs and termination, training and development. If the definition of career planning is based on these personnel functions, one could argue that most public administrations and private sector organizations accomplish these tasks. If, on the other hand, we think of career planning as the use of a formal plan and career path about which employees are counselled, it clearly does not exist to a great extent in the public service of Canada.

Degree of Participation in Organizational Direction

The organizational change literature emphasizes the value of participation in decision-making. Participation has its roots in the administrative principle of centralization, first espoused by Fayol, who viewed centralization in terms of the degree of subordinate participation in the decision-making process.[22] Since that time, many have argued that the notion of decentralization is strongly related to participatory decision-making.[23] Whether participation is real or illusory, the important principle is that employees feel part of a process, that their advice is sought, and that decisions are perceived to be made jointly with superiors.[24]

The contingency model of participatory decision-making suggests that there are several decision types (autocratic, consultative and participative) and that managers can use any style as long as it fits the situation.[25] Researchers have found a tendency for managers to involve their subordinates when the quality of the decision is particularly important, when acceptance of the decision by subordinates is critical for implementation, and when they can trust subordinates to focus on organizational rather than personal goals.

Although our survey did not delve into the participation of managers in the workplace, two questions were asked to determine the degree to which respondents met with their superiors and with their subordinates to discuss objectives and strategic planning. In this way, we attempted to get a sense of the perceived degree of democracy and participation in the workplace with respect to strategic decisions. The responses are shown in Table 6-6.

Table 6-6
Perceived Degree of Participation
in the Public and Private Sectors

Participation Indices		Levels below DM/CEO					
		1	2	3	4	5	Av.
Discuss objectives with superiors	Public	82.3[1]	59.4	52.4	46.0	38.5	57.2
	Private	75.0	65.3	71.6	66.1	70.0	70.3
Discuss objectives with subordinates	Public	93.6	80.4	70.2	67.0	64.0	76.1
	Private	81.8	77.7	77.6	80.2	76.8	79.3

[1] per cent who responded "agree" or "strongly agree"

Table 6-6 contains a few particularly interesting results. First, although the differences between the two sectors are not very large, the private sector respondents perceived their environment as generally more participative than the public sector managers; the vertical solitude was pronounced in the public sector. While 82 per cent of those one level from the DM indicated that they met their superiors regularly to discuss objectives and strategy, 39 per cent of those five levels from the DM said they did the same. As well, 94 per cent of those one level from the DM felt they met with their subordinates to discuss objectives and strategic planning, but only 64 per cent of those five levels below reported meeting with their subordinates. Looking at the two questions, we see that while 94 per cent of the managers one level below the DM said they asked their subordinates to participate, only 59 per cent of those two levels below, and hence the immediate subordinates, said they discussed objectives with their superiors. This difference is evident at all levels when the two questions are analyzed together. Ironically, it seems that in the public sector more managers at higher levels view themselves as being more participative than their immediate subordinates are willing to attest to.

Keeping in mind that supportive, participative, and democratic leadership styles are usually associated with increased job satisfaction, lower turnover and absenteeism, and less job-related stress and conflict, we cannot overemphasize the importance of participation in creating a healthy organization.[26]

Capacity for Change

One traditional measure of organizational health is the degree to which an organization is able to adapt to changing external and internal pressures. Relevant questions include: time elapsed before top management recognizes the need for change and acts on it; the extent to which dialogue is necessary to initiate change; whether change is driven from the top; and how much of the change is a shared responsibility.

Although few respondents in either sector felt that it was not possible to change things in their organizations, there were marked differences between the two sectors and across levels within the public sector. Only 8 per cent of the respondents in the private sector felt they could not change their organizations, but the percentage increased three-fold in the public sector (see Table 6-7). Moreover, among public sector respondents the percentage increased significantly as one moved away from the top, from a low of 10 per cent one level from the deputy minister to 38 per cent five levels away.

Respondents were also asked about the influence employees wielded in their organizations. The amount of influence one has in the organization can be tied to one's perception of the amount of influence one can exert, and these two items turned out to be highly correlated. Sectoral and hierarchical differences were dramatic in this instance. Only 20 per cent of the most senior managers in the public sector thought that employees had little influence, but 55 per cent of those five levels away from the deputy minister felt they did not have an opportunity to influence the organization. On the other hand, private sector managers indicated that they had influence on the affairs of their organization. On average, only 14 per cent of private sector respondents felt they could not influence their organizations. Even though the figure declined as one moved down levels in the private sector, too, except for those who were five levels below the CEO, in no way was this difference as significant or as large as the one in the public sector.

The results related to the propensity for change dramatically demonstrate the existence of the vertical solitude in the public sector, as job level was significantly related to the amount of influence managers believed themselves to have.

Table 6-7
Propensity to Change in the Public and Private Sectors

		Levels below DM/CEO					
Change Orientation		1	2	3	4	5	Av.
Not possible to change things here	Public	10.0[1]	19.9	26.9	31.0	38.0	23.9
	Private	5.8	6.8	10.4	13.2	10.0	8.2
No opportunity to influence	Public	20.1	35.0	41.7	47.4	54.9	38.4
	Private	11.6	13.8	17.6	19.3	10.7	14.1

[1] per cent who responded "agree" or "strongly agree"

Relating Work Environment Attributes to Outcome Measures: The Influence of the Working Environment on Work Satisfaction

To what extent do perceptions about the work environment influence feelings of satisfaction in the workplace? If certain job characteristics are important in job enrichment, if having autonomy and independence makes certain jobs more attractive, especially for people who have high growth needs, then we should try to see how work environments in the two sectors affect overall work satisfaction. The following analysis looks at how the various satisfaction indices were affected by selected aspects of the work environment. Second, we investigate whether job level mediated the relationship between work environment and satisfaction. As in previous chapters, we report on those aspects of the work environment that are most relevant in explaining the work satisfaction of managers.

Work Environment Attributes and Satisfaction

The most important work environment attribute contributing to job satisfaction is the degree of influence managers think they have. When we examine the relationship between our five work satisfaction indices and managers' perceptions about being unable to change things where they work, we see that the more they think they can influence change, the more satisfied they are (see Table 6-8). Intrinsic, departmental, job, and career progress satisfaction are all influenced linearly in both sectors by the feeling that one can influence change.

Table 6-8
**Relationship Between Work Satisfaction and
the Perception of Not Being Able to Change Things**

Indices of Work Satisfaction		Strongly Disagree	Disagree	Neither	Agree	Strongly Agree
Intrinsic	Public	81.5[1]	68.1	43.5	29.2	30.4
Satisfaction	Private	90.0	79.8	54.8	42.9	58.1
Extrinsic	Public	36.3	37.0	31.1	32.8	26.8
Satisfaction	Private	70.2	61.1	42.4	46.0	42.0
Departmental	Public	53.2	33.7	17.2	14.5	10.0
Satisfaction	Private	83.9	64.1	44.4	24.0	51.7
Job	Public	57.3	26.5	13.8	14.3	14.8
Satisfaction	Private	60.3	32.5	22.8	14.7	35.5
Satisfaction with	Public	53.2	35.9	19.0	14.5	13.2
Career Progress	Private	67.1	45.7	25.1	22.4	45.1

[1] per cent of respondents who are "satisfied" or "very satisfied" on the five satisfaction indices

By examining the responses of those who agree strongly that it is not possible to change workplace activities, we observe that fewer public sector than private sector managers were satisfied. Interestingly, extrinsic satisfaction in the public sector appears impervious to perceptions about influencing change, whereas private sector respondents who believed they could change their work environment felt they could influence extrinsic rewards. The differences between private and public sector respondents with respect to extrinsic satisfaction (Table 6-8) support this argument.

Closely related to change, and in many ways replicating the results depicted in Table 6-8, are the findings related to the relationship between influence on the organization and work satisfaction. Overall, the more respondents agreed that they had little influence on the organization the less satisfied they were according to all indices of work satisfaction (Table 6-9). As in the previous analysis, private sector respondents showed variation in extrinsic satisfaction depending on their perceived influence in their organization.

Table 6-9
Relationship Between Work Satisfaction and Having
No Perceived Opportunity to Influence Organization

Indices of Work Satisfaction		Strongly Disagree	Disagree	Neither	Agree	Strongly Agree
Intrinsic	Public	83.5[1]	73.5	52.3	37.3	25.2
Satisfaction	Private	91.8	83.4	63.9	46.8	33.4
Extrinsic	Public	40.5	36.7	33.3	33.4	26.6
Satisfaction	Private	71.6	61.9	52.3	42.6	39.0
Departmental	Public	55.8	39.9	20.6	16.4	5.8
Satisfaction	Private	80.6	69.5	50.5	35.4	22.3
Job	Public	58.2	31.4	17.6	14.9	12.6
Satisfaction	Private	60.3	36.5	27.2	19.0	11.2
Satisfaction with	Public	51.2	40.5	24.3	16.6	12.2
Career Progress	Private	67.6	51.2	29.8	20.9	22.2

[1] per cent of respondents who are "satisfied" or "very satisfied" on the five satisfaction indices

Extrinsic satisfaction was not affected by the degree to which individuals felt they could influence their public sector organization. Performance pay is obviously not a sufficient incentive to influence the amount of extrinsic satisfaction public sector managers experience.

Another important predictor of work satisfaction was feedback. In the survey we did not specify the source of the feedback.[27] Nevertheless, as Table 6-10 demonstrates, all satisfaction indices were very strongly related to the feedback question. In both sectors, the number of satisfied senior managers increased rapidly when feedback was a feature of the job. The fact that both extrinsic and career progress satisfaction increased when respondents reported higher levels of feedback suggests that most managers regard feedback as an important element in good management. Under neutral feedback conditions we would expect that intrinsic, job, and departmental satisfaction would increase, but that the other two dimensions would not be much influenced. The availability of feedback either creates a level of satisfaction that generalizes also to extrinsic and career progress satisfaction, or respondents may have interpreted promotions, career progression, and increases in extrinsic rewards obtained as instances of positive feedback.

Table 6-10
Relationship Between Work Satisfaction and the Possibility of Obtaining Feedback on the Job and Work Satisfaction

Indices of Work Satisfaction		To a very little extent	To a little extent	To some extent	To a great extent	To a very great extent
Intrinsic	Public	18.4[1]	27.3	51.4	74.4	84.6
Satisfaction	Private	22.2	43.4	68.2	86.8	94.6
Extrinsic	Public	21.1	27.1	32.3	40.7	48.6
Satisfaction	Private	34.0	39.0	46.9	65.8	74.1
Departmental	Public	6.5	9.3	22.8	38.5	61.2
Satisfaction	Private	25.9	33.7	53.6	73.1	79.8
Job	Public	4.0	7.9	15.2	37.9	67.4
Satisfaction	Private	11.1	7.1	21.3	43.8	82.6
Satisfaction with	Public	9.7	10.8	25.6	40.4	42.8
Career Progress	Private	23.0	14.7	36.2	54.8	68.5

[1]   per cent of respondents who are "satisfied" or "very satisfied" on the five satisfaction indices

The authority needed to accomplish work objectives seems to influence all facets of work satisfaction in the public sector; the pattern in the private sector was not as clear. As can be seen in Table 6-11, public sector managers showed increasing degrees of satisfaction for all five satisfaction indices, the more they perceived they had authority to accomplish work objectives. Although, in general, private sector managers also felt that way, quite a few were still satisfied even when they did not perceive themselves to have authority to accomplish work objectives. For example, 71 per cent were satisfied with extrinsic aspects when they did not have any authority, while 69 per cent were satisfied when they had the authority to accomplish their work objectives. With respect to career satisfaction in the private sector, those who felt they had no authority felt more satisfied than those who had authority. As with extrinsic satisfaction this may be because respondents might have progressed through their careers irrespective of the authority their jobs entailed.

Although we have presented only selected work attributes in this analysis, the data relating these attributes to satisfaction indices show clearly that most of the time a linear relationship exists between work satisfaction and the perceived working environment.

Table 6-11
Relationship Between the Authority to Accomplish
Work Objectives and Work Satisfaction

Indices of Work Satisfaction		Strongly Disagree	Disagree	Neither	Agree	Strongly Agree
Intrinsic	Public	17.0[1]	21.4	32.0	65.0	86.6
Satisfaction	Private	47.1	28.3	49.6	78.9	92.5
Extrinsic	Public	17.5	28.3	30.2	36.0	44.3
Satisfaction	Private	70.6	40.7	40.5	59.1	68.9
Departmental	Public	4.6	9.7	12.4	30.1	54.5
Satisfaction	Private	29.4	43.2	33.9	63.1	78.7
Job	Public	12.5	8.8	9.5	21.6	60.3
Satisfaction	Private	35.2	15.1	11.8	30.1	65.3
Satisfaction with	Public	3.3	16.8	14.5	32.1	47.3
Career Progress	Private	29.5	16.7	30.1	44.7	61.9

[1] per cent of respondents who are "satisfied" or "very satisfied" on the five satisfaction indices

Managerial Job Level, Work Environment Attributes and Satisfaction

We have argued elsewhere in this chapter that we expected to find evidence of the vertical solitude with regard to the authority questions because people who occupy senior management positions have more formal authority and greater organizational privileges than lower-placed managers. Nevertheless, it is still important to look at job level and some of the more relevant aspects of work environment to see the nature of the relationship. In this section we look at feedback, change orientation and amount of authority to see whether they are influenced by job level. These items were chosen after analysis demonstrated that they were the most important of the work environment attributes in predicting work satisfaction.

The possibility of producing change in an organization was the best predictor of work satisfaction. This finding is also tied to job level, as demonstrated in Figure 6-1. Even when managers believed it was not possible to produce change, EXs were more satisfied than SMs or SM-1s. Interestingly, the SM group felt slightly less satisfied than the SM-1s, when questioned about the possibility of producing change. It may be that frustrations caused by the inability to effect change or to influence events create more dissatisfaction for the SMs than the lower-placed SM-1s. The latter, who do not occupy senior managerial positions within the system, can tolerate better than SMs the fact of not being able to change and affect their environment. SMs who hold management titles do not have the authority to influence change and possibly feel some degree of frustration.

The authority public sector managers believe they have is influenced by their job level, which in turn has a bearing on their satisfaction. We analyzed the authority managers perceive they have to accomplish work goals, since we know that much of the authority to deal with human resources, such as promoting or hiring personnel, is held by central agencies. The data in Figure 6-2, displaying the relationship between authority to accomplish work goals, job level and departmental satisfaction, exhibit a pattern very similar to the earlier analysis on change orientation. The EX group was always more satisfied than the SM and SM-1s even when it did not perceive itself to have much authority to accomplish work goals. The SM-1 group also tended to be slightly more satisfied than the SMs at similar levels of authority.

Job level had less influence on intrinsic satisfaction when we factored in authority to accomplish work objectives. As can be seen from Figure 6-3, EXs were more intrinsically satisfied, regardless of level of authority, when compared to SMs and SM-1s. However, this difference was not as pronounced as the one found with departmental

Figure 6-1
Relationship between the Possibility of Changing Things,
Managerial Level and Departmental Satisfaction
(public sector)

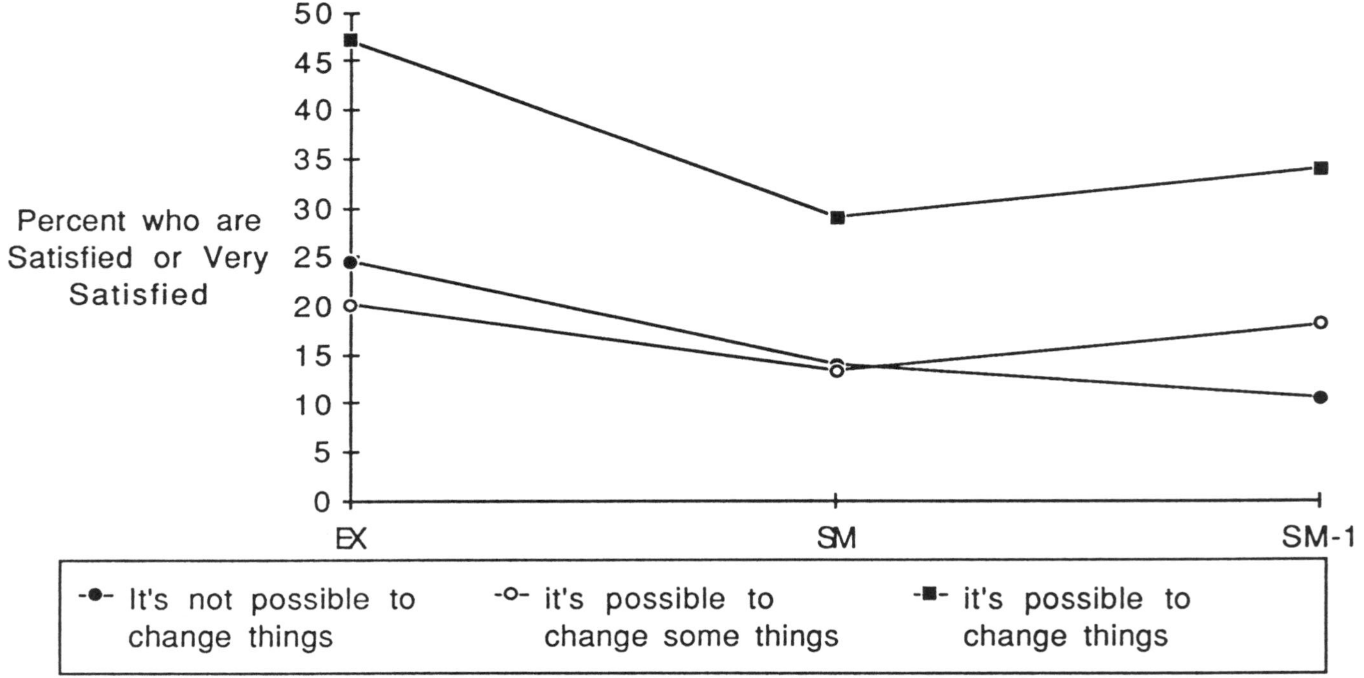

Percent who are
Satisfied or Very
Satisfied

EX   SM   SM-1

● − It's not possible to   -o- it's possible to   -■- it's possible to
     change things   change some things   change things

Figure 6-2
Relationship between the Authority to Accomplish Work Goals,
Managerial Level and Departmental Satisfaction
(public sector)

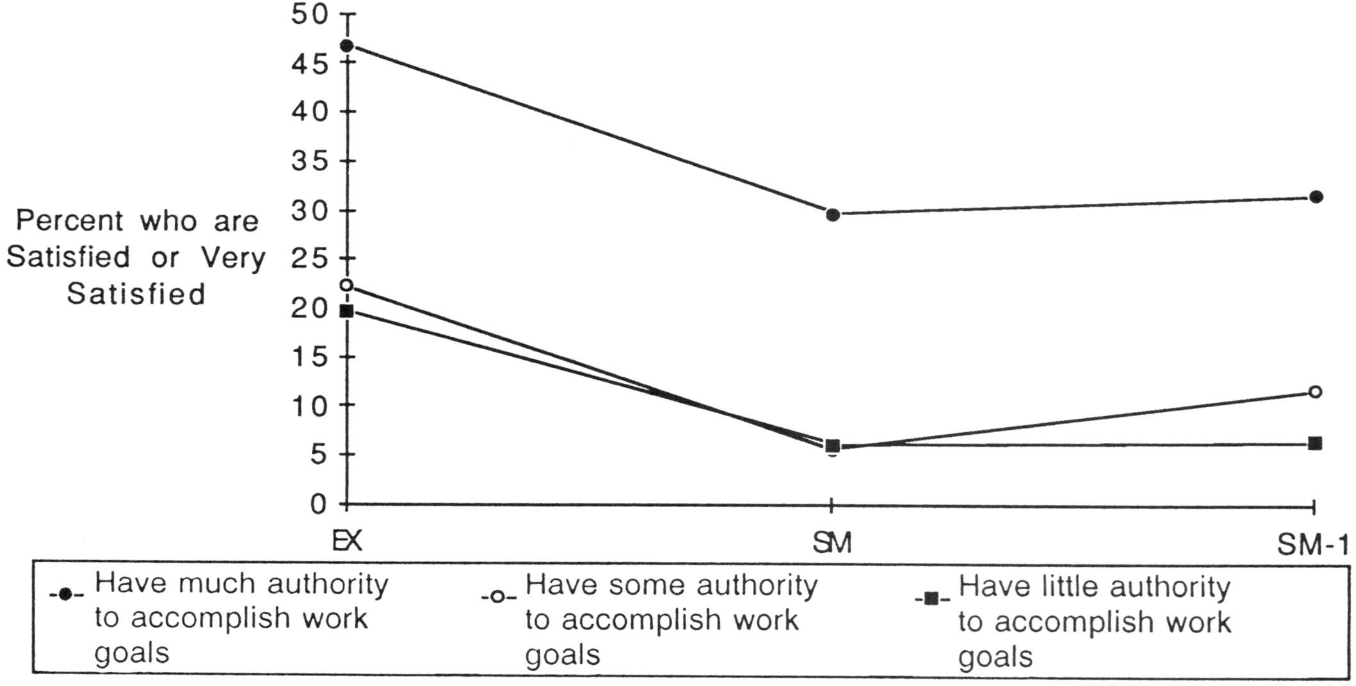

Figure 6-3
Relationship between the Authority to Accomplish Work Goals,
Management Level and Intrinsic Satisfaction

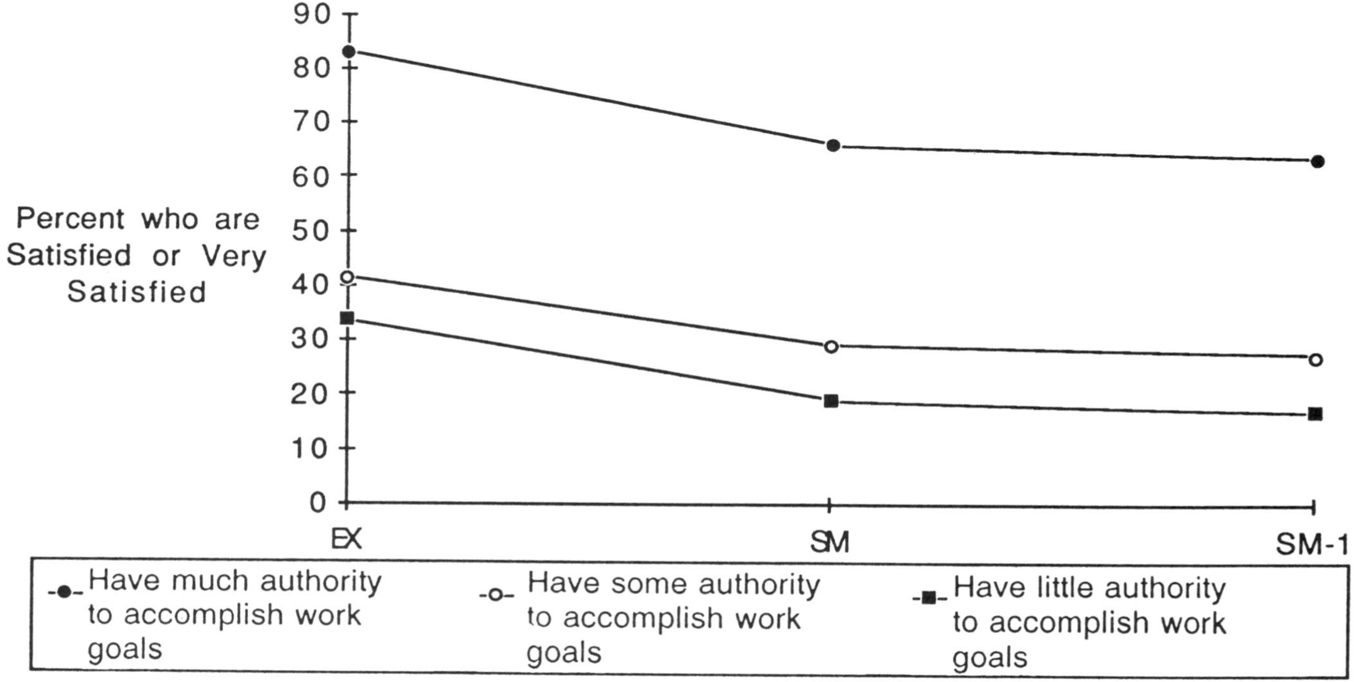

satisfaction. What clearly influences intrinsic satisfaction more is the amount of authority managers believe they have to accomplish work objectives.

One area where job level did not play much of a role was in the amount of feedback managers receive. Job satisfaction was clearly influenced by feedback but not by job level (Figure 6-4). When managers received a lot of feedback all three managerial groups were "satisfied" or "very satisfied" with their jobs. This level of satisfaction hovered around 94 per cent for the EXs and SMs and fell to 77 per cent for the SM-1 group. The level of job satisfaction decreased systematically for all three groups as the amount of feedback received on the job went down.

Work motivation and job design theories argue that feedback is crucial in creating a favourable work environment. Our survey data confirm that feedback is a significant determinant of work satisfaction for senior managers in the public sector irrespective of the type of job or position in the hierarchy.

Managing the Work Environment: The Need for Commitment

We argued in Chapter 1 that we believe performance and work satisfaction are closely related and that organizational effectiveness is an outcome of managing various contingencies depicted in the management model. The work environment influences organizational effectiveness in that model through the various satisfaction measures.

Our data have shown that a favourable work environment — one that fosters employee participation in decisions, feedback either through the job or through open communication, career planning, fewer personal or organizational constraints, and high levels of vested formal managerial authority — facilitates effectiveness and leads to work satisfaction for managers. As well, it appears that these aspects of the work environment tend to receive greater attention in the private sector than in the public service of Canada. Our analysis also revealed a vertical solitude when it comes to the work environment.

To discuss how environmental factors ought to be managed we look at some of the more salient issues analyzed in this chapter and point out some of the improvements that could be brought about. Our discussion revolves around the nature of the work, including feedback, career planning, and participation. We argue that a high level of commitment is necessary on the part of the most senior managers in departments and central agencies to bring about some of the changes we advocate.

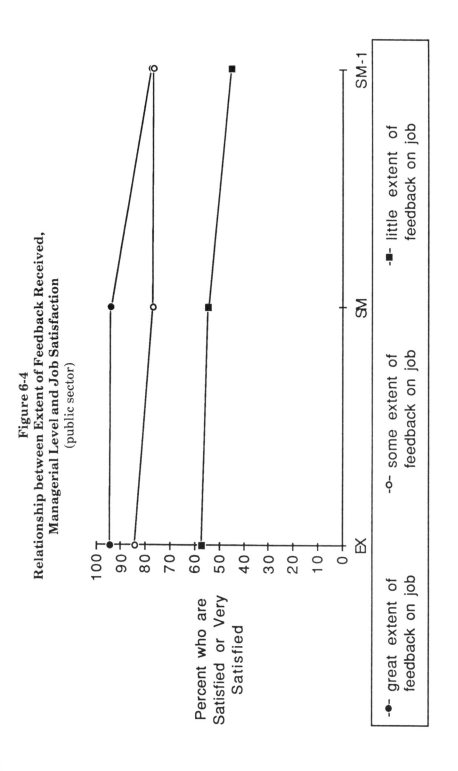

Figure 6-4
Relationship between Extent of Feedback Received,
Managerial Level and Job Satisfaction
(public sector)

Managing Feedback

One area that can easily be managed in the public sector is the provision of feedback. This requires several steps at the departmental level. First and foremost, some feedback ought to be built into managerial jobs, although this may be easier in operational than in policy jobs. Second, the performance appraisal system for managers should include a strong and serious feedback component, to allow managers to improve their performance. Finally, channels of communication must be kept open so that superiors can provide feedback to their subordinates.

We have underlined the importance of feedback and its influence as a motivational factor throughout our analysis. Unless feedback takes place openly and frequently, satisfaction levels of managers will remain low. We are uncertain as to the most appropriate way to manage the feedback process for it depends on the nature of each department, but we do know that it requires commitment and willingness on the part of the most senior managers in each department to create a climate where feedback is used positively to build and reward rather than sanction and punish. Feedback can become a very useful tool for organizational effectiveness; by receiving information on what they do well, being praised, and participating in some job-related decisions, managers, like any other employees will know that recognition is related to performance.

Managing Career Planning and Development

The lower levels of satisfaction in the senior management and SM-1 group indicate a need to re-examine careers and career progression. One important reason for the relatively low satisfaction scores is, as Morgan suggests, that changing demographic trends and restraint measures leave "nowhere to go" for many who have reached the SM and SM-1 level.[28] Their average ages are only a little more than two years lower than for the EX group.[29] Many are in their late thirties and early forties and are going to be in their present positions for many years.

Our survey indicated that in both the private and public sectors very little formal career planning takes place. It is difficult for us to compare career advancement and mobility among senior managers in the two sectors. Suffice it to say that downsizing, restraint and age pyramids all converge in the swelling SM cadre, which needs to be motivated in the years to come. By definition, the pyramid narrows at the top in all organizations. However, the relative youth of the SM and SM-1 groups makes the problem especially acute; unless more variety in career assignments can be programmed into the work cycle, psychological needs will not be met and work dissatisfaction will be exacerbated. We have already discussed the importance of task variety in providing additional job satisfaction.[30]

One option for the Public Service Commission is a new approach to career development, one in which senior managers have some certainty about how their careers will progress. This implies using lateral movement and slower progression as a way of preparing senior managers for more responsibilities. This approach to career development could also heighten the sense of caring on the part of the organization that seems to be missing in the public sector. By demonstrating organizational commitment, the Public Service Commission could reasonably expect to improve the current system.[31] The Japanese have been quite successful in using career planning. In Japan a lifetime career is offered by a particular department to those who pass competitive exams, followed by a variety of organizational learning assignments for younger senior public servants. Movement up the hierarchy is orchestrated.[32] Although we do not advocate the blanket importation of this philosophy, we strongly suggest that the Government of Canada look at how some Japanese practices could be adapted to our public sector culture.

Closely related to career planning is the practice of moving managers, executives and deputy ministers around in the system, often after brief periods of tenure. This is predicated on the belief that managing is a universal skill that can be transferred without regard to departmental culture and history, or management ability. Although our data do not point directly to the pitfalls of this practice, a recent study shows some of the negative implications of short tenure.[33] This concern has also been raised in the private sector, where the practice of transferring executives from one organization to another has been seriously criticized.[34]

It is clear that an explicit career planning policy must incorporate a strong training and development component to help retain managerial resources in the system and give managers the new skills and knowledge necessary to grow. The federal government, through the Public Service Commission, has spent considerable sums on service-wide training programs. Our data lead us to conclude that these programs have been responsive to the needs of managers; however, public sector managers have suggested in their survey responses that the training has not been adequate to their needs.

It is time to re-examine the federal public service approach to training and development. One could continue with courses of short duration for managers, to prepare them for certain functions, to initiate them into managerial positions, and to impart skills and knowledge, as is the case now. Alternatively, a more systematic approach could be adopted, with training tied to career paths and to developmental plans for employees identified as having management potential, and training and education provided both within the system and outside.

Managing Participation

The data have shown that managers at lower levels do not perceive the work environment to be as participative as the one their superiors describe. Several reasons may explain this discrepancy in perceptions, but only a few are plausible. First, mis-communication or insufficiently open communication may be at the root of the problem. A second reason is that participation, to the extent that it exists, may be more illusory than real. In other words, even when lower-level managers are asked to participate in decision-making, they do not really have any power to influence or change the outcome. Finally, the discrepancy in perceptions may be due simply to the fact that communication does not take place. The most senior managers may define those occasions on which they disseminate information in meetings as participation, whereas lower-level managers may believe that no such exchange occurs.

Participation in decision-making is not a panacea that would result quickly in a more effective organization and there are many decisions for which participation is not appropriate. It requires candidness, openness, and the ability of managers to communicate in a positive climate. Instituting a more participative climate within an organization also means that managers at lower levels, as well as supervisors and employees, must be listened to. Advice should be sought and participation made real, rather than illusory. A participatory work climate leads to reducing hierarchical rigidities and the misuses of power. We are aware, however, that especially in the public sector, trust is required for the system to become more open. The fewer opportunities for promotion create incentives for individuals and groups in the system to hoard information in order to use it to their advantage. Such behaviour seriously hampers attempts to open the system to more participation.

In the End: A Positive Work Environment is Indispensable

The discussion has shown differences between the private and public sectors in perceptions of work environment. In the private sector, managers feel they have more authority, participate more in decision-making, and receive more feedback. They also tend to perceive different constraints in the work environment than their public sector counterparts. However, the nature of work and the work processes in place are not perceived very differently. As for differences within the public sector, there are many, demonstrating the existence of a vertical solitude. Although we had hypothesized that such a solitude would be found in the private sector too, the data did not support this view. A positive perception of the work environment, such as that reported by private sector respondents, is indispensable because it influences how managers perceive their overall organization and undoubtedly has an influence on their self-image.

Notes

1. F.W. Taylor, *The Principles of Scientific Management,* (New York: Harper and Brothers, 1911).

2. E. Mayo, *The Human Problems of an Industrial Civilization,* (New York: Macmillan, 1933); F.J. Roethlisberger, *Management and Morale,* (Cambridge, Mass.: Harvard University Press, 1941).

3. H. Tosi and J. Slocum, "Contingency theory: some suggested directions," *Journal of Management,* vol. 10, (1984), pp. 9-26.

4. A.K. Korman, *Organizational Behavior,* (Englewood Cliffs, New Jersey: Prentice-Hall, 1977).

5. J. Pfeffer, and G.R. Salancik, *The External Control of Organizations,* (New York: Harper and Row, 1978).

6. L.D. Brown, *Managing Conflict at Organizational Interfaces,* (Reading, Mass.: Addison-Wesley, 1983); A.C. Filley, *Interpersonal Conflict Resolution.,* (Glenview, Ill.: Scott, Foresman and Company, 1975); K.W. Thomas, "Conflict and Conflict Management," in M.D. Dunette, (ed.), *Handbook of Industrial and Organizational Psychology,* (Chicago: Rand McNally, 1976), pp. 889-935.

7. J.H. Reitz, *Behavior in Organizations,* (3rd ed.; Homewood, Ill. Irwin, 1987).

8. For a review of job design strategies as they relate to motivation see, R.J. Aldag and A.P. Brief, *Task Design and Employee Motivation,* (Glenview, Ill.: Scott, Foresman and Company, 1979).

9. F. Herzberg, "One More Time: How do you Motivate Employees?" *Harvard Business Review,* vol. 46, (1968), pp. 53-62.

10. For detail on the so-called Topeka experiments, see D.A. Whitsett and L. Yorks, "Looking back at Topeka: General Foods and the quality of work life experiment," *California Management Review*, (Summer 1983), pp. 93-109; R.E. Walton, "Work innovations at Topeka: after six years," *Journal of Applied Behavioural Science*, vol. 13, (1977), pp. 422-433; R.E. Walton, "The diffusion of new work structures: explaining why success didn't take," *Organizational Dynamics*, vol. 3, (winter 1975), pp. 3-22.

11. R.J. Hackman, and G.R. Oldham, *Work Redesign*, (Reading, Mass.: Addison-Wesley, 1980).

12. See R.J. Hackman, and G.R. Oldham, *Work . . .*, for a discussion of the importance of feedback.

13. O.P. Dwivedi, "On Holding Public Servants Accountable", in O.P. Dwivedi (ed.), *The Administrative State in Canada*, (Toronto: University of Toronto Press, 1982), pp. 151-176.

14. Canada: Royal Commission on Financial Management and Accountability, (Chairman: A. Lambert), *Final Report* (Ottawa: Supply and Services Canada, 1979); G.F. Osbaldeston, *Keeping Deputy Ministers Accountable*, (London, Ont.: National Centre for Management Research and Development, University of Western Ontario, 1988); T.W. Plumptre, *Beyond the Bottom Line: Management in Government*, (Halifax, N.S.: The Institute for Research on Public Policy, 1988).

15. F. Herzberg, "The wise old Turk," *Harvard Business Review*, (September-October 1974), pp. 70-80.

16. For an overview, see H. Selye, *The Stress of Life*, (New York: McGraw-Hill, 1976); J.M. Ivancevich, and M.T. Matteson, *Stress and Work: A Managerial Perspective*, (Glenview, Ill.: Scott, Foresman and Company, 1980); V.A. Price, *Type A Behavior Pattern*, (New York: Academic Press, 1982).

17. J.M. Ivancevich, and J.H. Donelly, "Relation of organizational structure to job satisfaction, anxiety-stress, and performance," *Administrative Science Quarterly*, (June 1975), pp. 272-280.

18. S. Parasuraman, and J. Alutto, "Sources and outcomes of stress in organizational settings: toward the development of a structural model," *Academy of Management Journal*, vol. 27, (1984), pp. 330-350; R.V. Marks, "Social stress and cardiovascular disease," *Millbank Memorial Fund Quarterly*, (April 1976), pp. 51-107.

19. E.A. Locke, "Toward a theory of task motivation and incentives," *Organizational Behavior and Human Performance*, vol. 3, (1968), pp. 157-189; G.P. Latham, and G.A. Yukl, "A review of research on the application of goal setting in organizations," *Academy of Management Journal*, vol. 18, (1975), pp. 824-845.

20. A.P. Raia, *Managing By Objectives*, (Glenview, Ill.: Scott, Foresman and Company, 1974).

21. J. Walker, "Does career planning rock the boat?" *Human Resource Management*, vol. 17, (Spring 1978), pp. 2-7.

22. H. Fayol, *General and Industrial Management*, translated by C. Stors, (London: Pitman, 1949).

23. R.M. Steers, *Organizational Effectiveness*, (Santa Monica, Calif.: Goodyear, 1977).

24. L. Coch, and J.P.R. French, Jr., "Overcoming resistance to change," *Human Relations*, vol. 1, (1948), pp. 512-532.

25. V.H. Vroom, and P. Yetton, *Leadership and Decision-making.*, (Pittsburgh, Pa.: University of Pittsburgh Press, 1973).

26. A.C. Filley, and R.J. House, *Managerial Process and Organizational Behavior*, (Glenview, Ill.: Scott, Foresman and Company, 1974); R.M. Steers, and L.W. Porter, "The role of task-goal attributes in employee performance," *Psychological Bulletin*, vol. 81, (1974), pp. 434-452; V.H. Vroom, *Work and Motivation*, (New York: John Wiley & Sons, 1964); D.R. Denison, "Bringing corporate culture to the bottom line," *Organizational Dynamics*, (Autumn 1984), pp. 52-64.

27. In the survey we did not specify the source of the feedback, i.e., whether the feedback was provided by superiors or whether the job itself had built-in feedback mechanisms.

28. Morgan, N.S. *Nowhere to Go? Possible Consequences of the Demographic Imbalance in Decision-Making Groups of the Federal Public Service*, (Halifax, N.S.: Institute for Research on Public Policy, 1981) pp. 1-29.

29. These numbers were provided by the Treasury Board Secretariat in 1988.

30. See J.R. Hackman, and G.R. Oldham, *Work*, regarding importance of task variety in providing high levels of motivation and as a technique for enriching jobs.

31. On a practical note, we are not aware that clear succession plans are operative in the Canadian public sector, as is the case in Britain for instance, where the top level positions are evaluated and a short list always kept open for replacements, albeit not communicated to candidates.

32. S. Borins, "Management of the public sector in Japan: are there lessons to be learned?" *Canadian Public Administration*, vol. 29, no. 2, (1986), pp. 175-196; S. Nakamura, "Aspects of personnel policy in the Japanese public service," Paper presented at Informal Expert Meeting on Increasing Flexibility in Personnel Management in the Public Service, OECD, Paris, 8-9 February, 1988.

33. G.F. Osbaldeston, *Keeping Deputy Ministers Accountable*.

34. Y.K. Shetty, and N.S. Peery, "Are top executives transferable across companies?" *Business Horizons*, vol. 19, (June 1976), pp. 23-28.

Chapter 7

Conclusions

We embarked on this study because we saw growing informal evidence of increasing managerial and staff problems in the public sector and so sought to determine the causes of this malaise. At the same time, the study would offer a means of comparing managerial practices in both the public and private sector, with the aim of investigating the possibilities of transferring such practices. A well-designed, large-scale survey would shed light on the issues and could be a springboard for further data collection and action. In other words, the study could help managers focus on the problems of managing in the Canadian public service.

The research concentrated on a subset of four management factors in the public and private sectors and how they related to work satisfaction. A subset of five variables from the 17 possible choices were studied with regard to public and private sector differences, their relationship with work satisfaction and the impact that job level might have on the outcome of the analysis. These five variables were personal and work values, leadership, rewards, work environment, and culture. Given that we are working with data gathered during a given time period, we have hypothesized that these variables have produced the levels of work satisfaction which we report. We have made only a few of the possible analyses. At some point in the future, we will look at research questions which try to clarify the causality problems and which explore more complex linkages among the four factors in the future.

Both the public and private sector surveys yielded response rates of greater than 70 per cent. The high level of commitment to this survey, which was voluntary in the two sectors, indicates a great level of interest on the part of managers. The high response rates also increase the representativeness of the data.

At the outset, the study was designed to measure the managerial practices used in the public service and to see to what extent these practices differed from those used by a number of comparable managers in the private sector, with the aim of determining if the practices were transferable. As a part of this exercise, it was hypothesized that there would be some fall in the level of agreement or satisfaction as one moved down the hierarchy.

Our research revealed, on a consistent basis, two important findings. First, almost without exception, the private sector managers had a more positive view of the management practices in their organization than did their public sector counterparts, working at similar levels in their organization. Repeatedly, we found significant differences between the sectors in all factors in the management model—personal values, leadership style, allocation of rewards, the working environment, and corporate values.

The second result appeared with astonishing regularity in the analyses. We found, within the public service management cadre, divergent views among the five managerial levels with regard to almost all managerial practices. The differences were almost always dependent on where one worked in the management structure. This effect, which we have called "the vertical solitude", suggests that, as one moves down the bureaucratic hierarchy, managers are less satisfied and less positive about managerial practices in their organization.[1] As a counterpoint, we did not find this effect to any significant degree in the private sector.

The data also revealed that levels of work satisfaction among the SMs and SM-1s, regardless of the index used in the analysis, were substantially lower than those of their private sector counterparts and, in our opinion, were too low for managers occupying such pivotal positions in the organization.

While we had hypothesized that there would be differences between the two sectors, including the assessment of the efficacy of managerial practices in the two sectors, we were not prepared for the strong and consistent differences which characterized the overall findings. The results strongly suggest the existence of a phenomenon which is symptomatic of a serious problem in the management culture of the federal public service.

Subsequent analyses of the results demonstrated in a number of instances that the vertical solitude was not simply the direct result of a manager's job level. Instead, the data suggested that other factors explained the differences in perceptions between the executives and managers. In particular, it was found that, when those working at lower management levels perceived the same degree of leadership in their organization as those at the EX levels, their degree of work satisfaction was essentially the same (see Table 3-6). In effect, we suspect the explanation of the vertical solitude is not that low-level managers are always dissatisfied but that their ranking in the hierarchy denies them the opportunity to perceive instances of leadership, the ways in which rewards are allocated, and the inculcation of values.

In light of this analysis, it is more than likely that the vertical solitude is not a function of organizational layering or uninteresting lower level managerial jobs. Instead, the data suggest that managers and senior managers (i.e., those working four and five levels below the deputy minister) do not share the same type of management experiences as their corporate superiors. In those relatively rare instances where managers working five levels below the deputy minister indicated that they actively participated in making decisions or perceived the allocation of rewards as being very fair, there was little to distinguish their perceptions from those working at the assistant deputy minister level.

We think that the relatively low level of agreement and satisfaction at the lower end of the managerial structure adds an additional element of concern. SMs and SM-1s are among the most critical links in the management chain in the public service, since they play a pivotal role as "culture carriers" by passing on their perceptions of the needs and desires of those working above them to the many thousands of employees who actually deliver services to the public and various client groups. Given the relatively low level of work satisfaction among the SMs and SM-1s, we are concerned that many public servants working in contact with the public may not be performing at an optimal level of effectiveness.

In the beginning of this book, we raised a number of questions about the Canadian federal public service. Many of the findings go a long way in answering these questions. The issue of whether there is still a strong public service culture remains only partly answered because there are no historical data beyond individual recollections of the past glories of the federal public service that would serve as a useful measuring stick.

Despite methodological limitations, there is no doubt the data indicate that, at the lower management levels, there is confusion within the ranks as to the purpose and direction of the federal public service. However, despite the lack of a shared "corporate culture", we have also found relatively high levels of work satisfaction, particularly satisfaction related to the job. The data also suggest that public servants are very committed to the public, to the respondent's perceived clientele, and have strong feelings of personal accomplishment. We are therefore left with a somewhat contradictory view of the situation. While the culture measured in terms of values appears somewhat fragmented, there is ample evidence that the work force is committed and motivated to do a good job in support of the Canadian public.

We made the argument earlier that the principal culture carriers in the federal public service are the middle managers since they typically occupy key positions within their organizations. If the SMs are the culture carriers in most federal government departments, then one is left with the task of convincing SMs and SM-1s to share the same values and attitudes as those working above them in the government hierarchy. Since we have no data for the thousands of employees who work further down the organizational structure, we can only presume that the break in perceptions which we observed between the SMs and the EXs is the critical one. Unless this difference is bridged, there is no reason to expect that remedies such as improved internal communications will have much of an impact on the vast majority of government employees.

We are also aware from the findings that good performance is not reinforced by rewards. The primary motivational tools available to managers, i.e., rewards and promotions, do not appear to have much use within the system. In any event, recent financial and personnel constraint programs will make it more difficult to reward the superior performer. Given this new reality, motivation and morale problems will likely increase over the next few years.

One of the major barriers against the likelihood of a major reform of the federal public service management function is the relatively low cost of not acting. Most good policy analysis contains a "no-action" option which allows the analyst the possibility of deciding not to do anything to remedy the perceived problem. This option is a viable one in the case of public sector reform since there is little public pressure for change and those most affected by present circumstances are not particularly forceful in their demand for reform. In fact, as noted, the public has been served with a steady dose of anti-public service rhetoric over the last few years.

This lack of internal pressure means that the commitment to reform must be firmly implanted in the minds of those responsible for the health and nurturing of the public service. Unfortunately, there is a bias towards inaction since the responsibility for the development of the public service is effectively shared by at least three organizations—the Treasury Board, the Public Service Commission, and the Privy Council Office. This sharing suggests that, even if there is a commitment to producing a more effective public service, as much time may be spent in sorting out appropriate roles and responsibilities as in implementing true reform.

Since the private sector sample was from large, bureaucratic, client-oriented companies similar to many government departments, there was no reason to have anticipated such a wide variation in the findings between the two sectors. Our conclusion is that the differences in perceptions do not arise from inherent dissimilarities between the two sectors but from the way management and management skills are valued and rewarded in the public and private sectors.

It appears that senior management in the private sector believes there is a strong link between their profits and the quality of service to clients. Our data indicate that most of our private sector respondents have realized that providing good services results from managing people well. Private sector executives generally recognized that maintaining a highly motivated and well-directed work force was one of the most critical tasks of the senior management cadre and that good management practices foster and maintain motivated employees. This belief implies that the organization is committed to the development of leadership skills, reward structures and value systems, as a means to greater productivity, work satisfaction and, ultimately, profits. In the private sector, it is generally acknowledged that good management practices are critical to achieving corporate goals.

The public sector findings suggest a somewhat different view of management. In our opinion, managing in the public sector, as an activity, has not received the type of attention it has in the private sector. There is a range of possible reasons for this lower level of commitment but we suspect the problems of public sector management are more a function of tradition and job content than an explicit rejection of management principles. Over the years, management in the public sector has been preoccupied with efficiency concerns, as government cutbacks and changing priorities required managers to make do with relatively fewer resources. As well, several central agency rules and regulations place emphasis on procedural requirements, to ensure equity and fairness in all aspects of the management process. As a result, when it comes to deciding how to tackle a given public sector problem, much of the concern is to find ways of ensuring that the process is fair rather than that outputs are appropriate. This preoccupation with administrative processes has tended to put a premium on people who can find system-based solutions to problems, as opposed to those who can get the job done. The systems-oriented style of managing is the antithesis of what many regard as good management. There is a conflict between the value associated with accountability and the values of originality, experimentation, inventiveness, and risk-taking.

Another feature of the public service is the importance given to policy matters. One can argue that the emphasis among the executive cadre in the federal public service has been to encourage and, more importantly, to reward those especially adept at developing policy and "working it through the system". It is not surprising that, as Plumptre noted, "a corollary often associated with this belief is the view that administration—the implementation of policy—is both less difficult and less demanding than policy, and that it can be safely delegated to subordinates."

Given the emphasis on policy and process, it is not surprising that the system has disproportionately rewarded managers who have spent time working in the central agencies such as the Treasury Board Secretariat and the Privy Council Office and in a number of key policy departments. As a consequence, policy intensive departments often acted as a kind of spawning ground for candidates for the senior posts in the rest of the public service, providing officials with the exposure and contacts required for a successful career.

One other characteristic of management culture in the public service, which is in direct contrast to that in the private sector, has been the practice over the last 15 years or so of encouraging managers to use interdepartmental moves as stepping stones to the senior management ranks. The erroneous but commonly held view that people are easily transferable from one department to another, without attention to corporate culture or departmental history, has spawned a generation of EXs who, until recent restraint measures, never spent more than a few years in a given department. This practice is so ingrained in Ottawa that, until recently, the typical deputy minister's tenure was about 22 months in a given department. This example has not been lost on the senior public service manager.

The public service has long been aware that it is different from the private sector for reasons explained in Chapter 1. This difference has too often been an excuse for not paying attention, or giving sufficient credit to management skills. Ironically, the differences between the two sectors have made management skills in the public sector more necessary and, at the same time, more difficult to accomplish, given the fact that jobs are becoming more complex and more difficult because of the inevitable constraints and lack of freedom to manoeuvre and find innovative solutions. In short, the solutions to improving the public sector management dilemma must recognize the reality of public sector management while striking a balance between what is best for the public service and what is possible given the constraints.

We believe that all of these factors have played a role in developing the vertical solitude. The implications of the vertical solitude are profound for the Canadian federal public service. Only a severe breakdown in the development of the federal government's management cadre could have produced such diverse perceptions of managerial practices. The failure of public sector managers to share common views on such factors as organizational goals, corporate values, reward systems, and levels of commitment suggests that the essential link is tenuous between those people whose job it is to manage the organization and those who deliver the service or product.

Improving Management in the Public Sector: The What and the How

This study has empirically documented management problems in the federal public service. The data do not tell us directly what must be done and so the solutions which we offer are based on our observations of the current system and on the written suggestions of respondents.

It appears to us that the problems of public sector management should be addressed at three different levels. First, we must develop a better understanding of emerging work values and demands in Canadian society. Second, there is a need to better define what it means to be a manager in the federal public service today. Third, those at the most senior levels must develop ways of assuming more responsibility for management activities in their departments.

The work satisfaction issue presents an urgent and many-faceted problem. There is an immediate need for the federal public service to better understand the changing nature of work, defined in terms of job content and employee attitudes in Canadian society.

Public servants face increased workloads due to job enlargement. Access to more and better information means administrative decision-making is increasingly complex. The process itself has become more transparent, and this is placing additional pressure on administrators. Special interest groups have gained considerable legitimacy, allowing them to become more directly involved in administrative decision-making. Finally, instant two-way communication has brought its own levels of stress. All these factors have enormous impact on the service-oriented employees, who consequently differ markedly from their counterparts of a generation or less ago.

Managers are being asked to make more difficult and complex decisions. Many jobs which were once quite straightforward, like those of air traffic controllers and meat inspectors, have become stressful and complex. Staff cutbacks have placed a greater burden on those who remain. Moreover government-wide initiatives, such as access-to-information legislation and affirmative action programs, have opened up the government administrative decision-making process to a range of new players who have strong interests in the outcomes. The addition of so many outside sources of influence has inadvertently produced a more complex and cumbersome decision-making process. Increasingly, management is being forced to operate in an environment which provides a greater volume of information but demands quicker decisions. The old ways of managing are increasingly inadequate in this more turbulent environment.

In this context, the second step in dealing with the issues raised by this study is to attempt, through concerted action and commitment, to orient the managerial philosophy of the federal public service towards a better appreciation of the role of a manager in public administration. Without this change in attitude, particularly at the most senior executive levels, any change to the system will be ineffective.

This change in attitude will be difficult to bring about in the short term. Since the management function within the federal public service is still divided among three different central agencies (the Treasury Board Secretariat, the Public Service Commission and the Privy Council Office), there is a need for coordination to produce a single vision of what constitutes good public sector management. To accomplish this task, these central agencies will have to address questions about the federal government's obligations and policies regarding innovative management, as well as career development, training, employment equity, affirmative action, career paths, compensation, and risk-taking practices.

While we await the development of the new management philosophy there are a number of preliminary steps which can be undertaken.

First, dramatic efforts must be made to provide public servants with some form of public recognition for their contribution to Canadian society. The responsibility for this activity lies with the politicians and especially ministers, who provide the public service with its raison d'être, and with those senior public sector officials who are explicitly responsible for the management of the federal public service—the Clerk of the Privy Council, the Secretary of the Treasury Board, and the Chairman of the Public Service Commission.

Criticisms of the public service, especially by politicians during election campaigns, have placed unnecessary pressures on it. To blame the public service for the failures of political parties to deliver effective policies is inappropriate and misplaced. While the public service obviously plays an important role in framing policy it is not directly accountable for what a government does as part of its mandate. Therefore, as a second step, a clearer distinction must be drawn for the public between political and administrative decisions so that the appropriate accountabilities are assigned.

Third, it is probably unrealistic to expect that new Members of Parliament will have sufficient understanding about the public service and its place in the policy and administrative systems of governance. It may appear naive to suggest that they become part of the solution given their partisan orientation and the demands on their time from other quarters. In spite of this limitation, it must be fully appreciated that Members of Parliament can play a crucial role in defining the public's image of the public service. It is therefore imperative that the recent initiatives of the Canadian Centre for Management Development to offer some orientation to MPs continue.

The future of the public service is inextricably intertwined with the improvement in the quality of the political system and its players. Without a political vision of the public service, the public service as an institution is hampered in developing its own vision of the future.

All these actions will have little practical value, however, if the fundamental nature of public sector management is not changed dramatically. In both a corporate and a departmental sense, managing activities well has rarely been rewarded by the federal government for many of the reasons noted. However, a period of restraint and downsizing is the best time to change this attitude of disinterest. Managers must be shown that good management is as highly prized in the federal government as other skills.

Good public sector managers must be able to demonstrate an expertise in three essential activities: subject matter knowledge, understanding of the decision-making process, and managerial skills. Over the past 10 years or so there has been a tendency to reward those individuals who were particularly adept at understanding the decision-making system, at the expense of the content experts and the managers. Based on the survey findings, it appears that there has been too little attention paid to managerial skills.

Since the term "managerial skills" has so many meanings, it will become critical for those in authority to explain to their employees their definition of good management. In concrete terms, the emphasis on management skills will also require changes in the incentive and reward system. Managers are rational actors and the reward system will have to be structured so as to ensure that good management is rewarded and bad management is not. As an example, managers will have to accept the challenge by spending more time encouraging employee participation in decision-making, holding employees to account for their management behaviour, allocating rewards, and improving the quality of communication between the upper echelons of the department and those working lower in the hierarchy.

Given that information is the currency of power in any bureaucracy, it should be recognized at the outset that this new philosophy of management will require some dilution of power, especially at higher levels. We suspect, therefore, that by advocating better internal communication we are arguing for a more dramatic change than any structural change yet imposed on the federal government. We would expect initiatives in this direction to be resisted from the top, since they will challenge entrenched modes of behaviour and power-sharing.

This reorientation of emphasis on management skills must take into account the values and culture of the public service, its constraints and reward systems. Tackling these issues would be an important and ground breaking innovation, because we are not aware of any public administration that has systematically undertaken such change. Some local administrations have attempted to change their organizations, but their size is hardly comparable to the public service of Canada.[2]

Many change initiatives in large organizations are generated from the top. When they involve value change, the experience has shown that this approach is not very effective because employees who are affected do not participate in the change process.[3] A more effective way of producing change is a shared approach, where all levels of the organization are represented in both defining the problem and producing solutions. This latter approach is usually referred to as organizational development. Although the aim of this study was not to develop a blueprint for change, we conclude with a brief outline of this method.

Behavioural scientists have long advocated using organizational development to bring about system-wide change. Organizational development can be defined as an effort to improve an organization through collaborative diagnosis and the management of its culture. Organizational development follows a process of diagnosis, feedback, discussion and action. Initially, data are collected about the perceived problems facing employees in the organization. Data are classified and fed back to employees for their reaction as to validity and relevance. In essence, the employees decide which aspects of the data are important and require action. Once priority problems are identified, a collaborative effort is set in place to decide on the actions necessary to solve the problems.

The approach requires that the organization perceives a need for change, be involved in the planning and implementation of change, and that the process results in change in the organization's culture. Organizational development is not geared to accomplishing individual changes in people; rather it aims to change the total system.[4] A consequence of improving the system may be individual changes leading organizational members to espouse different values and attitudes and perform differently. By system-wide change we mean that, although the initial diagnosis may point to problems in authority systems, by the time the discussions have occurred and the feedback is terminated, members will have looked at corporate culture, analyzed leadership, investigated reward systems and commented on career planning and promotions, while minutely dissecting the communication channels in the organization. An organizational development effort rarely remains isolated to one issue.

We suggest that the task at hand is not to apply the organizational development process to the entire public sector but on a department by department basis. This is similar to its typical application in the private sector, where the approach has been used to improve a single organization. However, even working on a departmental basis, trying to improve the existing system using organizational development will be difficult since it requires a strong commitment on the part of all participants.

As mentioned earlier, organizational development is not a top-down approach to change but a shared and collaborative effort which especially requires the active involvement of top management. The task in the federal government must start at the top at a committee such as the Committee of Senior Officials (COSO) where there should be serious discussions to determine priority areas for change.

The agenda for discussion, whether at a committee such as COSO, or at departmental management committees, might include an examination of i) the culture of the public sector and the values and assumptions on which it operates; ii) the role of senior managers in all activities outside policy formulation and especially in relation to human resource management issues; and iii) the state of interpersonal relations and communication. At the departmental level the discussion on culture should turn not only on the broader public service culture, but also on how and whether the departmental culture fits into it.

The federal public service of Canada is a mammoth, fragmented, multi-purpose organization with multiple constituencies, many goals and objectives, and quite a few disgruntled and demoralized employees and managers. The change process would be incremental and relatively slow in producing results. It would require the commitment of all managers but especially the senior executives and their deputy ministers. It would also require the commitment of ministers to make this a continuous process of organizational renewal. Finally, it would require that managers move beyond the management rhetoric and respond to the results this exercise will generate.

The serious issue, throughout this study, lies in the confirmation of our research questions which concerned managers at the middle and lower layers of the public service. The study strongly confirms that they live in a world very different from the one at the top. This finding is significant because we believe senior managers at the middle and lower levels are the culture carriers of the organization. It is difficult to transmit a culture that one doesn't know or feels excluded from. This situation has developed over time because of the systemic peculiarities of the public sector. Most of it has occurred unconsciously. The time has come, however, for serious efforts to ameliorate the managerial climate of the public sector in Canada so that managers and employees can be satisfied to work within the system knowing that they can reach their full potential.

Notes

1. Because the survey was restricted to senior managers, we cannot speculate about the pattern of responses we would have found if the sample had included employees further down in the organization.

2. T.W. Plumptre, *Beyond the Bottom Line: Management in Government*, (Halifax, N.S.: The Institute for Research on Public Policy, 1988), p. 71.

3. M. Beer, *Organization Change and Development*, (Santa Monica, Calif.: Goodyear, 1980).

4. M. Beer, *Organization Change and Development*.

Afterword

The 1988 Survey of Managerial Attitudes: A Preliminary Overview

In the summer of 1988 all executives and senior managers in the government of Canada received a questionnaire asking them to participate in a survey of managerial attitudes. The survey was introduced to respondents as an ongoing study of senior management attitudes in the federal public sector in Canada which was begun in the summer of 1986. The participation rate in the 1988 survey was, once again, excellent. Seventy-two per cent of senior managers who received the questionnaire responded to it. This resulted in a sample of 3,006 senior managers (i.e. EXs and SMs) working in 65 departments and agencies.[1] This report contains a summary of the findings.

The 1986 survey was a comparative study of senior management attitudes in the private and public sector in Canada, whereas the 1988 version was a public-sector-only study with a much wider distribution within the federal public service. The questionnaire used in 1986 was somewhat modified for the purposes of the 1988 survey. While many of the original questions were included in the 1988 study, items specifically designed for public/private sector comparisons and those

---

[1] In 1986 senior managers (i.e. SMs and EX1s to EX5s) as well as the SM-1 group were randomly sampled from 20 departments and compared to a similar group of senior managers from 13 Canadian private sector companies. The public sector response rate to the 1986 survey was 73 per cent.

dealing with individual differences and personality were replaced by questions which measured perceptions of whether management practices had improved in two years. Also, a number of questions relating to respondents' views of their immediate supervisor were added. Including the various socio-demographic and open-ended questions on organizational values and communication, the final instrument was composed of over 150 items.

Respondents were asked, as they were in 1986, about managerial practices and their work environment, in order to get a sense of organizational climate and the degree of work satisfaction within the departments and agencies in which they worked. In this report, we have presented the results of the sample of senior managers who responded in 1986 compared with those in 1988.[2] We have also presented data collected in 1988 for which no comparison base exists, since these questions were introduced for the first time in 1988. In analyzing and interpreting the data, it is important to keep in mind that the 1986 survey was done in 20 departments only, while in 1988 it included 65 departments and agencies.[3]

The data have been presented by job level, because this variable revealed important differences in the 1986 survey. The EX5s and EX4s have been lumped; the EX3s, EX2s, and EX1s make up the second grouping; and the SM group the third. The purpose of this approach was to focus on the potential impact that working levels had on responses.

The preliminary analysis of the 1988 data leads to two general observations. First, in comparison with the 1986 data, in most areas surveyed managers' attitudes and perceptions were less favourable. The EX4-5 group was sometimes the exception to this trend; there were instances where their assessment of managerial practices saw improvement over 1986. Satisfaction with the organization remained unchanged. Second, in 1986 we had found that managerial level in the public sector appeared to have a very significant and consistent impact on the pattern of responses. The 1988 survey, once again, showed that job level was a very powerful determinant of respondents' attitudes towards, and perceptions of, their work and organization.

---

[2] The average for the 1986 numbers in this appendix does not contain the SM-1 results. They will, therefore, differ somewhat from those in the body of the book.

[3] A separate analysis of the 1988 data was done for the 20 original departments which participated in the 1986 survey. There were no important differences between the original 20 departments and the total population of 65 departments and agencies.

Culture, Leadership and Rewards

In both the 1986 and 1988 surveys, we asked senior managers to describe their departments and how they reacted to the leadership provided and perceived organizational rewards.

Senior managers' descriptions provide an image of departmental culture and suggest which values are emphasized. Table 1 shows the percentage of respondents in the three job levels who, to a large or very large extent, describe their organization (department or agency) as having the ascribed orientation. In general, the results show that perceptions related to organizational orientation did not vary in the two years. Service to clients continued to be the most widely endorsed orientation of federal departments and agencies. While orientation to employees is not perceived to be an important characteristic, it gained some ground since 1986.

Table 1
Orientation of Organization
(% responding "to a great" or "very great extent")

ORIENTATION TO:	EX4-5		EX1-3		SM		AVERAGE	
	1986	1988	1986	1988	1986	1988	1986	1988
Service to Clients	80.6	83.0	80.6	71.9	73.3	68.9	76.6	71.1
Employees	27.5	34.7	12.0	16.0	8.3	13.4	11.5	15.9
Innovation	38.1	38.0	23.0	23.6	22.1	22.4	23.9	23.9
Creative Management	39.8	40.6	23.4	18.3	14.4	15.5	20.1	18.3
Efficient Management	61.2	52.7	45.6	38.2	35.4	36.0	41.5	38.0

An important aspect of managing is the degree to which leadership is provided by senior managers in the organization. Respondents were asked a number of questions dealing with the issue of leadership. Table 2 shows the distribution of leadership scores in the surveys conducted in the two years. The data suggest an overall fall-off in the level of perceived leadership provided by the senior manager cadre in all three groups.

Table 2
Leadership in the Organization

LEADERSHIP ITEMS	EX4-5 1986	EX4-5 1988	EX1-3 1986	EX1-3 1988	SM 1986	SM 1988	AVERAGE 1986	AVERAGE 1988
% who agree or strongly agree:†								
Superiors discuss object-ives with subordinates	100.0	93.5	90.1	84.9	76.2	74.9	83.5	80.9
Superior encourages participation	83.8	73.0	72.5	60.0	63.5	55.9	68.6	58.9
Management committed to development of org.	88.9	80.3	68.8	57.2	54.5	48.4	62.8	54.5
% who chose "to a great" or "very great extent":								
Deputy Minister gives leadership	84.0	69.4	61.6	43.5	48.5	33.0	56.7	40.3
Management involved in long term planning	81.0	57.5	72.4	47.0	63.2	47.6	68.2	47.8

† Includes those who chose 4 or 5 on a 5-point scale

Rewards in the public sector are regulated by numerous procedures and policies. The constraints faced by many public administrations all over the world in the last few years have resulted in fewer rewards available for more public servants. Given that rewards are an important management tool, we asked senior managers for their reactions to a number of statements measuring their perceptions towards available rewards and related issues. The results for the 1988 survey are shown in Table 3, and compared to those of the 1986 survey.

The results demonstrate that rewards are perceived more positively depending on one's job level. This tendency, observed in both surveys, may be understandable by the fact that those whose job level is higher tend also to be the recipients of the rewards they are evaluating. On average, respondents viewed the allocation of rewards less favourably in 1988 than they did in 1986.

Table 3
Rewards in the Organization

	EX4-5		EX1-3		SM		AVERAGE	
REWARD ITEMS	1986	1988	1986	1988	1986	1988	1986	1988
% who chose "to a great" or "very great extent":†								
Doing job well leads to pay increases	45.5	39.9	25.2	18.1	14.6	10.5	21.2	15.9
Employees given fair consideration for openings	51.0	56.8	38.4	29.2	25.9	20.2	32.7	26.7
Promotions are based on merit	62.0	53.7	39.0	27.9	24.6	17.4	33.3	24.6
Generalists are rewarded more than specialists	35.9	32.0	31.1	29.7	33.3	29.6	32.7	29.8
% who agree or strongly agree:								
Good advancement opportunities (in organization)	25.5	13.5	23.7	12.7	18.0	10.8	20.7	11.9

† Includes those who chose 4 or 5 on a 5-point scale

The work environment and its constraints is very important to senior managers. Among important internal constraints in the public sector are restrictions on handling personnel issues and the inadequate degree of authority to hire, promote and set salaries. External constraints also have some impact on the respondents—a major restricting factor.

Satisfying Various Stakeholders

In trying to assess the impact of various external pressures, we asked managers to rate how important it was for them to ensure the satisfaction of a number of different groups with which they come into contact. The ratings provided can be viewed as an evaluation of the importance of the various stakeholders to senior public servants. The results of their responses are shown in Table 4, which summarizes data for both 1986 and 1988. The most interesting conclusion from these data is the degree of their stability over time. Senior managers, at all levels, perceive that it is especially important to satisfy their organization's clients, politicians and central agencies. Although these three groups dominate the immediate attention of senior public servants, the general public, various interest groups and the media come a close second.

Table 4
Degree to which Senior Management Cadre
Ensures Satisfaction of Various Groups
(% responding "important" or "very important")

IMPORTANCE OF SATISFYING	EX4-5 1986	EX4-5 1988	EX1-3 1986	EX1-3 1988	SM 1986	SM 1988	AVERAGE 1986	AVERAGE 1988
The organization's clients	92.9	94.8	87.8	85.1	83.6	85.6	86.0	85.9
The general public	75.8	78.6	72.3	69.1	64.5	67.4	68.4	68.8
Interest groups	62.6	72.9	69.0	65.1	63.9	60.1	65.6	63.3
The media	61.6	59.6	59.0	62.8	59.6	54.8	59.6	58.9
Politicians	94.9	92.8	90.9	90.7	87.6	84.5	89.5	88.0
Central agencies	59.8	73.2	75.2	73.1	74.3	72.4	73.3	72.8

The only difference of any consequence in senior managers' perceptions of their work environment from 1986 to 1988 is found among the EX4-5s, who gave more importance to satisfying central agency concerns and interest groups than they did two years earlier. Additionally, the variation in satisfaction across job levels, found for other items in the survey, was not evident in the responses provided to "ensuring the satisfaction of different groups" by the three job categories.

Changes in the Management Environment

The 1988 Survey of Managerial Attitudes was designed to measure changes in perceptions of senior managers in two ways. The first was by measuring the difference in respondents' answers to the same questions in 1986 and 1988. The second was to ask senior managers to reflect the changes over this two-year period. This next section contains the results of these questions. As well, questions were added related to respondents' perceptions of the managerial practices of their supervisors, which was identified as a critical factor in the 1986 study.

Table 5 shows opinions on whether activities are better managed now by senior managers than two years ago. Service to the public, budgeting and resource planning, and financial administration were viewed as being better managed. Career planning, staffing of vacancies in the management category and performance pay were perceived to be worse-managed. Without exception, proportionally more members of the EX4-5 group perceived that these areas were better managed in 1988 than members of the EX1-3 or SM group.

The Role of the Immediate Supervisor

The 1986 data indicate that leadership is an important attribute of good management. In Table 2 of this report we reviewed general perceptions of leadership provided by senior managers in the two surveys. To further clarify the issue within departments and agencies, respondents were asked to rate the extent to which their immediate supervisor devoted time to good leadership practices. Answers are in Table 6.

The results underline few important leadership issues with regard to the behaviour of immediate supervisors. Senior managers feel that their immediate supervisors ask them to produce high quality work, encourage them to participate in work-related decisions and inform them about the views of the minister and the deputy minister. However, when it comes to giving clear directions, creating enthusiasm about the work, and providing feedback related to performance, only a few more than half the senior managers rated supervisors as performing these tasks "to some extent", "a great extent", or "very great extent". It is also important to note that, as we descend the hierarchy, the immediate supervisor is perceived as devoting less time to such activities.

The data on the immediate supervisor, when added to the previous set of items presented on leadership, clarify some issues. Senior managers, as leaders, inform and involve their subordinate managers and demand high quality work from them. They are weaker, however, on the more behavioural and human relations aspects of leadership.

Table 5
Areas Better Managed Now in the Organization than Two Years Earlier

AREAS BETTER MANAGED NOW	EX4-5			EX1-3			SM			AVERAGE		
	Agree†	Neither	Disagree	Agree	Neither	Disagree	Agree	Neither	Disagree	Agree	Neither	Disagree
Service to the public	55.1	39.0	5.9	43.4	40.4	16.2	39.4	41.2	19.4	42.0	40.7	17.3
Internal communications	55.7	30.5	13.8	35.8	36.1	28.1	32.4	34.5	33.1	35.4	35.0	29.6
Support for career planning	39.4	35.1	25.5	17.1	38.6	44.3	12.0	35.8	52.2	16.0	37.1	46.9
Caring for employees	48.3	34.7	17.0	25.5	38.9	35.6	24.2	34.8	41.0	26.2	36.8	37.0
Financial administration	45.7	41.8	12.4	37.8	39.0	23.2	36.0	41.0	23.0	36.6	40.0	23.4
Budgeting and resource planning	51.7	32.9	15.4	40.1	35.4	24.5	35.8	35.9	28.3	38.8	35.5	25.7
Staffing of vacancies in the management category	31.5	46.1	22.4	14.6	48.4	37.0	11.8	46.7	41.5	14.3	47.4	38.3
Performance pay	36.2	41.3	22.5	21.8	45.5	32.7	13.7	42.0	44.3	19.0	43.0	38.0

† The results are based on a 5-point scale, ranging from "strongly disagree" to "strongly agree" with a neutral middle point. The "agree" column contains the percentage of respondents who chose "agree" or "strongly agree", the "neither" column shows the percentage who "neither agreed or disagreed", and the "disagree" column shows the percentage who "disagree" or "strongly disagree" that various activities were better managed than two years earlier.

Table 6
Activities to which the Immediate Supervisor Devotes Time
(% who endorsed "to a great" or "very great extent"
or who chose "to some extent")

MY IMMEDIATE SUPERVISOR	EX4-5 Great†	Some	EX1-3 Great	Some	SM Great	Some	AVERAGE Great	Some
Gives clear directions	24.8	41.9	17.7	35.0	18.4	35.6	18.5	35.7
Creates enthusiasm about the work	41.1	25.9	25.3	29.0	23.0	28.9	25.1	28.8
Provides me with feedback regularly	27.0	31.6	26.9	31.1	17.4	30.9	17.7	31.0
Demands high quality work	59.6	23.2	48.8	28.3	47.1	27.6	48.7	27.7
Informs me about views of Minister and DM	72.3	15.8	43.8	28.1	34.2	30.4	41.0	28.5
Is concerned about me as an individual	41.1	32.3	25.9	32.2	28.3	29.9	27.9	31.1
Encourages participation in decisions	66.1	16.7	44.7	31.2	45.0	29.1	46.0	29.4

† "Some extent" is the midpoint (3) and a "great" or "very great" extent represent the 2 positive alternatives (4 and 5) of a 5-point scale in which respondents were asked to indicate the extent to which the statement reflected their assessment of their immediate supervisor's managerial practices. Subtracting the percentage of those who chose these three options from 100% gives the percentage of senior managers who chose "to a little" or "very little extent".

Work Satisfaction

Work-related attitudes and perceptions usually have an effect on work satisfaction. As in the 1986 survey, we queried senior managers about different facets of work satisfaction and job morale. Whereas only 26 per cent of respondents had felt that there was to a great or very great extent a morale problem in their organization in 1986, this percentage increased to 40 per cent in 1988. Slight downward changes were also noted in the pride respondents felt in working for the federal government or their organization. A partial explanation for these lower satisfaction scores may be related to the fact that senior managers do not perceive much chance of getting ahead in the government through promotions.

While morale and pride among senior public servants had gone down a little, overall satisfaction with their own organization remained unchanged in the two surveys, as is shown in Figure 1. Levels of satisfaction with the organization diverged as one moved down the hierarchy, but remained stable in 1988. As in the previous survey, job satisfaction tended to be higher than organizational satisfaction.

Figure 1
Overall Satisfaction with Organization

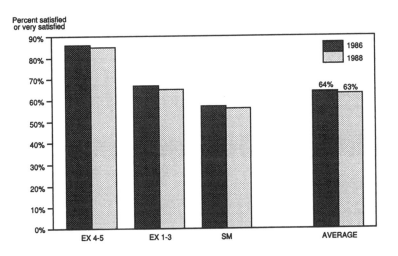

Concluding Comments

As suggested in the introduction of this report, we have once again found that levels of job-related satisfaction and other important indicators of organizational culture, leadership and rewards decreased as one moved down the senior management hierarchy of the public sector. The fall-off in levels of agreement between those working in the most senior levels of the public service (for whom the 1988 results in themselves are sometimes more positive than 1986) as compared with those working lower down the managerial hierarchy, such as SMs, continues to remind us that these groups work in different environments.

Two years is too short a span to reap the fruits of any reforms undertaken to better manage the human resource environment. It is clear that changes in managing human resources, in improving the leadership displayed by the senior management cadre, and in articulating a public sector culture will take a concerted effort on the part of numerous parties. Many departments have started such activities, but it is important to note that such efforts will require a long time before attitudes, perceptions and behaviours are changed. Five to seven years is typical for organizational change initiatives to take hold in large private sector organizations. Although there are a number of areas of concern highlighted in this study, the fact that two-thirds of senior managers are satisfied with their organization provides a strong foundation for remedial initiatives.

Related Publications Available
November 1989

Order Address

The Institute for Research on Public Policy
P.O. Box 3670 South
Halifax, Nova Scotia
B3J 3K6
1-800-565-0659 (toll free)

Peter Aucoin (ed.)　　　*The Politics and Management of
Restraint in Government.* 1981　$17.95

Nicole S. Morgan　　　*Nowhere to Go? Possible Consequences
of the Demographic Imbalance in
Decision-Making Groups of the Federal
Public Service.* 1981　$8.95

Jacob Finkelman &　　　*Collective Bargaining in the Public
Shirley B. Goldenberg　Service: The Federal Experience in
Canada.* 2 vols. 1983　$29.95 (set)

Gordon Robertson　　　*Northern Provinces: A Mistaken Goal.*
1985　$8.00

Nicole Morgan	*Implosion: analyse de la croissance de la Fonction publique fédérale canadienne (1945-1985).* 1986 $20.00
John W. Langford and K. Lorne Brownsey (eds.)	*The Changing Shape of Government in the Asia-Pacific Region.* 1988 $22.00
Timothy W. Plumptre	*Beyond the Bottom Line: Management in Government.* 1988 $24.95
Tom Kent	*Getting Ready for 1999: Ideas for Canada's Politics and Government.* 1989 $19.95
Gordon Robertson	*A House Divided: Meech Lake, Senate Reform and the Canadian Union.* 1989 $14.95
Edward E. Stewart	*Cabinet Government in Ontario: A View from Inside.* 1989 $14.95

DATE DUE